de Gruyter Studies in Organization 72

Communication, Power and Organization

de Gruyter Studies in Organization

Organizational Theory and Research

This de Gruyter Series aims at publishing theoretical and methodological studies of organizations as well as research findings, which yield insight in and knowledge about organizations. The whole spectrum of perspectives will be considered: organizational analyses rooted in the sociological as well as the economic tradition, from a socio-psychological or a political science angle, mainstream as well as critical or ethnomethodological contributions. Equally, all kinds of organizations will be considered: firms, public agencies, non-profit institutions, voluntary associations, inter-organizational networks, supra-national organizations etc.

Emphasis is on publication of *new* contributions, or significant revisions of existing approaches. However, summaries or critical reflections on current thinking and research will also be considered.

This series represents an effort to advance the social scientific study of organizations across national boundaries and academic disciplines. An Advisory Board consisting of representatives of a variety of perspectives and from different cultural areas is responsible for achieving this task.

This series addresses organization researchers within and outside universities, but also practitioners who have an interest in grounding their work on recent social scientific knowledge and insights.

Editor:

Prof. Dr. Alfred Kieser, Universität Mannheim, Mannheim, Germany

Advisory Board:

Prof. Anna Grandori, CRORA, Università Commerciale Luigi Bocconi, Milano, Italy
Prof. Dr. Cornelis Lammers, FSW Rijksuniversiteit Leiden, Leiden, The Netherlands
Prof. Dr. Marshall W. Meyer, The Wharton School, University of Pennsylvania, Philadelphia, U.S.A.
Prof Jean-Claude Thoenig, Université de Paris I, Paris, France
Prof. Mayer F. Zald, The University of Michigan, Ann Arbor, U.S.A.

Mats Alvesson

Communication,
Power and Organization

Walter de Gruyter · Berlin · New York 1996

Mats Alvesson, Professor, Department of Business Administration,
University of Lund, Lund, Sweden

Library of Congress Cataloging-in-Publication Data

Alvesson, Mats, 1956–
    Communication, power and organization : Mats Alvesson.
    (De Gruyter studies in organization ; 72)
    Rev. and expanded ed. of: Kommunikation, makt, organi-
    sation.
    Includes bibliographical references and index.
    ISBN 3-11-014622-3 (cloth : alk. paper). –
    ISBN 3-11-014897-8 (pb : alk. paper)
    1. Communication in organizations.   2. Leadership.
    I. Alvesson, Mats, 1956–   Kommunikation, makt, organ-
    isation. English.   II. Title.   III. Series.
    HD30.3.A44   1996
    658.4′092–dc20   96-6132
                                                              CIP

Die Deutsche Bibliothek – *Cataloging-in-Publication Data*

Alvesson, Mats:
Communication, power and organization / Mats Alvesson. –
Berlin ; New York : de Gruyter, 1996
    (De Gruyter studies in organization ; 72 : Organizational
    theory and research)
    Einheitssacht.: Kommunikation, makt, organisation ⟨engl.⟩
    Auszug
    ISBN 3-11-014622-3 Gb.
    ISBN 3-11-014897-8 brosch.
NE: GT

♾ Printed on acid-free paper which falls within the guidelines of the ANSI to ensure permanence and durability.

Printing: WB-Druck GmbH. Rieden am Forggensee. – Binding: D. Mikolai GmbH. Berlin. – Cover Design: Johannes Rother. Berlin. – Printed in Germany

Preface

In this book I explore a particular event in a single company, and hope that this exploration may promote a deeper critical understanding of organizational and management processes. Such an approach calls among other things for the development of a particular sensitivity to those power and dominance relationships that are so crucial a part of social life, not least in the organizational context. By developing an awareness of the more subtle aspects of power relationships it might become easier for those in subordinate positions to understand and therefore to resist, at least to some extent, the workings of power. Thus, unlike most of what is written about organization and leadership, this book aims to undermine rather than to enhance the exercise of power, to stimulate people to question rather than to reproduce power relationships (which does not mean to say that power relationships are either "evil" or avoidable). At a time when much is being written about management and leadership, and almost always from the standpoint of the upper ranks, it seems important that leadership should also be addressed in a critical perspective. It is my hope that this book can act as a counterweight to the dominating routes by which organizational and management processes are usually approached.

I also hope to contribute to an organization theory which places actions, situations and social practices at the centre of attention. This means that neither individuals (actors) nor systems (structures) are allowed to predominate, but that analysis and insights both concentrate on the actions and manifest organizational practices that characterise or are displayed by a particular situation. In such cases it is important to choose situations or practices that are meaningful, rich in content, and able to provide a good picture of typical organizational processes. In my view the situation addressed in this book, an information meeting in a fairly large industrial company, satisfies these criteria very satisfactorily.

The book starts from three theoretical sources of inspiration: cultural theory, which has a slightly more critical orientation here than is usual,

Foucault´s theory of power and Habermas´s theory of communicative action. In my view these rich sources of inspiration are still underexploited in organization theory. Much research has of course been done on organizational culture, but it often lacks a critical edge.

Two inputs in particular give rise to the present study. One was a research project undertaken jointly by Ivar Björkman and myself during 1990-92, which brought a cultural perspective to bear on companies. It was as part of this project that the information meeting discussed below was originally documented. The second input was an invitation to give a keynote speech at the Dublin Conference of the International Communication Association in June 1990, under the overall rubric "European Approaches to Organizational Communication"; as I was wondering how to write my paper, an appropriate empirical starting point appeared in the shape of this information meeting, which with excellent timing was being documented just at that moment. As this material seemed to lend itself very well to a critical interpretation, or rather to several such interpretations, I decided to address it in this way. Since Critical Theory, and particularly the variant represented by Habermas, often remains on an abstract conceptual and theoretical level, I felt that an attempt to link it to an empirical example might prove a fruitful, if not altogether an easy, endeavour. Perhaps my study may also inspire others to make close readings of social situations and actions, starting from the theoretical sources for which I break a lance in this book.

I would like to thank the following people who have commented on various drafts of this manuscript: Göran Ahrne, Rolf Lind and Richard Sotto, Stockholm University; Leif Borgert, University College of Falun/Borlänge; Stan Deetz, Rutgers University; John Forester, Cornell University; Owe Johansson, Gothenburg University; Astrid Kersten, La Roche College, Pittsburg; Robert McPhee, University of Wisconsin-Milwaukee; Stephen Payne, University of Eastern Illinois; John Roberts, Cambridge University; Bengt Sandkull, Linköping University; and David Silverman, London University. I would also like to thank Ivar Björkman, Stockholm University, for his comments and for his help with the empirical material for this book. It was Ivar who documented the information meeting which provides the empirical focus of the study, and who produced a first draft of the description of the meeting. Inga Collin has been most helpful in the process of editing the text.

The book represents part of the above-mentioned research project which has been financed by the Work Environment Fund, Stockholm, and I should like to take this opportunity to thank the Fund for their support.

November 1995   Mats Alvesson

Contents

1 Introduction

The subject of this book is organization, or organizing, in companies: how is it effected and how is the social order maintained in institutions of this kind? More specifically we will look at the way power, in symbolic form, is exerted over those at subordinate levels and how organizational processes produce and anchor taken for granted ideas and values in employees. This is of course a vast subject and I shall limit myself to demonstrating, with the help of one specific example, certain aspects of the way corporate management acts in order to maintain social relations in terms of power or, to put it in more "positive" terms, to create and maintain that preparedness for collective action which is the distinguishing feature of the organization: power relations are more than a simple question of oppression.

The point of departure and particular focus of the study is a specific and clearly defined event, an information meeting for middle level managers in a fairly large industrial company, which took place prior to a major reorganization. At first glance, it seemed to be a question of informing managers about the future organization of the company, and about the considerations underlying decisions regarding the new organization. This particular meeting could be seen as a less than crucial episode in the functioning of the company, but it nonetheless contains many valuable clues to the way in which this sort of social institution is run, maintained and changed. This specific event is, I think, highly illuminating. While the event can be viewed as a briefing on a pending (re)organization, it can equally well be seen as a way of (re)creating an organization by establishing and reinforcing certain views, ideas and attitudes among the employees. We could call it a process of *cultural organizing*. The cultural concept turns the spotlight on common ideas, meanings and definitions of reality. Other kinds of organizational process – those that focus on formal structures or material conditions – naturally also contain a cultural dimension. Even a formal reorganization of a fairly simple kind such as the introduction of new departmental boundaries, new routines, or new lines of communication call for some adaptations in the minds of those involved. Their ideas about formal structure must change or be changed; otherwise, total confusion would ensue. But a process of cultural organizing is directed primarily at commonly held ideas and meanings. Here, formal or physical conditions are not of central importance. According to modern organization theory and even according to some management practice, cultural organizing processes constitute a crucial element in organizations. Such processes are often referred to as "symbolic management" (Alvesson and Berg, 1992; Pfeffer, 1981a) or "management of meaning" (Smircich and Morgan, 1982).

Using as a basis the empirical material from the information meeting, two related and important organizational themes will be considered in the book: techniques of power and discipline, and communication in the organizational context.

Thus far, a tentative presentation, or perhaps an indication, of the preoccupations and aspirations of the book has been given. There follows a more detailed account of the aims of the study and of the frames of reference applied. No distinction is made here between aims and frameworks, which instead are presented together since they are also inextricably linked throughout the book. Then comes a section on multiple interpretations, and something is said about how best to approach the reading and interpretation of a body of material from different perspectives. The chapter closes with a few words on the cognitive or knowledge-constitutive interest that guides this study and a brief summary of the design of the book.

1.1   Aims and frames of reference

Three motives have led to the writing of this book: a desire to contribute to the stock of knowledge on power processes in organizations, to show the relevance of the works of Foucault and Habermas to empirical organization studies and to develop ideas on qualitative method. The mode of research proposed and developed here includes two elements: multiple interpretations and close readings of a specific situation. I will now elaborate on these three motives.

1.1.1 Motive 1: Power and cultural organizing

My paramount ambition has been to understand the power dimension in cultural organizing, more specifically to see how particular social situations can express and (re)produce cultural understanding and social relations in organizations, by influencing ideas about what is right, rational, natural and reasonable. Here the focus of attention will be on the broader communicative and symbolic content of situations which, at the superficial level, are technical and instrumental. Special attention will be paid to the power and ideology aspects of cultural communication: how the "neutral" conveying of information and use of language can reinforce asymmetric power relations and contribute to the disciplinary function that is so central to management and to many other manifestations of culture. The power element in communication means a forming and fixing of ideas, the selves of the participants and the preconditions for social interaction. I am thus interested in throwing some light on the aspect of dominance in the reproduction and development of commonly held ideas and meanings which are the essence of cultural communication. Implied here is an interest in the effects of this dominance on the identities of the objects of the operations of power and the constraints on the possibility of engaging in dialogue.

The study is thus based in part on cultural theory (which will be discussed in greater detail in Chapter 3). In cultural theory three ways are usually indicated whereby a culture – the ideas, meanings and symbols held in common by a collective – is sustained (Ortner, 1984). One such way is by socialising, whereby ideas, values, ideals and norms are transmitted from one generation to the next. Another way is by means of a finely meshed network of meanings and significations which pervade social practices and which "carry" the culture. Various practices such as ways of working, forms of social intercourse, etc., are imbued with meanings and symbols which both materialize and communicate culture as a dynamic whole – a whole, it should be added, that is far from free of inconsistencies, contradictions and fragmentation. A third way in which cultural ideas are created and recreated is in the form of special and culturally significant symbolically charged activities, events, words or material objects, that condense important ideas and assumptions and convey them forcefully to the members. Culture is thus given a particular form which reifies the broader ideas and meanings, for instance in the shape of rites, ceremonies and verbal symbols.

All three of these culturally productive and reproductive mechanisms are naturally important. This study is concerned with the third way. Presumably an information meeting in a contemporary company will fail to reach the same level of expressiveness as a "genuine" ritual or ceremony in a non-modernised society, but the transmission in symbolic form of the beliefs, values and feelings contained within seemingly "rational" and "neutral" activities, can certainly have its own importance. The significance of the implicit "non-rational" element in the organizational context has been noted in recent research on organizations, management and working life. (Surveys of the relevant literature can be found in Alvesson and Berg, 1992; Frost et al. 1991.)

By concentrating on the relationship between culture and power in relation to specific empirical material, I hope to contribute to a critical understanding of culture, and to give a more dynamic, processual view of culture than is the norm in mainstream organizational culture studies. Despite some work in this direction (reviewed in Chapter 3) the use of culture theory in organization studies tends on the whole to assume consensus and harmony. If conflict is noted at all, most studies focus on explicit conflict only. There is also a heavy emphasis on a stable set of ideas, values and norms which are viewed as characterizing the organization as a whole, rather than an appreciation of how cultural ideas and meanings are expressed in local settings. By focusing on power in processes of cultural organizing, it is possible to counteract some of the most profound biases in (mainstream) organizational culture studies. The emphasis on cultural organizing rather than organizational culture is also, of course, vital in my attempt to use culture theory productively.

The use of culture theory is supported by the use of the theories of Foucault and Habermas in the study of power and cultural organizing. However, the prominence of these authors in the present book is also contingent upon a different type of motive.

1.1.2 Motive 2: Linking Foucault and Habermas to empirical organizational research

The second idea behind this book is of a more general theoretical nature. Here my ambition has been to link Foucault´s notion of power and Habermas´s theory of communicative action to empirical organizational research. This purpose is related to the first aim, as these two social scientists have important things to say about the power/culture/ communication theme, but the idea of exploring the works of Foucault and Habermas in connection with empirical material also aims to inspire the use of these authors not only as a source of theoretical reflection, but also as an inspiration in empirical work.[1] Foucault (1974, 1980) is of particular importance in relation to organization theory, as he draws attention to the multifaceted and concrete nature of power. In modern societies, as Foucault himself has gone some way towards suggesting, it is organizations that provide the basis for the kind of power techniques which work by moulding those subjected to the power. Habermas (1971, 1984) in turn is pivotal because he challenges current perceptions of rationality and offers a constructive alternative. Modern companies are often presented as models of great rationality. At the same time it is a special kind of rationality that is being invoked, namely the instrumental or technical rationality which is concerned solely with maximising resource use and the means for

---

[1] By empirical I mean "real life" situations, talk and social practices in contexts other than those of the production and elaboration of academic texts. One should be careful about separating the theoretical and the empirical too strictly, for two reasons: all accounts of the empirical are theoretically constructed and all theoretical work is in a sense an empirical phenomenon – a researcher writing is as "real" as a manager talking and an academic text is as "empirical" as a corporate building or a product. Both theoretical and empirical work tend to deal with texts: empirical work revolves around interviews and interview transcripts, observation protocols, etc. Pointing out the problems of a strict separation between the empirical and the theoretical does not, of course, prevent the distinction from telling us something important in terms of different aspects, foci and logic. The empirical – at least in qualitative research – tends, for example, to be rather concrete and close to experience, while the theoretical is less so.

achieving goals – goals which themselves are taken as given. The discussion of goals and values is regarded as being "beyond rationality" (Alvesson and Willmott, 1992, 1996). To equate instrumental rationality with rationality in general appears increasingly absurd in light of the technological capitalist society´s combination of material affluence and ecological crisis. Habermas´s suggestion for a broader anti-technocratic discussion of rationality has created a focal point for current critical-constructive thinking that has great relevance for organizational theory. Foucault and Habermas help to make us more aware of important, yet scarcely obvious, facets of disciplinary and communicative situations, such as the information meeting to be spotlighted in this book. They therefore provide inspiration for politically meaningful interpretations of such phenomena.

Despite the considerable impact these two writers have had on social science, and despite some references to them in recent studies on management, organization and working life (for overviews, see Alvesson and Deetz, 1996; Alvesson and Willmott, 1992), their influence has so far been much less on the empirical side. In Habermas´s case it is sometimes even assumed that such a thing would not be sensible, indeed would be all but impossible, given the philosophical orientation and high level of abstraction in his texts. Such organizational studies as do refer to these authors are generally confined to the level of discussion or theory, rarely seeking explicit links with empirical matter, at least not with "primary" empirical material such as direct observations and interviews. People in management and organization studies, who are greatly inspired by Foucault, often do not seem to follow the major thrust of his work, i.e. the detailed empirical study of the technologies of power in operation. Within the Habermasian or Critical Theory field, Forester (1992, 1993) is quite exceptional in taking the master as a source of inspiration for empirical studies. My previous Critical Theory oriented work has been theoretical/conceptual, while this framework has on the whole been less prominent in my empirical (ethnographic) projects, or even absent from them altogether. My present text indicates an interest in testing and illustrating the possibility of using these authors in the readings of a particular body of empirical material, which more than anything else raises questions about the forms of power and communicative rationality.

Some readers may now be asking themselves whether two such dissimilar authors as Foucault and Habermas could be integrated. Many people see them as playing in two quite different leagues, which means that they should not really be brought together at all. One indication, however, that it is not impossible to be inspired by both authors at the same time, is their frequent appearance alongside one another in other writers´ lists of references. In one collection of articles devoted to the work of Foucault (Hoy, 1986), Habermas is the writer most frequently cited apart from Foucault himself. In another reader, using Habermas and Critical Theory as a primary point of departure, Foucault is the most influential reference apart from Habermas (Alvesson and Willmott, 1992). Mumby puts the idea of drawing upon both these authors as follows:

> While each may pursue different agendas, both are bound together by their desire to generate counterfactual conceptions of knowledge which run counter to the prevailing epistemological trends. Simply put, it can be said that whereas Habermas seeks the a priori conditions for the consensus that grounds truth, Foucault´s task is to seek out and encourage the conflict and dissensus that potentially leads to new and different consensuses about the order of things. It is in this sense, finally, that the works of Habermas and Foucault can be seen as existing in a productive tension, rather than mutual opposition. (Mumby, 1991: 37-38)

I do not intend to say any more, however, about whether, and, if so, how Foucault and Habermas can be made to agree, since my aim is *not* to integrate these two sources of inspiration into a common frame of reference. Instead I intend to draw on some of the theories and ideas of each in making various distinct interpretations. Consequently the differences and tensions between the two become a prerequisite rather than an obstacle to my project. My empirical material will thus be subjected to various theoretical readings: the Foucault-inspired and the Habermasian, as well as the above mentioned cultural-theoretical interpretation. This structure is contingent on the third theme of the book.

1.1.3   Motive 3: Multiple interpretations as a response to postmodernist critique

The third theme or purpose of this text is a little different from the other two. It springs from the current debate about modes of expression and the possibility of representing – i.e. depicting/mirroring – phenomena in research, and the doubts which have been raised about this (e.g. Deetz, 1992a; Calás and Smircich, 1987; Clifford and Marcus, 1986; Cooper and Burrell, 1988; Guba and Lincoln, 1994; Marcus and Fischer, 1986; Steier, 1991). Parts of this debate are expressed under the umbrella labels of postmodernism and poststructuralism; sometimes constructionism, rhetoric or reflexivity are the key terms. There is a reaction against the formerly predominant view that "reality" could be unproblematically represented in language and texts.[2] These last are regarded as being problematic in themselves. The act of writing and the resulting texts are no longer regarded as a marginal aspect of research, something that simply happens when the empirical work is finished, enabling its results to be communicated to others. Scientific texts are perceived not as vehicles of "truth" and "objectivity" distinct from imaginative literature, but as attempts – powerfully imbued with rhetoric – at constructing "truth" (e.g. Baker, 1990; Brown, 1990, 1994; Simons, 1989). In his introduction to a collection of anthropological texts Clifford addresses these questions. The authors, he says:

> ... see culture as composed of seriously contested codes and representations; they assume that the poetic and the political are inseparable, that science is in, not above, historical and linguistic processes. They assume that academic and literary genres interpenetrate and that the writing of cultural descriptions is properly experimental and ethical. Their focus on text making and rhetoric serves to highlight the constructed, artificial nature of cultural accounts. It undermines overly transparent modes of authority, and it draws attention to the historical predicament of ethnography, the fact that it is always caught up in the invention, not the representation, of cultures. (Clifford, 1986: 2)

These discussions are to some extent associated with alleged problems about the use of a coherent theory and a predominant voice (a certain theory or discourse) as the base for a good (in some sense) understanding of a phenomenon. The ambiguity of language inevitably pervades theory and the ability of theory to conduct itself in relation to what it claims to

---

2 According to Wellmer (1986) the poststructuralists mean that the links in the chain subject-representation-meaning-sign-truth must be broken down.

elucidate (handling "reality"). The postmodernists or poststructuralists have challenged the value of well-integrated theoretical systems and frames of reference in research, and of texts which purvey, as they see it, a totalising or even totalitarian view of how the phenomena can be understood.[3] Instead it is advocated that texts should express multiplicity: several voices must be heard (Calás and Smircich, 1987; Linstead, 1993; Lyotard, 1984, etc.). Plurality, diversity, unresolved paradoxes, ambiguity and challenges to order are celebrated while the ideal of representativeness is met with suspicion (e.g. Jeffcutt, 1993). I am not altogether happy about this rather heterogeneous trend and its somewhat vague recommendations, and agree with the following judgement:

> The recent concern with poststructuralist strategies of textual readings provides a mixed blessing for social research. The good news is that our interpretive powers may be enhanced, as might our sensitivities to the pervasive disciplinary structuring of discourses and thus to the relations of knowledge and power. The bad news is that these advances seem to be purchased at the cost of sweeping away crucial political and ethical questions of agency and praxis, reflective, politicized, theoretically engaged, practical judgments made in ordinary (but fantastically diverse) contexts. (Forester, 1988: 3)

---

[3] "Postmodernism" is rather an unfortunate expression which subsumes a whole host of somewhat differing views in a variety of fields, ranging from film and architecture to philosophy and sociology (Foster, 1984). The term is normally used in confrontation with "modernism", an expression which is applied just as freely and often in a remarkably broad sense. In the social sciences the concept of postmodernism is used primarily to indicate a certain view of theory, frames of reference or – following from this last – text and authorship, or to denote a particular period exhibiting certain putative social characteristics. The first of these uses has been touched upon above. Postmodernism as a concept pertaining to modern society or to "the spirit of the age" can be characterised rather unkindly as a view whereby culture, consumption, service, computers, images, simulation and fragmentation are regarded as "in", whilst industry, production, wage labour, "reality", overview, connections and totality are "out". These two concepts of postmodernism – as a metatheoretical concept and as a view of society with a (possible) empirical content – are not always kept properly apart, but it would be far beyond the scope of the present study to explore this question. For introductions, see Featherstone (1988), Sarup (1988) and, within organization studies, Alvesson and Deetz (1996) and Hassard and Parker (1993). Thompson (1993) has given us a good, albeit rather rough, critical survey of postmodernist variants in organization theory.

There is, in my opinion, a strong element of linguistic reductionism in much poststructuralist and postmodernist work. (All research includes an element of reductionism, but sometimes it seems particularly important to raise the issue.) To concentrate on scientific texts "as rhetorical enactments, with no ultimate logical or empirical warrant" (Brown, 1994: 13), for example, discourages empirical work as a significant input into the production of important insights relevant to a wider audience than that composed of intra-academic specialists. The whole project of social science tends to be defensive and minimized, narcissistically preoccupied with the researchers´ own texts and modes of producing them.

However, my somewhat critical view of poststructuralism and post-modernism does not preclude my recognizing an important lesson: the ideal of a well-integrated theoretical frame of reference should be treated with caution; it should also be recognized that such frames of reference can impede understanding and mislead the researcher or reader as a result of their totalising effect and their tendency to present reality as unambiguous and accessible to representation in the chosen theoretical idiom.[4] Rorty (1989) warns against an approach in which a "final vocabulary", a language providing the ultimate knowledge or wisdom, is used. Instead he proposes a position in which the researcher (1) "has radical and continuing doubts about the final vocabulary she currently uses, because she has been impressed by other vocabularies...; (2) she realizes that argument phrased in her present vocabulary can neither underwrite nor dissolve these doubts; (3) insofar as she philosophizes about her situation, she does not think that her vocabulary is closer to reality than others, that it is in touch with a power not herself" (p. 73). An openness to the appreciation of the values and limitations of different vocabularies and understandings is thus well

---

4 Postmodernist criticism of traditional schools of thought for using a totalizing approach should not go unchallenged, however. Reed (1993) points out that this critique "... may be guilty of grossly overestimating the totalizing momentum of modernist thinking and underestimating the fragmenting and localizing consequences of its chequered history as an integrative narrative" (p. 10). It is rather postmodernism that is guilty of a totalizing approach, with its attempts to paint a broad and clear-cut picture of "modern" concepts and scientific views, from which it is concerned to distance itself (Alvesson, 1995b; Kellner, 1988). Regardless of whether or not postmodernism falls into its own trap here, a word of warning to both postmodernists and others regarding the "totalizing" effect of a well-integrated, all-embracing and influential theory would not come amiss.

motivated. There is something to be said for caution when it comes to "monologic texts (that) employ a consistent and homogeneous representational style... and express a dominant authorial voice" (Jeffcutt, 1993: 39). This lesson can lead to a certain humility in face of the idea that truth, or "right" or "the best" interpretations, can be produced. In such a case a greater willingness to allow diverse vocabularies, interpretations and voices to make themselves heard in research texts appears desirable. The ambiguities of the social world should be recognized and, as far as possible, reflected in such texts (Alvesson and Sköldberg, 1996).

The idea of conducting multiple interpretations is well worth trying, and will be tried in this book. It is one systematic response to the postmodernist challenge. Within the frame of a broad critical-cultural orientation I make different readings of various theoretical sources which can represent different voices. These include, as noted above, cultural theory, Foucault's theory of power and Habermas's ideas on communicative rationality. Briefly, cultural theory implies a recognition of the way in which collectives and leading actors define and give meaning to the common social reality; Foucault's influence means investigating the way in which seemingly neutral situations contain a number of power techniques which mould or shape individuals through prescribing specific forms of subjectivity; and, finally, a Habermasian interpretation fastens on nuances in communicative action, particularly asymmetries and systematic "distortions" in speech situations. More on this topic is provided in Chapters 3-5.

I imagine that inside my word processor these sources of inspiration will approach one another – with the risk of a "totalizing" view and the opportunities for connections and convergence – and that something important and striking will come out of it for the reader. The latter qualities, involving some degree of coherence and direction in the enterprise, are associated with a (minor?) totalizing element involved in some degree of (non-intended) synthesizing contingent upon the idiosyncracies of the present author. After all, it is not Foucault or Habermas themselves who are hammering away at my keyboard. And I have no overweening ambition to place my interpretations as close as possible to the sources of inspiration. Methodologically speaking I have not attempted to put myself in Foucault's or Habermas's shoes or tried to interpret things in the way I think the "masters" would have done. This would not not have been possible, of course, but I might have tried to get as close to them as possible. Had I been a life-long student or devotee of any of the gurus, the situation would have been different and more strongly characterized by faithfulness. Rather than attempting to let Foucault or Habermas speak "through me", I have taken these thinkers as a source of inspiration for my own relatively independent interpretations of the issues discussed in this study. I am more interested in saying something interesting about organizational life than in being as orthodox as possible in relationship to the masters. My interest in Critical Theory (the Frankfurt tradition and associated scholars within what Burrell and Morgan (1979) refer to as radical humanism) and its concern with critical reflection and emancipation, keeps the interpretations from straining in too many different directions, and this seems to me more desirable than its opposite, namely the poststructuralists´ predilection for relativism, pluralism, fragmentation and ambiguity, their concern with language and what it may conceal rather than what it (more or less) represents (or does not represent), and their terrible fear of hoodwinking the reader by asserting authorial authority and interpretive precedence. Rather than joining the postmodernists in their excessive concern about "the totalizing force of reason" – where in fact they fail to distinguish between different forms of reason – I am more worried about abandoning the idea of a critical faculty able to resist those more limited forms of rationality that do function as a "totalizing" force in technological capitalist societies where fragmentation does not prevent the powers of ego administration from producing subjects in a specific direction (e.g. as consumers). It is important to distinguish between different concepts of rationality and reason, and to resist the trend that seeks to mix them together.

Having said this, I should add that I am not a true devotee of Habermas´s version of Critical Theory either. I am sympathetic to his work, but sufficiently well read in the critique of it, and appreciate alternative vocabularies such as Foucault´s and the postmodernists sufficiently to avoid writing this text in a pro-Habermasian manner. The limitations of human reason as well as the rational potentials of language are too obvious, as has been pointed out not only by psychoanalysts and postmodernists but also by Habermas´s "fathers" in the Frankfurt School (Horkheimer and

Adorno, 1947). Within the framework of a general critical orientation, I thus use the three theoretical approaches of culture theory, Foucault and Habermas in a basically positive and inspirational, but far from faithful and uncritical, manner.

1.2   On multiple interpretations

A few comments are now necessary on the basic idea and structure of this study. To interpret a given body of empirical material from different points of view is a potentially rewarding exercise – as I shall attempt to demonstrate in this book – but it very rarely occurs.[5] Maybe people are restrained by a distaste for eclecticism. But multiple interpretation is not the same as eclecticism. The idea is to make a number of distinct interpretations starting from different theories. The theories are thus not mixed together. Another reason for the absence of multiple interpretive research may be contingent upon the demand for space. The journal article is typically too short to allow the presentation of multiple theories and multiple interpretations of empirical material. A perhaps more significant "explanation" is simply that people do not even consider the possibility of it. It has not been institutionalized and does not appear in books on method.

In my opinion the multiple interpretation method has several advantages. One advantage, quite simply, is that it becomes possible to draw attention to several interesting angles. We can make more interpretations and gain a richer understanding. The empirical material can be used more efficiently. Naturally it is not impossible that an integrated frame of reference based on different theoretical sources might allow for the same "mass" of inter- pretations (an equally wide view over different aspects), but presumably part of the interpretive capacity is lost when several theories are merged into a single frame of reference. Because the frame of reference becomes so

---

5   One exception is Martin (1992; Martin and Meyerson, 1988), who bring different cultural perspectives to bear on a studied company. An attempt at a multiparadigmatic study of a fire brigade by Hassard (1991), using the Burrell and Morgan (1979) model, led to four different foci and rather disparate descriptions of different parts of the organization (cf. Parker and McHugh, 1991). Borgert (1994) also uses Burrell and Morgan's paradigm model and interprets a failed consultancy project from four different perspectives.

general that it loses some of its edge the resulting synthesis may be capable of directing attention with adequate sharpness towards one or two parts of the object under study but is unable to command a wide-angled view, in other words to direct attention to several aspects/interpretations of the object. Another advantage is that the text offering multiple interpretations acknowledges and actively draws attention to the indeterminate and open character of social reality, encouraging the readers to make their own interpretations. This becomes easier if alternative interpretations and points of view are provided, as these may something that a specific frame of reference is not capable of elucidate doing. The boundaries and blind spots of a particular theoretical perspective emerge. A certain internal criticism thus appears in the research text. That there are interpretive possibilities which are not tied to any particular theory already used by the author consequently stand out more clearly. The "totalising" effects contingent upon the use of a single frame of reference and its attendant language, which cause so much worry to the postmodernists, are thus to some extent reduced. The research text is then characterized by disclosure and an active readership is facilitated and encouraged. All this also means that the reflective character of research becomes more pronounced (Alvesson and Sköldberg, 1996).

An important question concerns the way in which the chosen theoretical sources of inspiration should relate to one another. The choice of references should be such that the combined approach will be as "interesting" as possible. Naturally the capacity and preferences of the researcher set the definitive parameters on what is possible and pertinent. On this point I differ from the view expressed in Morgan (1986), namely that the greater the number of perspectives that the researcher and practitioner can command, the better (more comprehensive, more complete) the understanding that can be achieved (see Reed, 1990, for a criticism of this argument). In my view, a qualified understanding (including that which seeks to take ambiguity seriously) calls for concentration and a good deal of work on the theory or theories in use; it is also necessary that the theory or theories be entrenched in the interpreter´s person and in his or her political-ethical position. There are thus normally limits to the theories – which ones and how many – that a researcher can successfully command, at least in the context of interpretive and discursive studies which call for a deeper feeling for the theoretical framework employed than is required in rational-analytical approaches. Within these limits I believe it is important that the sources of inspiration promote interpretations that allow for cross-fertilizations as well as a certain friction. The theoretical sources should be more or less distinct and able to promote separate interpretations, i.e. be capable of directing attention towards different aspects. In this way limits are also set on what a particular theory is able usefully to elucidate. But interpretations deriving from one theory should also facilitate interpretations based on some other theory.

An important issue concerning the possibilities of making multiple interpretations is the problem of paradigm incommensurability (Weaver and Gioia, 1994). This term, originally used by Kuhn (1970) is interpreted in various ways. Some choose a strong case, saying that it means the impossibility of communication between different paradigms (Jackson and Carter, 1991). Others emphasize a weaker version, indicating that it just means that complete translation of languages and strict comparisons of theories from different paradigms in relationship to data are not possible. (Data are never neutral but fused by paradigmatic assumptions and the vocabularies used, as data never emerge independently of a theory – academic or commonsensical.) Even if a weak case of incommensurability is accepted, the problems of getting theories based on different para-digmatic positions to come to terms with each other should not be underestimated. Meaningful cross-communication between paradigms is a difficult but not an impossible enterprise (Bernstein, 1983; Weaver and Gioia, 1994). With some effort it is probably possible to not only communicate across paradigms but also operate analytically in a satisfactury manner within an area which includes parts of one´s own paradigm and certain interfaces with other paradigms (Bernstein, 1983). Gioia and Pitre (1990), for instance, talk about transitional zones between paradigms that enable crossovers. With considerable effort it is also possible to learn positions dissimilar from the original one, in the same way that one can learn a new language (Rorty, 1992). We can expand and change our intellectual horizons. Paradigms are not hermetically sealed (Willmott, 1990). The important thing here is to recognize that there are no true or incontestable representations of paradigms and boundaries between different paradigms (Deetz, 1996).[6] All efforts to define paradigms and paradigmatic boundaries emerge from a specific position within the field, that one tries to define as if one could transcend the field and view it from an independent position. A more fruitful way than emphasizing firm paradigmatic borders and assuming unities within the various authors, schools and texts ascribed to a paradigm – particularly in the quite messy and rapidly changing discipline of organization studies – is to address the degree of intellectual distance between various positions. The distance is a matter of different vocabularies, variation in political commitments, research agendas, communities of researchers, etc. The greater the distance between various theories involved, the more demanding becomes the enterprise of understanding and using them productively.

This means that it is often wise to be cautious about using a wide span of theories. Providing interpretations from "completely different" paradigmatic positions could produce interesting results, but may become difficult and rather unrewarding, under normal conditions (Deetz, 1996). Almost by definition very few people could do it, and the result could easily be superficial. To be able to master two different world views and conflicting epistemological positions at the same time, is no mean achievement in itself.

Another problem concerns the constructed and theory-laden nature of empirical material. Because (complex) empirical material can be perceived and described in such completely different ways, different paradigms may easily produce several empirical objects – not only several interpretations of one and the same object. (See Hassard, 1991, for an illustration.) (An organization perceived as a production system refers, at least in part, to something other than the organization as a culture or a political arena.) It is then hardly a case of "multiple interpretations", but rather of different, albeit overlapping, studies drawing upon the same empirical input on a superficial level (an organization), only while the various studies focus on

---

6   Difficulties in finding unambiguous paradigms in the social sciences are revealed by the fact
    that authors who have tried to determine the paradigms of sociology have come to answers
    ranging anywhere from two to eight (Eckberg and Hill, 1980). Those who have agreed on
    roughly the same number of paradigms often have quite different ideas about what the
    paradigms are based on.

and interpret at least partly different empirical phenomena, more or less disguised by being connected to the reifying and common-sensical label "organization". This is not a prominent problem, given the situational focus chosen in this book, as the various perspectives of the multiple interpretive approach do not guide the empirical work towards investigating different parts of the organization.

Multiple interpretation research thus calls for a balance between two principles and several considerations. We have on the one hand the ideal of scope and heterogeneity. If a researcher masters a broad intellectual spectrum it is definitely a benefit in multiple interpretive research which can overcome some of the limitations indicated here. On the other hand it is probably more usual that the researcher´s paradigmatic base-camp reduces the number of alternative theories that could be absorbed and exploited in a qualified manner. Somewhere along the line the researcher runs the risk of turning amateur, or is forced to spend a lot of time and effort mastering the different vocabularies and their paradigmatic underpinnings, including different political-ethical positions.[7] In addition, with too wide, an intellectual spectrum, it becomes difficult to address the same empirical material.

Another issue concerns the quality of the text produced. Typically the reader is happy if the text hangs together, so that it does not just appear as a collection of different studies lumped together. This normally calls for a certain degree of coherence. On the other hand, a thrilling feature of multiple interpretation is the potential to expand thinking and to learn to interpret material in new ways. This element of transgression, including the aesthetic quality of the unexpected, should encourage considerable space for breaks in the text. Once again, we have two contradictory principles to balance against each other. There is great scope for variation and innovativeness in finding a good solution, due to the theoretical

---

7 However, depending on life trajectory and familiarity with various bodies of literature, there are considerable variations in terms of the interpretive repertoire mastered by various scholars, so it should not be ruled out that some people can combine quite different intellectual frameworks in multiple interpretative research. One possibility in working over a long intellectual distance is to collaborate between researchers with various backgrounds and commitments, and try to learn from the differences.

preferences, the range of interpretive possibilities and the creative skills of the researcher.

The theories and interpretations included in such a balanced text should produce a coherent whole: the reading experience should not be frustrated by violent breaches of style or contradictions in approach. There must be some reason for the appearance of the various interpretations in the same text. One aim could be to include elements of both tension and integration. Alongside interpretations which are mutually supportive or can at least coexist, some room should be left for those that point in other directions. The assembly of theories should encourage both cooperation and competition. It is important that the theories and interpretations pave the way for mutual criticism indicating white spots and debatable interpretations associated with the various perspectives. The texts should complement one another so that the phenomenon is illuminated in a fruitful way, and so that the authority of statements based on different theories can be challenged. The researcher, too, will thus be inspired to self-reflection and self-criticism. (For further ideas on reflexive methodology, see Alvesson and Sköldberg, 1996.)

1.3   On knowledge-constitutive ideals

My approach is based on an interpretive and emancipatory scientific ideal. In most instances emancipatory research is based on an interpretive stance, although the mix of objectivist and interpretive elements varies considerably. (The main exception is structuralist Marxism, which is based on a more objectivist scientific position.) Many interpretive studies have no critical or clearly emancipatory ambitions. Interpretive researchers often assume that there is a social consensus and that individuals voluntarily, as it were, develop meaning and create existential understanding. The aim is often to understand their way of relating to the world around them, without any wish to (critically) interfere with established meanings and ideas. This is usually referred to as the actor-orientated perspective, according to which the researcher seeks to understand the world from the subject's point of view. Here the key issue is the meanings that individuals impute to their own situation and actions. Critical-interpretive research, on the other hand, assumes that social contradictions, and thus basic tendencies to social conflict, do exist, and that power relations and ideologies interfere with the potentially free development of meaning and understanding. Ideas about social reality are regarded as being in part the result of various kinds of dominance relationships, which block awareness and understanding of the possibilities for action. This implies that, in important respects, the way people behave and think is not conscious or grounded in reflection. Thus in my approach I venture beyond the subjects´ own perception of reality. Whereas the interpretive ideal implies a conception of knowledge based on trust, critical emancipatory research views reality and consciousness with suspicion (Rao and Pasmore, 1989).[8]

1.3.1   The Critical Theory project of emancipation

The idea of emphasizing social science as a critical project aiming at stimulating reflection has been expressed most powerfully in Critical Theory, e.g. the Frankfurt School and related authors. It works within the Enlightenment tradition – a tradition originally dedicated to changing institutions such as the Divine Right of Kings, the Church, feudal bondage and prejudiced and superstitious ideas. Its project is to combine a philosophical understanding of the human basis of seemingly divine or superhuman (e.g. scientific) authority with an empirical investigation of contemporary ideas, dogmas and prejudices. A fundamental claim of the proponents of Critical Theory is that social science can and should contribute to the liberation of people from unnecessarily restrictive traditions, ideologies, assumptions, power relations, identity formations, etc., which inhibit or distort opportunities for autonomy, for the clarification of "genuine" needs (priorities) and wants, and thus for greater and lasting satisfaction (Fay, 1987; Fromm, 1976; Habermas, 1971, 1984; Horkheimer and Adorno, 1947; Marcuse, 1964, etc.). The combination of "philosophy" with "empirical investigation" is of fundamental importance. Without philosophical reflection, empirical study can do no more than solidify and legitimise existing dogmas and prejudices. It appears to mirror

---

[8] For comparisons of interpretive and critical research, see e.g. Alvesson and Willmott (1996), Burrell and Morgan (1979), Mumby (1988), Putnam (1983) and Putnam et al. (1993).

solidify and legitimise existing dogmas and prejudices. It appears to mirror reality. But it achieves this effect by disregarding the way behaviour and beliefs (e.g. of employees) are historically and culturally conditioned, and by paying no attention to the way research methodology and instrumentation are involved in producing and sustaining a construction of reality. Central to Critical Theory is the emancipatory potential of reason to reflect critically upon how the reality of the social world, including the construction of the self, is socially produced and therefore open to transformation. Its task is to combine philosophy with social science to facilitate the development of change in an emancipatory direction.

In Horkheimer´s (1937: 220) seminal formulation of Critical Theory, "critical thinking", is understood to be

> motivated by the effort really to transcend the tension and to abolish the opposition between the individual´s purposefulness, spontaneity, and rationality, and those work-process relationships on which society is built. Critical thought has a concept of man as in conflict with himself until this opposition is removed.

This alienated state of consciousness is regarded as irrational, in view of the fact that human beings are the producers, and not simply the receivers or products, of this knowledge. More specifically, Critical Theory challenges the dominant, common sense view of individuals as insular seats of consciousness, which exist independently of the historical processes through which a (bourgeois) sense of being an autonomous individual is generated. In the absence of democratic control of the institutional media, including industry and science, through which the consciousness of individuals is formed, the representation and self-understanding of this consciousness as being free and autonomous is seen as an expression of "false-consciousness". Accordingly, a key objective of Critical Theory is to challenge those forms of knowledge and practice which serve to sustain the illusion of autonomy, and to replace it with a structure of social relations in which "autonomy" is transformed from a pillar of bourgeois ideology into a practical reality.

This books shares with Critical Theory the understanding that the value of science, including social science, resides in its potential to develop conditions (material and symbolic) that are beneficial to human beings. The tradition of the Enlightenment, out of which modern science emerged, holds out the promise of applying the critical powers of reason to exposing and removing contemporary forms of "unreason", superstition and dogmatism. In the field of management, one powerful dogma, challenged by "softer" philosophies of management, has been the belief that man is economically rational, and that Taylorism provides the one best way of designing and managing work. The challenge illustrates another central thesis of Critical Theory: that science – recall Taylor´s description of his principles as "scientific" – can be used to legitimise new dogmas. With reference to the "softer", behavioural approaches to management, Critical Theory enables us to reflect critically upon their scientific credentials and practical limits (for overviews, see Alvesson and Willmott, 1992, 1996). Uncritical acceptance of their understanding of human needs, Critical Theory suggests, amounts to the development of a new dogma which preserves conditions of work that deny, or place socially unnecessary restrictions upon, processes of self-determination.

1.3.2   A critical-interpretive approach

In the present case my approach thus embraces the critical-emancipatory mode of research but with a perhaps more pronounced interpretive orientation than is common among proponents of Critical Theory. In this field a strong theoretical-philosophical orientation tends to give priority to ideas associated with intellectual tradition and theoretical reflection (armchair research), rather than using detailed empirical observations as a significant input in thinking, even less using it as the central element in research. As part of the interpretive empirical orientation of this book I am concerned with meanings and significations of a specific empirical setting.

The interpretive approach means that I am not interested in what empiricists believe to be unambiguous facts, robust data and causal connections. My approach is rather a question of uncovering new meanings, of questioning the apparently obvious. My ambition is to contribute to a kind of conceptual cornucopia, a richly textured open-mindedness, combined with a wide-angled view (cf. Asplund, 1970). A "good" interpretation means indicating a possible and richly textured way of understanding something. The interpretation should distance itself from the obvious and self-evident. Geertz (1973: 20) illuminates the nature of interpretative work well, when he says that, "Cultural analysis is (or should be) guessing at meanings, assessing the guesses, and drawing explanatory conclusions from the better guesses."

The relation between interpretive work and "objective reality", i.e. descriptions of social conditions about which everyone happily agrees, then easily becomes ambivalent.[9] On the one hand conceptual openmindedness requires that conventional ideas about reality are challenged. (This applies in a very high degree to critical research.) A breaking free from the blockages and limitations imposed by taken for granted conditions is thus encouraged. The interest in emancipation gives the interpretation a sharper edge as it aims to inspire critical reflection and rethinking of conventional, dominating ideas and understandings. On the other hand the person receiving the interpretation must feel that it seems to make sense in relation to the empirical material which inspired it. Ideally, readers who are most likely to be confronted by the interpretation – the members of a studied organization or people belonging to a studied more general category (managers, for example) – should feel that it can in some useful way illuminate their own situation. (This does not mean that we should automatically question an interpretation which a reader has rejected; there may well be a political or psychological reason for this, particularly in the case of critical research.) Thus a good interpretation – especially if it is guided by an ambition to liberate – enables both a clarification and a challenge to social perceived reality and to the individual´s existence.

Deetz and Kersten (1983) have developed a model for critical interpretive research that indicates the major elements of this kind of enterprise. It includes (as subgoals) understanding, critique and learning. By under-standing is meant – in terms of our immediate interest – an awareness that organizational arrangements and conditions do not consist of objective, concrete, unchanging structures beyond the reach of human action; rather, they are very human creations, and they are sustained by idea and action patterns which can be changed. Critique means recognizing that

---

9   As Hacking (1982: 61) writes: "There is perfect commensurability, and no indeterminancy of translation, in those boring domains of 'observation' that we share with all people as people. Where we as people have branched off from others as a people, we find new interests, and a looseness of fit between their and our commonplaces."

organizations as social constructions are neither neutral nor value free; instead they reflect asymmetrical power relationships and partisan interests. The political character of social conditions is thus demonstrated. Learning stands for the enhancement of reasoning and thinking capacities, which can pave the way for change. Ways of interpreting and acting that offer alternatives to dominating ideas and concepts open the way to emancipation on the individual or collective level, i.e. to a reflective, autonomous attitude and the change this can engender.

So, the present text is linked to the critical interpretive approach with its emancipatory epistemological position. But it must be emphasized that what comprises liberation, and what can stimulate independent thinking and thus (sometimes) increase the possibilities for action, is neither unambiguous nor self-evident. Like other forms of knowledge, those aiming at emancipation are not without their contradictions and dangers.

1.3.3   Some problems with the ideal of emancipation

A particular difficulty with this research ideal is what Benton (1981) refers to as the "paradox of emancipation", e.g. the insistence on the ideal of autonomy for a group seen by the researcher as victims of manipulation and "false consciousness", and thus not being aware of their own interests. As a result this idea can easily transform the researcher's task into one of creating emancipation and autonomy from above. The researcher acts as an authority liberating people from false authorities.

> If the autonomy of subordinate groups (classes) is to be respected then emancipation is out of the question; whereas if emancipation is to be brought about, it cannot be emancipation. I shall refer to this problem as "the paradox of emancipation". (Benton, 1981: 162)

Of course, the project of emancipation can be expressed in less rigid terms. One could say that people have reflective capacities at the same time that they live in a complex world, in which forces of domination, contingent upon dominant actors and cultural traditions, as well as unintended outcomes of actions and institutional arrangements, all serve to constrain these reflective capacities and thus to limit the scope for considering a broad set of values and logics of action. Critical research may thus provide knowledge which does not try to offer the ultimate way to liberation, but contributes alternative interpretations and inspires a rethinking of fixed self-conceptions and taken for granted ideas and priorities. This would mean a "softer" and more modest approach to emancipation, free from the arrogance of some older versions of Marxist thinking, for example. The purpose is to open up thinking rather than to suggest a specific route to take or a particular solution to embrace.

It is important to be open to the idea that any attempt at emancipation contains within itself at least the seed of its opposite, namely new blockages arising from the fact that criticism is unable to clarify its own limitations. The way we denote a phenomenon is always in a certain sense arbitrary. By singling out certain forms of power and dominance, we are failing to single out others. By characterizing certain phenomena in the vocabulary of power and domination, we discourage the consideration of other less "negative" meanings, for example those associated with concepts and forms of understanding such as leadership. By drawing attention to a particular field of action, we are diverting attention from another. Combating one manifestation of power or ideology can prepare the way for another, perhaps contained within or helped by the very approach adopted. Defining clear boundaries between repression and emancipation can confuse the sometimes uncertain relationship between these two indeterminate entities. I am not implying here, as some postmodernists seem to do, that emancipation or greater individual autonomy are nothing but fictions. But we do have to remember that even projects based on the best intentions should not be protected from suspicion and critical reflection. The arrangement of this book, with its focus on multiple interpretation, offers some defence against what we could call "over-confidence" in emancipation. Foucault is particularly important here.[10]

---

[10] Some fundamental ideas about how to combine the emancipatory ideal in research with an awareness of the risk that the approach can lead to paradoxical results, may be found in Alvesson and Willmott (1996, Ch. 7) and Deetz (1992a).

1.4   Plan of the book

The book is designed as follows. Chapter 2 starts with a discussion of method and focus in (qualitative) organizational studies. After a very brief description of the company in which the studied event takes place, I describe and discuss the event itself – an information meeting for managers, prior to a reorganization. The event is presented as far as possible in uninterpreted form, apart from some factual explanations. But an "uninterpreted" description does not mean that it is a question of "pure" or interpretation-free data (such a thing is hardly possible, for without some form of interpretation no body of empirical material is meaningful). My aim has been to describe the situation with relatively little filtering, and without seeking to pick out any non-obvious aspects or pointing the reader´s understanding in any particular direction. We could perhaps say that the empirical input is "uninterpreted" in the sense that it has been interpreted with the greatest restraint, or only in so far as was necessary to understand the material and make it comprehensible to others.

In the next chapter I introduce some ideas about organizations in terms of social construction, culture, symbolism and ideology, thus outlining a general critical-cultural approach to organizations. On a basis of this approach I then interpret the information meeting as one element in the ongoing creation and recreation of the organization. In Chapter 4 I say something about Foucault´s conception of power, and this provides a basis for a more distinct reading of the empirical data. I then discuss Habermas´s theory of communication, which permits an assessment of the event and the organization itself in terms of systematically distorted communication and communicative rationality. Finally, in Chapter 6, I suggest some important conclusions and compare the three perspectives that I have been using. This chapter also includes a section on resistance and countervailing power. I also discuss some possible advantages of the multiple-interpretation approach applied in the book.

2 Information meeting about a new organization

I am now going to acquaint the reader with the Multi Group, a large Swedish company that is probably fairly typical of its kind. I am not interested primarily in the organization as a whole, nor in its particular field of business; instead I will be looking at an information meeting that was arranged in the company for low and middle-level managers. But before proceeding to the event itself I should like to comment briefly on this choice of focus and make some general methodological-theoretical remarks. After the account of the meeting I will add some specific comments on method – comments which are easier to grasp after the event has been presented.

2.1 From structure and actor to situation and communication

Attempts at understanding organizations have traditionally concentrated on systems and structures, i.e. regularities in social patterns. Organizations were seen as "supra-individual" entities, which are real and accessible to study, separately from the individuals who compose them – as real and accessible, in fact, as those individuals themselves. Organizational variables such as goals, adaptability, formalization, centralization, specialization and technology, together with subsystems such as administration, authority, corporate culture etc., have been thought to capture an organization's character and way of functioning (e.g. Donaldson, 1985; Mintzberg, 1983).

During the last twenty years or so and in opposition to this predominant structuralist-functionalist stance, an approach has been emerging which emphasizes the pivotal role of the actors who populate the organizations and whose particular meanings, situational definitions, goals and intentions represent the core of all organizational activity. The adherents of this view advocate a kind of "methodological individualism", whereby understanding must start from the way individuals interact with their surroundings based on the way they give meaning to their situation. This is often referred to as the actor- or action-orientated approach (Arbnor and Bjerke, 1977; Silverman, 1970). The task of the researcher is to try to see the world from the actor´s point of view.

The main criticism of the first of these approaches is that the organization is reified, given a concrete "thing-like" character.[1] It is also personified, regarded as possessing goals, needs, powers of action etc. – characteristics which many claim to be the preserve of the individual (Johansson, 1990). Czarniawska-Joerges (1994) notes that the most common metaphor for an organization seems to be a super-person. A more general criticism is that the adherents of this approach often adopt inappropriate research procedures ("positivism"), that their language is only tenuously related to the real world it describes, at best glossing over the underlying reality and ignoring the fact that micro-events are the empirical reality of human actors: "Our lives are micro. Whatever human experience is, high points, low points and every other existential dimension, it happens to us in micro-situations" (Collins, 1988: 244).

The criticism raised against the second and generally more actor-orientated view is that it is reductionist; all social phenomena are liable to be seen as the result of the actions of individuals. Hardly any room is allowed for collective or institutional concepts, or for dependency relations or social dynamics at the supra-individual level. Whilst the structuralist-functionalist view is generally criticized for its determinism, the actor-orientated view may be criticized for its voluntarist and idealized view of man. It is sometimes also claimed that micro-orientated research all too easily becomes trivial. Neither approach appears particularly suitable in a critical-

---

[1] The critique of reification can be taken to great lengths, including the suggestion that we should abandon abstract concepts and notions altogether and concentrate on what can be concretized and directly observed. Sandelands and Drazin (1989) have argued, for instance, that the language used in organizational theory is pervaded by general and questionable terms that give a very vague indication of what the words actually refer to. They recommend a reorientation towards more concrete, observable phenomena. Sköldberg (1992) has countered this view, claiming that these authors are guilty of naïve empiricism, whereby only such phenomena as are directly observable may be studied. He points out that action, for instance, which has an inner, mental dimension that cannot be observed, would fall outside the range of what can be studied, if the demand for concreteness and observability as a condition for conceptualization were taken far enough.

emancipatory perspective (cf. Burrell and Morgan, 1979; Knights and Willmott, 1989).

Various attempts have been made to handle the tension between the system and structuralist pole on the one hand and the actor orientation on the other. Among them, we find Giddens´s structuration theory (Giddens, 1979), which is quite popular in the context of organization studies (e.g. Riley, 1983; Weaver and Gioia, 1994; Willmott, 1987); organizational cultural theory, which has become even more popular over the last decade (Alvesson and Berg, 1992); and a number of ideas about focusing on social practices (e.g. Reed, 1985). All these approaches seek to link together the actor and structural levels, or in some other way to release us from the reification/reductionist trap. In terms of micro and macro, we could state that anything micro is seen as "part of the composition of macro; it exists in a macro context, which consists precisely in its ramifications to and from other micro-situational events spread out in space and time" (Collins, 1988: 244).

The overall picture becomes more complicated if we include recent arguments which oppose the idea of the individual as autonomous and consistent, as a bearer of meaning and intentionality. Instead the subject is perceived as constituted by discourses – more or less systematic forms of knowledge, ways of reasoning and definitions of reality entrenched in social and linguistic practices – and as fragmented in relation to the multiplicity of its constituent mechanisms and processes (e.g. Geertz, 1983; Linstead and Grafton-Small, 1992; Shotter and Gergen, 1989; Weedon, 1987). This idea is often launched, like so much else, under the banner of poststructuralism (sometimes labelled postmodernism):

> Language is the central focus of all post-structuralism. In the broadest terms, language defines the possibilities of meaningful existence at the same time as it limits them. Through language, our sense of ourselves as distinct subjectivities is constituted. Subjectivity is constituted through a myriad of what post-structuralists term "discursive practices" practices of talk, text, writing, cognition, argumentation, and representation generally. ... Identity is never regarded as being given by nature; individuality is never seen as being fixed in its expression. (Clegg, 1989a: 151)

It may not perhaps be necessary to dislodge the individual quite so emphatically from the centre – i.e. locating the origin of action and the creation of meaning so strictly outside the individual (in language and discourse) – as has become popular in certain circles, but it does seem reasonable to show at least a little scepticism regarding the consistency and non-ambiguity of the subject in relation to meanings, values, ideals and discourse processes etc. Postmodernists also criticize the idea that systems at the supra-individual level, such as organizations, are well integrated and stable. These, it is claimed, are better understood as fragmented, ambiguous and indeterminate (e.g. Cooper and Burrell, 1988). The significance of themes of ambiguities – inconsistency, variation, uncertainty and con-tradiction – has also been emphasized by researchers who are not best described as postmodernists, e.g. March and Olsen (1976) and Martin (1992). These authors see ambiguities as empirical phenomena – some-times reality is ambiguous, sometimes it is not (or less so); or they see it as a theoretical interest – ambiguity is something worth investigating. They do not proceed, as the postmodernists do, from a privileging of indeterminancy as an ontological assumption which defines the very nature of the subject matter and the paradigmatic position of the researcher. One may push this line of thinking more or less far. If indeterminancy is strongly stressed, empirical work becomes highly problematic and perhaps even almost meaningless, as social reality does not stand still to be portrayed. But weaker and more empirically open and less ontologically "fixed" versions of the indeterminancy/ambiguity issue also are possible. Leaving variation in positioning aside, we thus have a third dimension alongside the structuralist and actor-orientated approaches, and this complicates any solutions which seek to synthesize the two. The "robustness" and coherence of the "system" as well as the human subjects cannot be taken for granted.

I shall be trying to deal here primarily with the structure-actor or micro-macro problem, but one possible way out of this particular dilemma can to some extent at least also reduce the problem of the clarity-indeterminateness dichotomy at the system and subject levels: namely, by starting from a concrete situation in an institutional context. From this angle of approach the micro and macro concepts meet (Knorr-Cetina, 1981). The individual actors are clearly present, while the organizational context finds equally clear expression. The institutional concept is "micro-anchored"; in other words the organization as a context is manifestly linked to the individuals who act within it and to the actions performed (Collins, 1981; Johansson, 1990). By focusing on a particular event the organizational processes are placed firmly in the centre. By adopting this focus we move the spotlight away from any assumptions about the consistent and unambiguous nature (or the opposite) of the actors or the institutional context. Interest can turn on the multiple and indeterminate aspects of organizations and the actions of subjects within them. Of course it is also possible, given a situational focus, to emphasize the actor as central, or to see what is happening as an expression of structural properties. But the general idea is to avoid such reductionism and to take account of several aspects without giving priority to any of them. In the terminology of Kenneth Burke (1989) consideration is given to the act (what took place?), the agent (who performed the act?), the scene (what is the context in which it occurred?), the purpose (why was it done?) and the agency (how was it done?). Even though one may – indeed must – give these different elements different weight and attention in particular cases, any specific element should not be viewed in isolation from the others and allowed to dominate the description and analysis completely. The agent, for example, should be seen as partly shaped by the scene (context) in which he or she acts, while the scene (for example the organization or its environment) is affected by the agent(s) involved and by their acts.

Admittedly, much more is needed than a situational approach, or that which the present book hopes to offer, in order to live up to the challenges of the many versions of postmodernism (and of many other authors not marketing themselves under this label). But I have no intention of giving complete satisfaction to the adherents of that movement. As mentioned in Chapter 1, my purpose is to propose a modest response to some of the points made by postmodernists, grounded in the empirical and theoretical commitments of critical-interpretive research as outlined above.

A particular situation – a meeting, a job interview, a decision process, an event, a problem or task delimited in time and space – can thus be interpreted from different angles of approach. Here, as I explained in the introduction, I have adopted three such perspectives, all of which attempt to overcome the actor/structure dichotomy. They represent different conceptions of the individual and the "nature" of the individual – if indeed it is possible to speak of such a thing.

2.2   The advantages and disadvantages of a situational focus

The drawback of this focus on a particular event is that such events are limited in time, space and representativeness. By tackling themes that are expressed in the situation but which are not solely limited to it either synchronously or diachronously, we risk giving a somewhat selective impression of the organizational context of the phenomenon under study. A certain amount of contextual knowledge is needed, but the suggested focus implies that such knowledge is primarily limited to facilitating an understanding of events but should not be used for far-reaching generalisations inside or outside the organization. The particular event under scrutiny can hardly be used as the only springboard for an account of the whole history of the organization (the broad organizational pattern). Nor does it tell us very much about outcomes or causalities. Moreover, this focus means that the insights and ideas of the organization´s members are not directly exploited to the same extent as a stronger actor-and-meanings orientation would allow.

Nonetheless this angle of approach does have considerable advantages. Interpreting a particular event means acquiring a limited but, one may hope, profound and enlightening insight into certain aspects of the organization of social relations in companies. Of particular importance is that the approach emphasizes the processual aspects. As several authors have suggested there is a need for a sociology and an organization theory of verbs, and to study modes of ordering rather than social order (e.g. Hosking, 1988; Law, 1994). The strongest methodological advantages of the approach here suggested are that it allows for (a) the detailed description of (b) naturally occuring events. A lot of empirical work is in various ways artificial, and too remote from "core empirical phenomena", and may therefore tell us little of what actually goes on in an organizational context.

This problem is especially noticeable when laboratory experiments and questionnaires are used. Laboratory experiments in social science may tell us a lot about how students, the commonly studied group, behave in a simplified and artificial setting, but the relevance of this to an under-standing of more complex processes in "real" organizational life is highly uncertain. Responding to abstract formulations in questionnaires is also far removed from actions, events, feelings, relations, articulations of opinions, etc. as they emerge in everyday life situations. That a person put an X by one of five response option in a questionnaire, may say very little about what that person feels or thinks or how she behaves in the various situations he or she encounters, and which the questionnaire tries to mirror. Questionnaires may be appropriate for getting information about simple issues where the meaning can be standardized and quantified, such as physical length, biological sex, income, formal education, chronological age and year of employment. When it comes to more complex issues, respondents typically interpret the questions and response options in varying ways, which cannot possibly be controlled by the researcher. Social reality and the psychology of people cannot be translated into abstract, standardized forms, and language is not transparent or capabel of functioning as a simple means for the transportation of standardized meaning (Deetz, 1992a; Potter and Wetherell, 1987). Instead, meaning is related to context. Consequently, the questionnaire method can hardly produce reliable knowledge on complex issues. The relationships between the questionnaire issue, the responses to it, and the empirical phenomenon it is supposed to mirror are simply too ambiguous. The critique of question-naire research, for example, in leadership research – an area which overlaps the preoccupations of the present study – has been severe. Several authors have called for a radical reorientation away from the elaboration and measurement of abstract constructs to the analysis of leadership processes as practical accomplishments based on a qualitative approach (Bryman, 1996; Hosking, 1988; Knights and Willmott, 1992).

A qualitative approach is often exclusively or mainly made up of interviews, which are relatively loosely structured and open to what the interviewee feels is relevant and important to talk about. This approach has the benefit that a richer account of the interviewee´s experiences, ideas and impressions may be considered and documented. Interviewees are less constrained by the researcher´s preconceptions, and there is space for negotiation of meanings so that some level of mutual understanding may be achieved, making the data richer and more meaningful for research purposes. Nevertheless, there are some serious problems connected with interviews. As Silverman (1989, 1994) has stressed, the value of interview statements is in many cases limited in terms of their capacity to reflect reality "out there" as well as the subjective world of the interviewee. This is partly because the statements are liable to be determined by the situation, i.e. they are related to the interview context rather than to any other specific "experiential reality", and partly because they are affected by the available cultural scripts about how one should normally express oneself on particular topics (see also Potter and Wetherell, 1987; Shotter and Gergen, 1989, 1994, etc.). An interview is a social situation, a kind of conversation – and what is said there is far too context-dependent to be seen as a mirror of what goes on outside this specific situation – in the mind of the interviewee or in the organization "out there". Interviewees speak in accordance with norms for talk and interaction in a social situation. The research interview is thus a scene for a conversation rather than a simple tool for the collection of "data". Silverman (1985, 1989) objects to the naïve and rather romantic view of research, which believes that genuine experiences can be captured with the help of unstructured interviews. He claims that "only by following misleading correspondance theories of truth could it have ever occurred to researchers to treat interview statements as accurate or distorted reports of reality" (Silverman, 1985: 176). Like people in general, people placed in an interview context are not just "truth tellers" or "informants", but "use their language to do things, to order and request, persuade and accuse" (Potter and Wetherell, 1987: 32). Although the authors quoted, and other discourse and conversation analysts, probably underrate the potential of the interview method and the capacities of the interview subjects, the drawbacks and risks of the method are obvious in the type of investigation we are discussing here, which involves aspects which interviewees may be unaware of, or which for other reasons they find difficult to articulate. As we shall see in Chapter 4, we have particularly good reason to avoid depending on interviews, when we adopt a Foucault-inspired approach.

A study design focusing on the observation of a naturally occurring event avoids – or, more usually, reduces – the researcher´s dependence on the perceptions, understandings and accounts of respondents. Interviews, or less formal, and, more spontaneous, talks between researcher and informants, are usually an important complement to this method. In this case the constraints and difficulties associated with statements produced in an interview context are counteracted.

An ambitious alternative to relying solely on a set of interviews is to carry out an ethnography, which typically employs several methods, of which the most important are (participant) observations over a long period of time, and interviews. An ethnography often includes the study itself as well as reports of a set of events/situations which have been observed by the researcher. The situational focus may thus be a crucial part of an ethnography. In fact, the situation which is focused on in this book was observed as part of an ethnographic study which also included other observations of a variety of situations, interviews, analysis of cultural artifacts, historical documents, etc. The focus of this ethnography however, was not the part of the company which was the scene for the event in the account that follows, but a division within the company to which only some of those present at the scene belonged.

The situation stands on its own as an object of study, but the ethnographic work which forms the context of the observation and documentation provides the researcher with sufficient background knowledge and pre-structured understanding to grasp the preconditions of what is happening. Local knowledge facilitates the interpretations and reduces the risk of misunderstanding and over interpretation.

Another important problem connected with studies based on a set of (open) interviews, but especially with an ethnography, which is avoided or at least reduced in studies with a situational focus, concerns the possibility of reproducing the empirical material in the published text. The output of a set of (open) interviews and long-term observer participation which aspires to describe a complex reality, is always difficult to transcribe in research texts. We have every reason to be wary of the realistic or naturalistic mode of writing "in which the production of understanding and construction of the text are hidden by a form of account that purports to present what is described simply ´as it appeared´; this being treated, with more or less conviction, as ´how it is´" (Hammersley, 1990: 606). Along with a whole host of other problems, briefly indicated above – for instance that interview answers are often partially determined by the interviewer, and that the interviewees are inclined to follow scripts allowing themselves to appear moral and rational – the presentation of the material inevitably becomes a question of selection and discretion. This is in particular a problem of broader studies utilizing extensive interview and observation material. Only a very small portion of all that has been said by the interviewees, or that has been observed over a period usually of several weeks or months, can be reproduced in a publication or even fully considered in an analysis. If, let us say, 25 interviews, are conducted, taped and carefully transcribed, this will easily produce 500 pages of transcripts. Of that material perhaps 5-10 per cent, at most, may be presented directly in a research book, and less than 1 per cent in a journal article. It becomes necessary to be highly selective in what is emphasized in the analysis and documented in the text. In order to present a coherent description and analysis the rich varieties typical of interview accounts must be treated with a certain bias, so that the inconsistencies and ambiguities presented to the reader are kept to a reasonable level.[2] To achieve a text that gives a good account in the sense of "mirroring" a reality represented in all this empirical material may be very difficult – even if we disregard the problem of treating language as though it stood in a one-to-one relationship to other phenomena.

With the approach suggested here the situation is quite different. To produce an account of a specific, isolated event is not without its problems; we can hardly expect a perfect reflection of a clearly defined episode. But it is not quite so difficult to produce an account that will be recognized and accepted as providing adequate coverage by people who took part in the event and whose memories are good. In our present case this task was also made easier by the fact that the essence of the information meeting consisted of words (talk). To reproduce words in words (a text) is not too difficult in terms of representation, even though the interpretive element is significant and some information disappears on the way. Consequently the purely random – and thus fictive – element is not necessarily so noticeable. In saying this I do not mean to understate the problem of reproducing the empirical material in the present case, but simply to point out that it is less evident than it is in certain other contexts – for instance in studies which are based on a number of interviews and/or long-term observations and which also purport to throw light on a broader organizational spectrum.

---

2 The problems associated with the practice of using categories to order empirical material, thus coping with variety and "rationalizing" the processing of data, are analysed by Potter and Wetherell (1987). The authors show that this practice of reducing variation draws upon selective readings and the suppression of diversity and inconsistencies. The practice is often necessary for reasons of space and efficiency, but it highlights part of the problem of working with a large body of empirical material.

This last method necessitates so much selection that the relationship between the empirical reality and its subsequent presentation in a research report may well be tenuous, to say the least, and the researcher´s selection of the empirical material presented wholly determines the final text.

Another advantage of studying particular concrete events (naturally occurring interaction) is that these easily lend themselves to multiple interpretations. All kinds of empirical material can of course be given this treatment, but the theoretical control exerted for instance in interviews (what questions are asked and what answers are followed up?) or ethnographic studies (which of all the possible observations are registered?) is much stronger, and can hardly avoid favouring or disfavouring the different theories (interpretive repertoires). It is, of course, impossible to collect or – to use a metaphor better suited to empirical work – to construct and (selectively) present extensive material which is not strongly structured by a theoretical framework (possibly in the sense of a set of taken for granted ideas), the idiosyncrasies of the researcher associated with sex, age, life history, etc. and, in the case of interviews, the interaction dynamics constructing the interview situation, whether the researcher wants it or not (Alvesson and Sköldberg, 1996). Such a construction process is less active and less salient in the approach suggested here, as data are not constructed in interviews, questionnaires or laboratory settings where the researcher must actively produce responses for something to happen. Arguably, the "bias" in describing the event in focus in this book is relatively weak. Given the ideal of multiple interpretations, it is also desirable to be able to give a reasonably brief account of the empirical material, and thus to allow scope for different interpretations; concentrating on a specific event could perhaps encourage a certain brevity in the account. These advantages should not be overrated, however, as the suggested link between limited focus and multiple interpretation is pretty tenuous.

2.3   On this study

The study of organizational processes as manifest in concrete events can bring out many aspects of interest and importance – and can do so as well if not better than the more traditional analysis of stable, objectified and reified structures.[3] It can also add something significant to cultural studies, which tend to give priority to relatively stable and coherent sets of shared meanings, values and ideas. At least, the detailed study of situations which illustrate significant elements of organizational life could be an important complement to the more traditional kinds of studies – whether structural, behavioural or cultural in orientation.

Not all events, social situations or sequences of events are suitable for intensive study. What are the criteria for choosing a particular situation in organization research for such a project? The chosen situation should be rich in content, in the sense that it touches on important themes in the organization such as hierarchical relations, legitimacy, ideology, principles of control, leadership, group formation and/or conceptions of rationality. Some meetings and events may be concerned primarily with technical matters, so that interesting organizational themes will not feature prominently (or are anyway very difficult to interpret). Another important point is that the situation should not be too complex, unclear or ambiguous. It must allow the researcher to make interpretations that appear reasonable. A situation that is very difficult to unpack will lead too readily to very speculative and uncertain interpretations. Here we might of course wonder, to whom does the empirical phenomenon appear unclear or difficult to interpret? A genius may not experience it in the same way as a more ordinary researcher. (Consider Freud, and the empirical material with which he worked.) A third criterion is that it should be possible to present the situation in such a way that the reader can make his or her own interpretations and evaluate the conclusions and claims of the researcher – and possibly use the case for research purposes other than those of the author. This brings up the the whole question of authority in the relationship between author and reader. One could say that (social) science has a problem with authority in the sense that the reader of the the research report simply has to rely on the scientific authority of the researcher. Research texts often appear authoritative, by placing the reader in an inferior position relative to the researcher-authority, who can claim familiarity with all the "data". If the empirical material were presented in

---

3   It should be noted, however, that several recent approaches to organizational structure treat these less "rigidly" than has traditionally been the case, incorporating material, social and cultural aspects (cf. Fombrun, 1986; Ranson et al., 1980).

an open way, this would immediately reduce the problem of the researcher´s authority, i.e. it would mean that the reader did not have to rely so entirely on the researcher, but could check interpretations and validity claims against the empirical material.[4] Two issues are involved here. One concerns selectivity in the account; as noted above, it is a clear advantage if the author does not have to be very selective in the account but can present it in its entirety. Another concerns the amount of background information about the setting that is needed to understand what is going on. Many situations involve action and talk which, before they can be adequately grasped, call for a lot of local pre-structured understanding, in addition to general cultural background knowledge. This, of course, reduces the reader´s chances of reacting constructively to the text and being critical of the author´s interpretations and/or calling for a lot of authorial explanations, all of which tends to create greater asymmetry between author and reader.

I feel that the information meeting described in detail below fulfils these criteria relatively well. I have chosen it for intensive study using a multiple interpretation approach from quite a large number of situations observed and documented in the course of three ethnographic studies made over a period of several years. The meeting touches upon a number of important themes, allowing for plenty of interpretations – which is the main reason for venturing to base a book upon it. As I see it, the meeting illustrates particularly well how "organizing" sometimes, one may even say, frequently, operates in contemporary bureaucracies and, more specifically, how relations between superiors and subordinates are created and recreated.

The meeting is about communication (in a broader cultural sense rather than a technical or factual). More generally, communication can be seen as

---

[4] The problem of the researcher's authority is only reduced in the sense of downplaying the extent to which the reader has to trust the researcher without being able to check whether or not the empirical claims are reasonable. The reader can directly evaluate the empirical material and is not forced simply to trust that the researcher is providing a fair and informed empirical account. On the other hand, the approach suggested here may reduce the legitimacy of the researcher, as the reader has an excellent opportunity to challenge the interpretations offered. The authority of the researcher may thus be questioned more easily, compared to researchers relying on the claim of "having been there" – which is the basis for the anthropologist's claim to authority – or of having done a fair bit of number-crunching and producing statistical tables. In these last cases the reader is in a weak position for evaluating the empirical basis of the research results.

a crucial aspect of organizations, something to which the growing corpus of literature on the subject of organization and communication can testify (see, e.g. Allen et al., 1993; Deetz, 1992a; 1995; Jablin et al., 1987; Putnam and Pacanowsky, 1983). It is important to note that communication should be regarded not simply as the transmission of information, but in a wider sense to include the very creation of meaning and understanding.

> In an organizational context, communication is the process through which meaning is created and, over time, sedimented. Communication – as an institutional form – articulates meaning formations which, when habitualized over time, provide the background of common experience that gives organization members a context for their organizing behavior. Communication is thus not simply the vehicle for information, but rather is the very process by which the notion of organizing comes to acquire consensual meaning. Organizing is therefore continuously created and recreated in the act of communication among organization members. (Mumby, 1988: 14-15)

Thus communication does not simply reproduce the organization and pass it on; it also creates it. Communication and organizing are thus in a certain sense facets of the same phenomenon – an idea that was crucial to my choice of the information meeting as the point of departure for the present study.

An interest in the communicative and cultural aspects of the exercise of power and of power relations thus motivates a focus on organizational processes, and the study of a particular event then seems a natural choice. Geertz (1973) points out that anthropologists do not study villages; they study in villages. In the same way this book represents a study *in* an organization rather than *of* an organization. The distinction is not razor sharp, but it is important to remember that understanding an organization does not necessarily mean focusing on the organization as a whole or any formally defined part of it. It may be possible to understand what goes on in organizations and workplaces better by concentrating on clearly defined concrete phenomena, as opposed to the formal frameworks and aggregated activities that together can be said to make up the organization. This also makes it easier to avoid reifying the studied object. So it is claimed, at any rate, in the growing body of criticism directed at macro-sociology – in which is included much traditional organizational theory (Collins, 1981;

Sandelands and Drazin, 1989; Sandelands and Srivatsan, 1993; Silverman, 1975).

The decision to emphasize a specific situation and to study it in detail does not mean that the researcher can neglect everything else in the local setting. Normally some kind of background knowledge of the broader aspects of the local organizational context is called for. In addition some time is needed for exploration, to find situations that lend themselves to this kind of study. An ethnographical study may be necessary. In the present case, the ethnography of which the observation of the situation focused in this book was an offspring, provided sufficient local knowledge – an understanding of local practices and patterns of meaning – to allow a fairly good appreciation of the level of meaning for those present. The risk that the study would express the attitudes of a "tourist" rather than an anthropologist was thus negligable. (The situation and organizational context were hardly an example of an alien, exotic setting; rather they exhibited cultural patterns which to a considerable extent characterize the societal culture of which I, the researcher, am also a part and am familiar with from other research projects and experiences of organizational life.) The approach could be described as a partial ethnography, combining a broader base of knowledge with a rather narrow empirical focus.

Only a few, short interviews on the reactions of the participants in the specific situation studied were held, however. To be honest, this was up to a point a mistake, and was due to the fact that it took some time before I looked more carefully at the account and decided to make it the topic of an intensive study. However, and more importantly, there are, as remarked earlier in this chapter, good reasons to question what interviews can really reflect in terms of the "true" meanings which people attribute to various phenomena. Here I could add that it seems as though most of the (relatively few) organization studies that concentrate on intensive interpretations of a particular situation include only marginal interview statements about the participant´s views on the matter; rather, they rely on the researcher´s ability, given a sufficient degree of ethnographically produced local knowledge, to interpret what is expressed in terms of the exercise of power (see Knights and Willmott, 1987, 1992; Mumby and Stohl, 1991; Rosen, 1985).

Bearing these various considerations in mind, let us now turn to the empirical material.

2.4   A short description of the Multi Group

Once again I must point out that my main focus of interest is not the organization which provides the context of the study; it is rather a particular event that occurred within that organization. The information meeting – and thus also an important organizational process – can be understood in broad outline without a lot of background information. A short description of the company will thus suffice. (All names and some other insignificant facts have been changed to preserve the anonymity of the company and the people involved.)

DMT, the organization studied, is an independent operation in the Multi Group, a major Swedish-based international industrial company. The organization includes the oldest parts of the company, which date back to the beginning of the century, as well as other units established or acquired later. DMT is engaged in the manufacture and sale of tools and other products for industry, often in small batches. The organization employs about 3,000 people who were divided at the time of the study among seven units, roughly the equivalent of divisions.

The Multi Group has a long history which, together with a series of earlier successes, particularly in the international arena, has given many employees a certain pride in being part of it. They recognize that their company is well known and has a reputation for quality. Staff turnover at the white-collar and managerial levels has been traditionally low. This is partly because the company has looked after its personnel, according to informants, and partly because certain categories of employees have developed skills for which there is little demand in other companies, and this means that the market for their labour is largely internal. Large parts of the organization have always been and to some extent still are located in one place, Northtown. The traditional core of the company´s operations has always been here, but during the last decade there has been some expansion and relocation elsewhere; there is some anxiety amongst the staff that other parts of operation will also be moved. Rumours of relocations and cutbacks come and go. To some extent the market for DMT´s products is a stagnating one, and the top management of Multi has been dissatisfied with the profitability of DMT, although the company as a whole is doing well. A series of rationalisations and reorganizational measures have been introduced, and some staff cutbacks implemented. As is customary in Sweden, where labour market legislation and tradition make it difficult to lay people off, this has been effected mainly by natural wastage and as a result of agreements of various kinds. Recent recruitment on the white-collar side has been low. The average age of the office staff has been rising, and many of these employees have been with the company for a long time. There is a mood of mild depression among large groups of staff, but more "positive" sentiments such as "corporate pride" can also be heard.

For a long time there has been talk of decentralization in the company, and some measures have also been realized. Certain units are expected to function more independently, to foster greater profit responsibility. One result of this is that the middle levels are conscious of a bigger distance between low-level units and the higher levels in the hierarchy. A middle manager of fairly advanced age puts it like this:

> Now you can´t go any higher than your own boss, as the units have been made smaller, and there´s been a lot of delegation downwards. Previously someone up there (HQ) might have something to say about things. Now distances upwards in the company are much greater. The top managers are just names to us here.

Twenty years or so ago, according to interviewees, top management had a much higher profile. Now it seems to have other priorities which it sets above employee contact and communication within the company. The feeling of distance between top management and the lower and middle levels is illustrated by the following snippet of conversation overheard at a coffee break between a plant manager and one of his team:

> I met Fritz – he couldn´t possibly be on his way to a DMT management meeting, as he was wearing a sports jacket and no tie.

His listeners laughed. It should be mentioned that the speaker was wearing a jacket himself, and no tie, while the the Managing Director of DMT, whose style the joke implicitly referred to, is a well-dressed gentleman who drives an expensive car – points that are not missed in a company like this, where style in dress is generally rather restrained and the general furnishings and so on are pretty Spartan. The joke reflects the perceived difference in social reality between different levels. Meetings connected with the DMT 1,2,3 project (a major programme of change) are very much a top-management preserve, particularly that of the MD of DMT who initiated it and now runs it, and they symbolise a culture markedly different from that of the day-to-day world of middle management in manufacturing.

This marked hierarchical segmentation, particularly in relation to higher levels, is partly due to the nature and size of the operations and to the attempts to emphasize the relative independence of the various units. But the sense of hierarchy – perceived distance between levels – was also reinforced by the experiences of markedly detached and thus hierarchy-enhancing behaviour of many top managers. This is unlikely to be intentional and their behaviour can rarely be described as authoritarian, but it hardly contradicts the general impression that top management lives in a world of its own.

> They sit in splendid isolation in large rooms behind closed doors. Not the sort of place you barge into just like that. It´s another world. Quiet corridors. They never come down here or go round talking to people. They meet their own immediate bosses, but they never come down and sit with us. That´s what the staff would like. Everybody says so: Just think if he could come down here and mingle, make a habit of it, sit in with us for a bit instead of always sending for us to his office. My boss was always sent for. Martin (the head of DMT) never came down here. They may sometimes put in an appearance, but if so it´s after we´ve gone home. If one of them´s ever spotted here, it´s certainly noticed. (Unit manager´s secretary.)

Nevertheless this same Martin, who we will soon be meeting again, is regarded by many people as a man with plenty of ideas and the ability to make changes. Someone suggested, though, that he talks more than he acts. Quite a few interviewees talked about a certain sluggishness in the organization, but without offering any shared opinion about its causes or what could be done about it.

After this brief description of the organization – the context for my study of the information meeting – I hope the reader feels prepared to move on. No more preamble is necessary; let us instead proceed to the meeting itself.

2.5 The information meeting[5]

Most people have been waiting a long time for this moment. The participants have been told that they will be given information about the new organization. In the two months during which the company has been under our eye, the staff has shown frustration at the general lack of information about the shape of the expected changes. Questions to which people have been seeking answers include: what is going to happen to individual employees, what section will I belong to, will we be given new assignments and what is going to happen to the Northtown area? Expectation and tension permeate the atmosphere. Various rumours have been going round about the future. Some people have received advance information, others have not. Now, however, everything is finally going to come out into the open. The meeting is important to different people in

---

[5] The first draft for this section was written by Ivar Björkman, who was also the observer at the meeting. Notes were made during the meeting and were supplemented afterwards. It should be noted that the theoretical bias which always accompanies observation – expectations and frames of reference influence how we perceive events – did not in this case originate to any great extent in the perspectives which were subsequently brought to bear on our analysis of the material. The project in which Björkman and I were jointly involved (and of which the observations at the information meeting are a biproduct) was not directed to any great extent by critical perspectives (our approach was a more general anthropological one). There are both advantages and disadvantages to this procedure, compared to the case in which the theoretical perspectives used in interpreting the material are adopted already at the observation and documentation stage. The advantage of our method is that the material is not structured according to the theoretical perspectives adopted, which means that these last do not automatically dominate the interpretation as well, and that other theoretical perspectives can be brought to bear freely at the interpretation stage. The drawback in our present case is that the material documented in this manner was not the result of the sensitivity to important dimensions which the perspectives applied in the study could have offered. It is possible that important aspects of the empirical material could have been better documented if these perspectives had steered the observations, and that even more qualified interpretations would then have been possible.

Finally I should add that the documentation is presented in this section in its entirety. The reader thus has access to the same written material on the meeting that I myself have had. (On the other hand I do possess some background information, but this is not essential to an interpretation of the meeting.)

different ways. Top management and the managers who have been called to the meeting are all directly affected in one way or another. Many are anxious because changes have now been made in the organizational plans which were presented earlier. A few months ago employees could read in the organization´s personnel magazine that "our goal is that units X, EDB and Y will become independent companies as from next year".

Today, however, it will be revealed that this structure will not be adopted. The reason for the changes have not been made clear, but it is obvious that the earlier plan for structural changes was decided in something of a hurry. For example, at a top management group meeting for EDB a month earlier it became clear that the management of DMT had not yet decided what products would be covered by EDB, or whether EDB as an organizational unit would be part of the new organization. This was a piece of information which it had not been envisaged would be presented to the EDB people at that time, but which leaked out and aroused strong reactions.

The reorganization which is due to be announced has been initiated and led by John Martin, MD of the DMT business sector for the last two years. At a marketing conference a year ago he promised to "double the sector´s turnover in three to five years".

The DMT 1,2,3 project (a broadly based rationalisation scheme) is one of the tools which will be employed in an attempt to realise a number of ambitious objectives, one of which is to fulfil Martin´s promise. At the present meeting one of the most important cornerstones of the project will be put in place, namely how the organization will be structured within the newly formed DMT.

The meeting has been fixed for a weekday afternoon and is expected to take two hours. The chosen location was built with just this type of activity in mind. It is designed rather like a cinema; it is equipped for comfort and the acoustics are excellent. There are more participants at the meeting than there are seats to hold them, so extra chairs have been placed in the aisles. The number of participants corresponds exactly to the number invited (so exactly that the unexpected presence of the observer meant that the speakers had to play a kind of musical chairs as there was always one seat too few). In other words everyone who was supposed to come, came. The observer´s previously unannounced participation resulted in another incident, which illustrates the tight control over attendance: he was approached by the DMT personnel manager, inquiring in some puzzlement who he was. The managers who have been convened, about a hundred in all, come from the various units in DMT which are affected. All the Northtown managers are present, while other units are represented by senior managers only. Many people sit with note-books at the ready, to record what is said. Almost all are men. The few women present are all personnel managers.

The meeting is chaired by John Martin. He is dressed in an apparently casual but expensive style. Instead of a jacket he is wearing a dark blue cardigan which matches his trousers. And he has a matching silk tie to complete the overall effect. He began his career with the organization by running the sales company in Holland before becoming head of DMT. Before that he worked for a company which manufactures and sells articles of clothing. By starting out in a sales company before getting assignments on the home front, he has up to a point followed the traditional route to a top job at Multi. At the same time, though, he has not had to take the usual long route up through the company, but was promptly promoted to a top job. Internal promotion is more common in the company. Some of the managers interviewed had their own views on this.

> Martin doesn't know our business properly. He's spent most of his life selling socks and underwear.

Before the meeting starts, Martin paces restlessly around. He opens a window and says "Christ, it's hot in here", walks a little more and continues: "Now we'll have to lock the door because soon there won't be any seats left." When everybody has arrived, he takes up his stand by the overhead projector. He starts by asking a question: "Why are you here? Well, it's because you're all managers at DMT."

Throughout his presentation he uses the overhead projector as an aid. He repeats the text on the overhead picture. The pictures are highly professional. There are no scribbled diagrams. The first picture shows the DMT 1,2,3 project and asks a question: What would be the best possible way of organizing DMT? Martin puts the same question to the meeting. Nobody answers, and no answer is really expected. The next picture shows the graph describing developments since World War Two, divided into the periods 1945-65, 1965-85, 1985-1990 and 1990 onwards. The vertical axis shows the increase in volume in Swedish kronor, while the horizontal axis represents time. Martin says that in the first period it was just a question of selling, it was a seller´s market: "It must have been wonderful to have been MD then." The company had no difficulty in making money after the war. The lines on the graph point upwards without interruption. In the next period, 1975-85, development flattens out. "Markets were generally stagnant, it was a buyer´s market." From 1985-90, the development curve moves slightly up again. "In this period we conducted a strategic review and came to the conclusion that the cobbler should stick to his last. We also became convinced that we were going to grow." At this point Martin raises his voice noticeably: "Both by increasing market shares and by acquiring competitors. Today, we´re on the way." Once again he raises his voice: "The 2 in DMT 1,2,3 stands for doubling our turnover." He has an original and dramatic style. Sometimes, he raises his voice to a pitch not unlike a sergeant addressing new recruits when he wants to emphasize something. His charisma is reinforced by extreme variations in his tone of voice. He likes to speak clearly and simply. Making money, getting bigger, thinking positively, seeing life as a challenge – all these ideas keep coming back again and again. To some extent he can also distance himself from his role as managing director by making jokes.

The next picture to appear shows the organization´s development in three phases as part of Multi. Before 1968, the Multi Group consisted of one company plus some wholly owned sales companies. In 1968 Multi split into three product companies – Water Power, DMT and Vehicles. This organizational form was retained until 1980 when it was decided to transform the product companies into profit centres, that is to say they also became responsible for sales through the sales companies. "Today we have three business centres, one of which is DMT."

The next picture shows DMT today. The overhead display shows a 5.5 billion kronor (about USD 1 billion) turnover and production in 17 countries. At this point Martin emphasizes that Northtown is no longer the global centre of manufacturing, however it is nonetheless the world centre for DMT. By this he means that although the Northtown area was previously the centre for manufacturing in DMT, even further back it was the centre for the entire Multi organization, but this is no longer the case.

The rules of the manufacturing game are different today, and so is the real world. Because Northtown is the world centre for DMT, this is where the managers of the business sector are to be found. This is where the major decisions are taken, as today´s meeting illustrates.

Martin then embarks on the business concept and strategy which are shown on the next picture. The strategy is that DMT should be number one in every individual business segment. "Why?", he asks. The first reason, he thinks, is psychological; people are more inspired by trying to be number one rather than number two. However, in Martin´s opinion the most important reason is something else:

> If we are number one, then we can always be as good as or even better than our competitors. We have more money to spend on being as good as or better than our competitors. At the start of the 1,2,3 project we asked you: Can we do better? The answers suggested (1) that we are too slow in responding to market demand, (2) our areas of responsibility are unclear, (3) we spend too little time on long-term planning, and (4) our decision process is too slow. When we asked you, this is what you said.

This rhetorical technique, with questions and answers, is continued as the next picture comes up:

> How are we going to organize ourselves to meet the future? What do the customers want and what do the employees want? The personnel want responsibility, interesting jobs, influence, results and the opportunity to develop. We must have a fast-moving and flexible organization and this means we must have a decentralised organization.

As he talks about the messages on the screen Martin harps continually on decentralization.

The next picture shows the new organization structure in a horizontal dimension, with Multi at the far left, followed by the three business sectors, with the division level in DMT to the right and finally the Business Line within each division. The spaces in the Division and Business Line areas are not filled in. Step by step the audience are given information about what is going to happen. This method of drawing the organizational chart horizontally is also applied in other contexts, for example in the presentation of the new organization in the DMT news sheet. The horizontal picture presents an organizational "reality" which agrees with the message that the decentralization of the organization is desired.

Martin calls the next picture a philosophical puzzle. It indicates the philosophy which is at the root of the way the company organizes itself, some fundamental ideas about what determines the structure of the organization. Every piece of the puzzle has a message, and together "the pieces signal the overriding ideas governing the way we organize ourselves". The puzzle, which consists of four pieces, sends the following messages. Puzzle-piece 1: Every product should be given the best possible conditions for development. Puzzle-piece 2: Every division is an independent company. Puzzle-piece 3: Business lines are built around products. Puzzle-piece 4: Short decision paths, decentralized responsibility for profits. The picture shows the various pieces separated from each other. But it is clear that they fit together, that they are made for each other and that together they form a whole. At the same time the picture shows that other pieces can be added to these four, but the four basic pieces are the very core of the puzzle, constituting the overriding concept.

Let us for a moment enter the mind of a member of the audience, as this picture gives him or her an opportunity to summarize the basis for the reorganization. If these pieces are not included, then it is not possible to build on them. Every future organizational piece of the puzzle depends on these four pieces. This gives a feeling of certainty – the puzzle pieces must guide future action. The form of the puzzle also suggests that the organization is not complete, and that it would be possible to go on building on it for ever since it has no boundaries.

Martin now shows a new picture with the empty organizational spaces filled in; he tells the audience the names of the three new divisional heads. One by one these people stand up. Others, in staff positions at DMT, also stand up and are introduced. All these people are sitting in the front row.

The important thing, Martin stresses, is that people are to decide as much as possible themselves. He does not mention any specific individual or group, but the remark could be interpreted as meaning each one of us, within ourselves, has a force or a drive that should be tapped.

When he comes to the next picture, Martin says: "What are we going to do next?"

1. Business responsibility from 1 April.
2. Appoint managers who report to the divisional head at end of March.
3. Advertise all positions at beginning of April.
4. Appointments in mid-May.
5. Joint functions retained in present form to year-end.

When he comes to point 3, Martin encourages everyone to apply for the new positions so that job rotation can start. Rotation is encouraged because, it is assumed, it makes for a more flexible organization. Individuals extend their knowledge and competence, which makes it easier for them to move around in the organization. Although this applies officially to all positions, it does not in fact do so. Those who are affected are the administrative, marketing and technical personnel at Northtown, and any other non-factory staff. Other personnel are not affected at all. This is something which was not mentioned at the meeting, except in response to a question that was asked by a member of the audience (see below).

The next picture emphasizes "Business as usual", that is to say the customers are not supposed to notice that a reorganization is under way; this is an internal matter.

Before taking a break there is a chance to ask questions. Someone in the audience asks whether all units are to advertise their appointments. The female personnel manager responds by saying that the questioner´s own unit is not affected by this item, and she adds: "You don´t need to feel worried." The questioner retorts: "I´d like to see it as an opportunity and not as a cause for anxiety" (laughter). Martin comments: "It´s nice that someone can make jokes about the organization."

In the break refreshments are served – fruit juice. Everybody collects outside the hall; people stand about in small groups, mostly discussing what has been said but there is some talk about other matters. People say "hello" to those they know, and perhaps exchange a few words. The break lasts 15 minutes and ends when the doors to the hall are opened and people begin to move back inside.

After the break it is time for the three divisional heads to introduce themselves and their new organizations. First comes Walter Lundberg, who is responsible for Industrial Equipment. He has a considerably calmer and softer style than Martin. He says a little about who he is and what his last position was. He displays on a board a list of points as follows:

1.   Manufacturing, marketing and sales of the division.
2.   Customers.
3.   Manufacturing in (cities).
4.   Number of employees, including sales companies.
5.   Turnover.
6.   Head office.

These points are on the left. The relevant expenditure figures are on the right. Walter goes through the points and comments on them. Underlying the screen projection, in the background, is a map of the world, which suggests to the audience that the organization is operating in a global perspective. The next picture shows what the organization looks like. Just like previous organizational charts, this one is horizontal. The organizational break-down is built up in the same way in all three divisions. Here, too, Lundberg runs through the details on the overhead display. To conclude his presentation, he says: "As an old hand in production, I think this is going to be fun."

The next speaker is Hans Beronius, who is responsible for Extra Equipment. His presentation style appears tense and curt, or as one of the participants commented afterwards in an interview: "His manner seems to be stuck on artificially." Rumour has it that Beronius and Martin do not really get on. When Beronius says that the division is to be centred on Antwerp, Martin can be heard saying: "What´s he doing now – pulling rabbits out of a hat?" – which could be interpreted as a joke, but it may also signal a personal tension between the two men. Another interpretation of this comment might be that the question of the division being brought together in Antwerp is a sensitive one. It will mean the loss of 40 or 50 jobs in Northtown, something which is being currently negotiated with the union. Beronius uses two pictures similar to those shown by Lundberg, although the data is naturally different. Beronius repeats what is written on the screen, adding a few brief comments.

The next speaker is Gunnar Johnsson, who is responsible for Building Tools. His style appears decisive, focusing on clear objectives. His decisiveness shows in his forceful manner. As one of the employees at the Northtown factory put it: "He seems to be in a hurry, he rushes past with long strides." Previously, Johnsson was head of Baluba, an independent company in the Multi organization, and in this he differs from the two other divisional managers who come from units in DMT. Johnsson pushes his own line, for example by using his own overheads showing the Baluba product range. But he also shows some of the same type of pictures as the others. His division includes an agency for the product range, and Martin chips in: "There´s something special about working with consumer products at Multi. Are snow blowers having a good season?" This question is directed at someone in the audience who is responsible for consumer snow blowers (for clearing paths), and the joke is that there has not been much snow this year. Back from the hall comes the riposte: "You can use them for clipping your hedges" (laughter). These consumer products do not fit in with the Multi strategy, something that both Martin and Johnsson bring up. But apparently top management has said that the company is to continue selling them. Johnsson adopts Lundberg´s punchline and says "It´s going to be fun working with the new organization". Martin points out that this particular division, EDB and Baluba, has an obligation to make even more money. "Your turnover is a billion kronor at the moment, and you´ve promised two billion, Gunnar. So now I´m going to sit back, smoke a cigar, and see how things go." Then Martin says: "Responsibility, and being able to measure results, that´s what makes things fun."

After Johnsson´s presentation, there is an opportunity to ask questions. Two are raised. One is about the location of the Building Tools head office – will it be in Northtown or somewhere else? Johnsson says this has not been decided yet, and he must talk to everybody involved first. Martin comments: "Everything has good and bad sides, that´s something you´ve always got to be prepared for." The other question is about how managers are to inform the sales companies. Martin and the female personnel manager reply that tomorrow morning the personnel in the Northtown area will be given the same information that everybody has heard here today, while the other organizations in the field will get their information in a special document and from the DMT news-sheet, which has a new issue coming out in three days time.

Martin tries to encourage the audience to ask more questions – all questions are welcome – but they seem to have dried up. He concludes by saying: "If there is anybody who wants to meet outside afterwards, we can continue our discussion if there is anything you want to take up or that you may be wondering about." He then brings the meeting to a close. Copies of the organizational charts which have been shown on the overheads are available at the exits for anyone who wants to take one away. Most people then leave the meeting to return to their usual jobs.

2.6   A commentary on method

Before commenting on the meeting itself, I shall mention briefly two points of methodology and say something about the advantages and problems connected with this particular event as an object of study. The stickler for methodological correctness might claim that our meeting cannot be regarded as "raw" empirical material accessible to a variety of inter-pretations, pointing out that it has already been interpreted. The same stickler might also demand that unprocessed material in the shape of exhaustive reports of everything that was said should be made available to the reader. In theory, I agree on both counts, but there are objections on metatheoretical and above all on practical grounds.

As is being increasingly recognized, every observation is determined by paradigmatic, cultural, social and political conditions which affect expectations and conceptualizations of the phenomena that can be perceived (Alvesson and Sköldberg, 1996; Deetz, 1992a; Steier, 1991). Different vocabularies, associated with the different language communities of different theoretical schools, frame issues in their particular ways. We do not simply see and represent reality in an objective, neutral fashion. It is commonly recognized that "facts" are theory-laden. Thus in a sense interpretations are always made before anything is written down in the shape of notes etc. This undermines the ideal of "raw" empirical material as a representation of reality "as it is", and allows greater scope for other ideals, such as expressing oneself economically or giving freer rein to interpretation. However, we could distinguish between different levels of abstraction and ambition in the interpretation, and it might be felt that less of these on my part would have been preferable in the present case, leaving the readers with more room to make their own different interpretations. On the other hand I do not feel that the material as presented here should restrict the readers´ chances too much. I myself can envisage several other interpretations apart from those reported in the following chapters, i.e. interpretations that do not contradict those made here but which highlight other aspects or dimensions. Different meanings, as we know, can be imputed to any complex phenomenon (Asplund, 1970). The inclusion of everything that was said during the meeting plus accounts of behaviour, gestures, etc. would involve an enormous mass of text, almost as great in volume as this entire book, which I am sure the readers would not appreciate. Without some help from the author in the shape of inter-pretation and explanation, parts of what takes place would be incomprehensible to the reader. (In reading detailed accounts of commun-icative interaction as described by conversation analysts, it is often difficult to follow what people are saying and to make sense of the interaction.) Nor do I think the reader would relish the exhaustive documentation that would be necessary for him or her to make up his or her mind on such stirring issues as whether a statement should be interpreted as a joke or not.

Another more practical reason why it was impossible to provide full transcripts is that a tape-recorder was not used to record the meeting; instead, notes were taken at the time and elaborated immediately after-wards. The choice of an ethnographic research approach in the research project in which this event was documented, called for note-taking as empirical technique. It is an approach relying on participant observation in situations where there is seldom any advance knowledge about what exactly will be happening. This necessitates flexibility and mobility of a kind that is not required for the study of recurrent situations in fixed settings. Occasionally, too, observer access may be conditional on not using tape-recorders. Thus we often have a trade-off between research that gives priority to flexibility and access to a variety of situations – conditions that favour "relevance" in the results – and research based on the scrupulous documentation of situations, with the attendant risk of triviality

– as the detractors of micro-sociology are quick to point out (Collins, 1981). I believe that the meeting discussed here includes material of sufficient importance to generate interesting interpretations of power and communication in companies. I have therefore chosen to use this specific event as the empirical material for the present book, rather than any of the many well-documented events reported in my other research projects.

The nature of the empirical material allows for "close" readings. Nonetheless the absence of exhaustive transcripts disallows the type of minutely detailed reading – whereby a couple of minutes of talk can generate a vast amount of text – to which the discourse and conversation analysts devote their attention. My own view is that the study of slightly broader themes is preferable to the study of tiny details, at least in the context of management and organization studies. Where ideals and priorities are in conflict, I therefore prefer what I feel to be "important" and "interesting" events above detailed documentation, and "close" above "myopic" readings. Of course, there is no need to decide once and for all which approach should be preferred. There is good reason to encourage a broad range of organization studies based on various degrees of concentration and faithfulness to more or less rigorously documented texts.

As has been seen, the information meeting is clearly structured from above, with most of the participants having a very passive role. Would another type of situation, where most of them had taken an active part rather than just listening, perhaps have been a better object of study, indicating more – or more interesting – dimensions of corporate life? However, as I pointed out above, this meeting corresponded to my criteria for a suitable focal situation. A structured situation is easier to account for without being forced to invoke a lot of background information. Even if such information is provided, it is often rather difficult for someone who has not been present at an event involving a poorly structured set of interactions, to understand what is happening and to make their own interpretations.

Apart from this motive for chosing the situation described here, I don´t think there is any reason to give priority either to top-down situations like this one, or to less asymmetrically structured situations in which activity and voice are more evenly distributed. Organizations exhibit processes of power in talking-down situations as well as in more interactive ones. Both need to be studied. Here I contend that it is not uncommon, and certainly not insignificant, that subordinates are put in situations where passivity is expected of them and is also actively produced. As Hardy (1994: 230) notes, "situations of obvious inequality where no conflict would appear to exist are promising venues for study". The study of this phenomenon represents an important area for critical organization and management studies (cf. Knights and Willmott, 1987; Rosen, 1985).

2.7   Comments on the meeting

The following chapter will introduce interpretations of the content of the meeting. First, however, I shall say something about the way it was perceived by a few of those present, and then add a few short comments of my own.

No attempt will be made in this study to evaluate the consequences of the meeting – which would hardly be possible anyway – or to evaluate people´s attitudes towards it. To isolate particular events and then try to measure the effects of these on abstract dimensions such as opinions and attitudes is not a very fruitful enterprise according to the perspectives advocated in this book. The idea of stable attitudes and opinions is very problematic. As convincingly demonstrated by Potter and Wetherell (1987), statements on attitudes seem to vary even in the context of one and the same interview, and this is over and above the problems already mentioned about what interviews can reveal. As will become clearer from the interpretations in the following chapters, there are also other reasons for questioning the value of asking those present for their views on details of the information meeting. Answers provoked by such a procedure would probably have led our respondents to reflect upon various aspects of the meeting. This in turn might have provoked responses lacking in the greater spontaneity which followed attendance at an event, where the communication did not encourage reflection or questioning. The meanings developed in the "real" situation would thus probably differ from the meanings developed retrospectively and reported in an interview context.

Another question concerns the distinction made by the advocates of realism that is between the real and the empirical (Outhwaite, 1983). Something may have an effect, although it is not possible to observe it. The effect is then real, but not empirical. This is probably often the case in complex settings where a multitude of mechanisms and processes create effects which never become fully observable. Perhaps, for example, the information meeting might have had the effect of making people more positive towards the change, while attitudes to the reorganization remained negative. Without the meeting, they might have been even more negative.[6]

However, a couple of informal interviews with some of the employees who attended suggests that their response to the meeting was generally positive. The meeting had pepped them up, as someone put it. In an interview some time after the meeting someone else described Martin as a "wonderful guy – a sergeant-major and an actor rolled into one". But we also got some indication of the perceived hierarchical distance between Martin and the lower-level managers in another interview, when we asked what the interviewee thought Martin meant by saying that it was fun to be able to measure results. Our respondent replied: "It may be fun at his level, because you get more time over for playing golf." More generally, though, we have to conclude that the staff responded pretty positively to the meeting. It seems to have made it somewhat easier for people to accept the reorganization. As to any other ideas about concrete effects, we can only speculate, so from now on I shall concentrate on interpreting the meaning and direction of what the meeting expressed, rather than the strength of its impact or its causal effects.

To some extent the meeting can be regarded as a reflection of the organization and of what is usually referred to as the corporate culture – the shared meanings, ideas, values, norms and symbols that to a greater or

---

6 One could of course consider a series of attitude measurements over time in order to see whether a specific event is followed by changes. Apart from the problems associated with such (quantitative) measurements discussed above, it is likely that any effects of a particular effort to change attitudes – such as the information meeting – would coexist with a large number of other changes in the organization and in the rest of the world thus making it difficult to draw any conclusions about causalities. One could add that the time and effort of researchers could be spent in more meaningful ways than in conducting a series of attitude measurements for the sake of trying to examine possible effects of a specific intervention such as the information meeting.

lesser extent characterize a company.[7] A social event of this kind can tell us quite a lot about the cultural context in which it occurs (the corporate culture), while purely personal relations (the idiosyncrasies of key actors) and more temporary concatenations can also come into it, and should make us wary of drawing farreaching conclusions about cultural aspects on the basis of particular events. The MD of DMT has only been with the company for two years, and can therefore hardly be regarded as an unadulterated product of its culture. More significantly, there is no one-to-one relationship between a specific situation and the whole of a company. As sites for the production and reproduction of patterns of meaning, formal organizations exhibit great variations between different groups and situations (Alvesson, 1993a).

The meeting does indicate, however, that the following values and virtues are fairly widespreading the organization, or are at least highly valued in certain parts of it on some occasions: exactitude, order, rationality, predictability, subordination and hierarchy. The meeting was carefully planned, there was hardly any room for unexpected elements or deviations from the programme. The number of seats corresponded exactly to the number of those attending (except for the researcher). Punctuality was important. The display boards had been professionally drawn and the general run-through well prepared. Nothing unexpected occurred – there was no (overt) opposition, debate or questioning. These clues accord with the impression of the organization that I formed on a basis of interviews and observations.

In the following chapters I will develop these and other themes in some interpretations of the meeting as a construction and reproduction of the organizational "reality" – "real" in the sense that it is an expression of a

---

[7] The concept of "corporate culture" can be misleading, in that it is often thought to imply that all the employees in a company share the same ideas, values and norms. It is doubtful whether this could be said of many companies. Because of the division of labour and the multiplicity of groups in companies, the cultural patterns are likely to be much more differentiated and multifaceted than the concept of corporate culture implies (Alvesson, 1993a; Martin, 1992; Martin and Frost, 1996; Van Maanen and Barley, 1985). To a limited extent, however, certain broadly shared views and attitudes may characterize various organizational conditions, for instance, relations between higher and lower managers. It is probably wise to avoid reifying such views and attitudes and instead relate them to on-going productions and reproductions of culture in events, social accounts, stories, vocabularies, etc.

number of people´s attitudes to and definitions of this reality and, partly because of this, that it includes certain patterns of behaviour which entail and/or regulate the production and distribution of material objects. Here I am less interested in the exact relationship between the "corporate culture" of Multi (DMT) – insofar as it makes sense to conceptualize meanings, values and ideas in this way – and what is expressed by the meeting. What interests me more is the cultural and symbolic communication of which the meeting, as a whole and in its parts, is composed. As an example of an organizational event which exposes issues of corporate language, organizational communication, power, leadership etc., it may have more to offer to an understanding of similar kinds of organizational situations and processes irrespective of the specific organizations, than to an understanding of a wide spectrum of aspects in the company in which the event took place. A lot of what goes on in a specific organization may only be able to tell us something about a highly selective portion of organizational life in that particular organization. As we have noted, organizations exhibit considerable variation in action patterns, cognitions, events, values, etc., and it may often be misleading to describe them in terms of averages and standard patterns. But a specific situation may also be enlightening as regards some of what goes on in many contemporary organizations in Western business and possibly even in the public administration sphere. I have used this case in lectures for practitioners, and many of them seem to find that significant elements in the event are familiar to them. This of course reinforces my perception of the information meeting as a good case for producing knowledge of general relevance. Case studies should not generally be linked too auxiously to the prospect of empirical generalization, but should concentrate on developing interpretations and insights of broader theoretical interest. Here, however, it is an obvious benefit that the empirical material should not be too idiosyncratic, i.e. it should not represent too specific an organizational context. To view the meeting as a culture-constituting (reproducing) action, in which attempts are made to create and maintain certain common perceptions of the organizational reality, can be regarded as an analytical strategy for opening up whatever the event can reveal as being of wide significance to an understanding of certain parts of organizational processes and events. This line will be followed up in Chapter 3, while Chapters 4 and 5 will explore other lines of interpretation.

3 The meeting as a culture-constitutive process

As I explained in Chapter 1, three types of interpretation will be applied to this empirical case. The interpretations and the theories or frames of reference which lie behind them are presented below in separate chapters. In the first of these I briefly outline a cultural and social-constructivist approach, reinforced by ideas from Critical Theory.

3.1 Culture, domination and the social construction of reality

The cultural approach in organization studies proceeds from the assumption that the ideas, the definitions of reality and the meanings which are shared in common by a group (a company, a work group, etc.) are a – perhaps even the – central feature of organizations. This approach draws attention to the question, "how is organization accomplished and what does it mean to be organized" (Smircich, 1983: 353). More or less integrated patterns of common ideas and meanings constitute the core of structures which denote relative stability in an organization. They have their roots in, and are influenced by, various social and material practices. They do not persist unchanged, but are recreated, reinforced (and sometimes weakened or changed) in a multitude of different situations, in everyday language, in actions and in material structures – and in a multifaceted network of symbols, meanings and significations (Alvesson and Berg, 1992; Frost et al., 1985, 1991; Hatch, 1993; Martin, 1992; Smircich, 1983, etc.).

These structures – which include hierarchic and other relationships and the acceptance of objectives, rules and various frameworks for operations – are based on the absence of questioning, or at any rate of serious questioning, of existing social conditions. In this case, basic conditions tend to be taken for granted and the social world will be regarded as natural, neutral and legitimate (Deetz, 1986; Deetz and Kersten, 1983; Frost, 1987). There is little room for any conscious awareness that social reality can be experienced and understood in radically different ways, and that an infinite number of approaches are possible. This acceptance calls for selectivity in the view of experienced social conditions, and "complementary" selectivity in interpreting and assessing what is heard and seen. There are limits to the openness and rich variety with which this social reality could be appreciated, and to the ways in which what is real, unreal, good, bad, sensible, problematic, not subject to influence, changeable, etc. could be classified. If a given social system is to function and to be reproduced, the ideas and meanings involved must thus be limited and a great many alternative interpretations – alternative in relation to the dominant interpretations – must be excluded from, or at least marginalized, in human consciousness and public life. This is partly what culture is about, and these selectivity mechanisms are characteristic of socialization processes in society at large and in organizations. The creation and recreation of meaning is not primarily located in the heads of people, albeit something must happen there to for culture to "work". Rather it comes in the form of a traffic in significant symbols, which guides thinking, feeling and social interaction. Meaning, from a cultural point of view, is social and public. Its natural habitat is the marketplace and the town square, according to Geertz (1973: 45), and, one could add, meetings in a company. In these last, for example, we can study how selectivity and control in the construction of meaning is accomplished.

3.1.1   Culture and power

Alongside the restrictions associated with cultural "belongingness" – constraints associated with language, tradition, taken-for-granted assumptions and ideas specific to a particular group or society – other factors too are at work. This limiting and freezing of ideas about reality is contingent upon two things: existential reasons – we need a coherent picture of the world; and practical constraints – it is far too time-consuming and distracting to be constantly wondering about different ways of interpreting the world. But power relationships also come into it. A view of reality is largely the result of negotiations between actors involved in asymmetrical power relationships. The actors in these relationships have access to different resources – material and symbolic – and have different possibilities when it comes to deciding how reality is to be defined.

Perhaps this is the most crucial aspect of power, at least in modern society (Frost, 1987; Lukes, 1978).

A great many different theories and definitions of power exist, but I will refrain from surveying them here. (For discussions and criticisms of the various concepts of power, see e.g. Beronius (1986), Clegg (1989a), Clegg et al. (1996), Hardy (1994) and Lukes (1978)). Briefly, most of them can be located on a scale ranging from theories which try to define power as something delimited and measureable, such as the classic definition of power whereby A makes B act in a certain way despite resistance on B´s part, to theories which look at more complex phenomena and emphasise structural relations and the influence of ideas, preferences, self-images etc. The problem about the classical theories is that they simply disregard the complexity of power, and focus instead on individual and behavioural factors. Another weakness of traditional conceptions is the connection of power with competition and conflict. Power is seen as a matter of defeating and preventing opposition. This is sometimes referred to as instrumental power (Pfeffer, 1981b). Critics have argued that power is also – and particularly – significant when not brought to the surface:

> If we define power as the capacity for a personal or impersonal instance (Instanz) to bring someone to do (or to abstain from doing) that which left to himself he would not necessarily have done (or would possibly have done), it is immediately obvious that the greatest conceivable power lies in the possibility to preform somebody in such a way that, of his own accord, he does what one wants him to do, without any need for *domination (Herrschaft)* or for *explicit power (Macht/Gewalt)* bringing him to do or abstain from doing. It is equally obvious that a being subject to such shaping will present at the same time the appearances of the fullest possible spontaneity and the reality of a total heteronomy. Compared to this absolute power, any explicit power and any form of domination are deficient and exhibit an irrepairable failure. (Castoriadis, 1992: 275)

The following empirical observation endorses this view:

> The most important kinds of power were already constituted as being those occasions when A´s didn´t have to get B´s to do things because B´s would do those sorts of things anyway. Simple empiricism would not be sufficient to reveal this. (Clegg, l987: 65)

It is important to recognize that power is most relevant in explaining the absence of conflict. Power does not only produce visible effects, but it is also vital to an understanding of inaction: why grievances do not exist, why demands are not made, why conflict does not arise and why certain actors appear as authorities whom people voluntarily obey (Lukes, 1978). Here it makes sense to talk about symbolic or ideological power. Another critique concerns assumptions about the deliberate nature of power. Rather than assuming power to be intentional, an instrument held by the powerful over the powerless, it is the structural and systemic character of power that is emphasized. Ideologies and mechanisms may exercise power beyond the intentions or control of the elites, who benefit from dominating forms of power but who are also subjected to them. Managers, for example, may be subordinated to cultural ideas and values which they take for granted. Intentions are not necessarily central. Power may thus be in force even if particular agents such as managers have limited control over it, and some of its functioning and effects are unintentional.

There thus seems to be a strong trend away from "episodic, agency, causal, mechanical conceptions of power as if they were the whole of power" (Clegg, 1989a: 186). In different ways, Critical Theory and Foucault have both been important to this development. Yet a great deal of power research continues to use a mechanical approach, presumably partly because it is most convenient for empirical studies.

One of the drawbacks of the modern comprehensive theories is that power becomes difficult if not impossible to delimit or define. Foucault (see chapter 4) contends that this lies in the nature of the phenomenon. There is little point in trying to produce a precise definition in such a case. Instead we must, like Bachrach and Lawler (cited in Hardy, 1994: 220) "ask not what is power but to what does the notion of power sensitize us". More important than formal definitions is thus a line of thinking which provides a focus and a sharp edge in reasoning and interpretation.

Sometimes culture theory, especially in the context of management and organization studies, is accused of being consensus-oriented and of avoiding or trivializing issues of power and politics. This, of course, is not an inherent characteristic of culture theory but is a result of the way many researchers have chosen to work with the concept of organizational culture.

A large proportion of organizational culture studies – especially in the USA – is governed to a greater or lesser extent by a technical interest in knowledge. Similarly it has been observed that culture studies have acquired an increasingly functionalistic orientation (Calás and Smircich, 1987), focusing upon concerns of immediate interest to practitioners, such as the economic value of controlling culture and the means for doing so (Barley et al., 1988). This literature has a pro-managerial orientation, based on the assumption that management acts in the common interest. By managing culture, e.g. creating ceremonies, rites, slogans, specific expressions, etc., it is possible to facilitate various potential outcomes: greater work satisfaction, social cohesion, commitment to the work and the workplace, less opposition and conflict, improved communications, the maintenance of appropriate behaviour or a change of behaviour patterns in accordance with technological changes or a new corporate strategy (Dandridge, 1986; Deal and Kennedy, 1982; Kilmann et al., 1985; Pondy, 1983, etc.). These outcomes are viewed as positive and this kind of research typically wants to produce knowledge of relevance to managers in supporting their actions for the benefit of the entire company. The assumptions about integration, harmony and consensus are thus strong (Martin, 1992).[1]

Many of these studies are in a sense dealing with issues of power, without explicitly addressing this topic and without taking seriously the potential negative consequences for subordinates of being the objects of cultural control. The fact that certain actions and arrangements sustain and

---

[1] Trice and Beyer (1985), for example, appear to assume that top management is the legitimate interpreter of the appropriate ideologies and values in an organization, and various means for controlling the ideas of subordinates are suggested. Non-managerial organizational members enter into this text only as objects of managed rites or as a conservative force which might, according to management, jeopardize the needed cultural change. Except for recognizing that management might also resist genuine change, the major problem, according to Trice and Beyer, concerns the risk that management's efforts are not successful enough.

The risk that management might have the "wrong" values and ideology or that it would be unethical to counteract possibly legitimate resistance to cultural change, is hardly recognized by Trice and Beyer, presumably because it is assumed that the cultural significance of managers in organizations is great, and that this group supports the common good and is hence in the right moral position to decide upon "desirable" values and ideals.

reinforce asymmetrical relations of power falls outside the scope of functionalist studies of organizational culture, making it vulnerable to charges of political naïvety and of hiding issues of power behind a technical and functionalist vocabulary. However, as will be seen below, there are also organizational cultures with a distinctly critical orientation.

The notion of symbolic power indicates the centrality of culture to an understanding of power, and vice versa. Culture may be related to (surfaced) conflicts as well as forms of domination that have prevented or minimized opposition and conflict:

> ... culture comprises various levels, directions, and forms of interpreting the world, the coexistence of which may result not only in a plurality of perspectives on the world but also in an explicit and structured conflict of such interpretations. (Arnason, 1992: 248)

However, culture may act as a force that reduces politically aware forms of social interaction, based on the autonomy of interpretation. This applies particularly in the context of asymmetrical relations of power. But even the taken for granted character of cultural ideas associated with tradition may freeze understandings of social reality and leave dominating rationalities, goals and values unquestioned. As Arnason (1992) puts it, "the elaboration and closure of interpretive contexts can serve to legitimize the withdrawal from or the minimization of interactive contexts" (p. 249). Culture can thus de-politicize what exists – often to the benefit of dominating groups and interests.

3.1.2   Cultural control and management of meaning

The creation and utilization of existing as well as novel ideologies and symbolic means of control are crucial features of management and leadership (Alvesson, 1993b; Czarniawska-Joerges, 1988; Kunda, 1992; Rosen, 1985; Willmott, 1993, etc.). In modern companies symbolic power is particularly salient, compared to technical and bureaucratic means of control. Sometimes symbolic power takes the form of systematic efforts to establish a certain world view, a particular set of values and/or emotions among corporate employees. Ray (1986) refers to corporate culture as "the last frontier of control". Critics have called this management strategy "cultural engineering" (Alvesson and Berg, 1992; Kunda, 1992). Ideas about what exists, what is good and what should be accomplished are being communicated by management. The purpose is to attain a monopoly of the definition of appropriate values and ideals.

> Through the careful design and dissemination of corporate values, employees are exhorted and enabled to acquire "a love of product" or the equivalent, as their sense of purpose. (Willmott, 1993: 522)

A slightly different approach involves the management of meaning. This is not necessarily tied to large-scale efforts to manage corporate cultures, but is part of the everyday leadership. This is regarded as symbolic action. Attention is drawn to certain things, and away from others. Language is carefully used. Objects and issues are framed in a particular light, encouraging certain understandings and sentiments, typically reflecting managerial interests and objectives – which sometimes overlap with what may be seen as the interests of broader groups, and sometimes not. This control is centred around the ideas and meanings that management wants employees to embrace (Barley and Kunda, 1992; Beckérus and Edström, 1988; Pfeffer, 1981a; Smircich and Morgan, 1982). Consequently, it implies the counteracting of a multiplicity of ideas and meanings which could hamper cooperation and the reproduction of the system (Willmott, 1993). Thus the managerially biased presentation and creation of social reality reduces the number of available variations in the way things can be perceived, when the possibilities of describing understanding and evaluating workplace conditions and objectives are being negotiated. The crucial issue of power does not thus consist of large-scale, visible moves, whereby resourceful actors decide for oppositional, or weaker actors, rather it is the creation or shaping of particular ideas and understandings whereby the ground rules of the organization are accepted.

> Generally, dominance is manifested not in significant political acts but rather in the day-to-day, taken for granted nature of organizational life. As such, the exercise of power and domination exists at a routine level, further protecting certain interests and allowing the order of organizational life to go largely unquestioned by its members. (Deetz and Mumby, 1986: 376)

According to this view, dominance is exercised chiefly by ensuring that the current social reality is regarded as natural, rational, self-evident, problem free, sensible, etc., and the leading actors as good and legitimate representatives of this reality (in our case the organization). Thus, the power aspect is of crucial importance in organizational communication:

> Communication provides the means through which power can be exercised, developed, maintained, and enhanced. Communication structures, channels, networks, and rules are avenues of power ... Thus the communication medium is never neutral. The structures and rules of communication established in an organization favour some actors over others. (Frost, 1987: 507)

Managers may be seen therefore as agents of power creating or reproducing shared meanings, ideas and values through acts of communication which freeze social reality or, at least, counteract an open, questioning approach to how it should be negotiated.

3.1.3   Openness, closure and ambiguity of culture

That certain definitions of and ideas about the social world have arisen and later come to dominate, mainly or partly contingent upon powerful actors´ (management) efforts to define significant ideas, meanings and values, does not mean that this conception of the world exists for all time, and is stable and predictable. A possible weakness of the culture concept is that it may indicate unity and coherence. This is most pronounced in consensus-oriented organizational culture studies, but also, many critically oriented authors tend to attribute strong powers to management and emphasize a farreaching and stabilizing impact of managerially biased ideas on other organizational members. Still, an interest in actual or potential conflict and contradiction makes unity and coherence less salient features in critical approaches to organizational culture.

An emphasis on integration, unity and coherence (Schein, 1985), is not a necessary focus in cultural analysis (Alvesson, 1993a; Martin, 1992). This approach can certainly take seriously the fact that the social world is also complex and contradictory, and thus dynamic, and that basic conflicts may exist (Benson, 1977; 1983; Deetz and Kersten, 1983; Fombrun, 1986).

Changes in external conditions and inner processes both have an effect here (Gray et al., 1985). Moreover the ambiguous and indeterminate aspects of meaning also have to be taken into account (Deetz, 1992a; Linstead and Grafton-Small, 1992; Martin, 1992). The fixation on certain interpretations and the denial of the precarious, open and negotiable character of the social world which has been touched upon above, requires among other things that these ambiguities and contradictions are dealt with, perhaps denied, trivialized or "compartmentalized", i.e. are placed in separate pockets of consciousness so that confrontation can be avoided. For the supporters of a given social system it is a question of handling contradictions so that they do not lead to any questioning of the system. Managers and leaders are concerned, among other things, with bridging over or masking such contradictions. Naturally the leaders and others who support the system are not doing this out of narrow conservatism or rigidity; they may well represent new orientations and dynamism within certain boundaries. A certain degree of ambiguity is not only impossible to avoid, but quite tolerable, indeed welcome, from a managerial point of view (Pondy, 1983). The point is, however, that contradictions implying possible radical change, and any potential willingness to accept the possibility of such change, are counteracted. Once again it is a question of influencing the prevailing conception of reality in a desired direction and of achieving particular definitions of reality and particular attitudes; this in turn implies reducing the possible interpretations of a social reality which can theoretically be perceived in an infinite number of ways.

The organizational reality may appear to be based on consensus, since the ideological conditions conceal contradictions and marginalize oppositional voices. These last do exist, but they make little impact as they are not supported by dominating power interests and do not therefore prevail (Mumby, 1988). Tendencies towards ambiguity, variation and frag-mentation as regards meanings and attitudes, seldom represent any distinct threat to the dominant ideologies, when they do not directly challenge these; nonetheless they do represent a problem. The impact of dominating ideologies is limited in time and space. Because there are no automatic mechanisms for spreading the élite-supported ideologies, these will be subjected, more or less regularly and consciously, to systematic treatment in the form of cultural engineering and symbolic management. These modes of control may be far less successful than managerial or radical researchers claim, but they still have a significant impact as modes of ordering which then counteract tendencies to contradiction, conflict, disclosure and ambiguity in organizations.

3.1.4   A brief critique of culture theory

A substantial critique of organizational culture studies has been developed over recent years. Much of this critique is not relevant, or at least not central, to the position outlined here, as it departs in many ways from the mainstream, functionalist organizational culture studies based on assumptions of integration and consensus, with an emphasis on broad, coherent patterns and an identification with a management perspective on organizations. This critique is echoed in the more critical and dynamic cultural understanding of organizations outlined above. However, I would like to mention two points from the debates within and against culture theory which I feel are relevant to understanding the limitations of the approach chosen here.

The first concerns the robustness or fragility of the basis for meaning-creating processes. Unlike functionalist approaches, the view proposed here assumes that meaning patterns in organizations are not organic, neutral, functional or relatively stable, but are contingent upon operations of power. Contradictions and opposition are thus potentially present forces. It could be argued that a critical approach attributes considerable power – and thus a certain degree of robustness – to the meaning-creating capacities of management as well as to other capitalist institutions. An even stronger emphasis on the open nature of cultural phenomena than that proposed above could be considered. As Arnason (1992: 255) puts it: "the world does not appear as a totality of pregiven component parts but as a context that simultaneously constitutes as well as relativizes and at the same time includes possibilities of experience and of thematization."

A second, related point concerns the degree of homogeneity in the hegemonic interests and the impact of management groups as agents of symbolic power, as well as the uniformity and the degree of meaning stabilizing in the communicated messages. Difference, diversity and variation in management groups in terms of interests, objectives and action patterns could be emphasized. In a postmodernist perspective, but also in light of some empirical studies, such a view appears more motivated than the one favoured by managerial/functionalist or radical/critical organizational culture researchers (Linstead and Grafton-Small, 1992). Management and meaning are both plural and fragmented, according to this view. "Culture then is continuously emergent, constituted and constituting, produced and consumed by subjects who, like culture, are themselves fields of the trace, sites of intertextuality" (p. 345). The idea of stable, shared meanings, accomplished through successful management action/cultural engineering would thus seem quite insensitive to the fluid, fragmented and indeterminate nature of cultural phenomena.

The approach suggested in this chapter takes these points into consideration, to some extent, but does not follow the postmodern route that privileges diversity and fluidity as analytical themes and de-emphasizes the presence of social order and domination in corporate contexts. Postmodern language is seductive, but difficult to apply to empirical material, and I suspect that it is not very successful (or at least is harder to apply) in grasping "lived experience" in many contexts, e.g. in bureaucratic settings (such as that studied in this book).[2] The focus of the present text on a specific event avoids or reduces some of the pitfalls that a postmodernist approach correctly criticizes, such as a strong belief in homogeneity and organization-wide patterns, since generalizations across different organizational situations are only made very tentatively. Nevertheless, the critical points presented above will, I hope, alert the reader to some of the blind spots of the perspective adopted here.

3.1.5 Summary

Thus I consider that the empirical situation described in Chapter 2 can be interpreted, in common with organizational circumstances in general, on a basis of the following frames of reference. The organization can be envisaged as a view of reality held in common – albeit sometimes

---

[2] It may do better – be easier to apply – in terms of appeal to lived experience in the context of the mass media and possibly also in the work settings characterizing certain high-tech companies and other "image-sensitive" organizations (Alvesson, 1990).

precarious, uncertain or challenged – which is constituted and reconstituted in social processes. Organization is a matter of the creation and re-production as well as the challenge and destruction of shared meanings. Normally, the first two will dominate. Without common views about reality, organization is hardly possible. But the precarious nature of common frameworks and meanings must be borne in mind. Thus, the organization requires constant organizing and the maintenance and the reinforcement of certain patterns of ideas. Symbolic forms and expressions are important in this context. They contribute to the freezing and limitation of views of reality, so that an ambiguous and "open" world is given a definite and basically unquestioned meaning. These limitations are tied up with existential, practical and political circumstances. Relations of power and dominance – usually in implicit form – are highly relevant in this context. At the meeting which we are examining, the spotlight was very clearly on such relationships. Power – in the sense of processes and techniques which control meaning and define reality – is a key dimension in my interpretation of the meeting. But it is now time to return to the meeting itself.

3.2   The information meeting in a critical-cultural perspective

The meeting is extremely interesting, according to my opinion, not least because it offers us some idea of how the regulation (or perhaps the attempted regulation) of ideas and meanings (organizational creations and recreations) may be effected in an organization of a certain type. I will examine a number of elements and offer some suggestions and inter-pretations of how these elements can help us to understand crucial aspects of organization (organizing, regulating), and how leadership and dominan-ce are exercised. I shall focus particularly on the symbolic, ideological and power aspects, which are especially interesting in a critical-cultural perspective.

3.2.1   Reorganization as usual

The character and duration of the information meeting are worth noting, since they tell us something in themselves. Two hours of the working day were devoted to the meeting (and the time limit had to be adhered to), a hundred managers were invited to a venue that was familiar to them, and there they were given some specific information and subjected to persuasion (as well as being given a little pep talk and other things as well). This suggests that the reorganization was not considered to be of extreme importance. Instead, an atmosphere of "business as usual" was promoted, not just for the customers´ benefit – which is explicitly stated – but also for the managers who had been invited to attend. Nothing that was said was particularly striking, either. And, in any case, people in this company are used to reorganizations.

Thus, the meeting does not express any serious attempt to involve those present in the reorganization, or to breathe new life or a new spirit of personal concern into the organization. Perhaps there is an attempt in this direction, but the ritual elements get the upper hand. Perhaps the low level of expectations helps to explain why many of those present are not particularly enthusiastic about the change; there is also a rather passive attitude. The change in the organization appears to be more of a ritual, rather than a transformation or a reform. The familiarity of the venue, the packaging of the meeting, the time restrictions, the rather familiar messages – all these factors suggest continuity, change along a certain predictable line rather than a break with the past. It is primarily a question of structural change, of changes in organizational frontiers and reporting obligations, in the basis for controlling results, etc. There is no great element of cultural change, that is to say any attempt to radically redefine the participants´ view of the company and its operations. Thus, to a large extent, the symbolism conserves the system (see Dandridge et al., 1980). The meeting could thus be interpreted as an event reducing negative feelings and potential hostility to the organizational redesign rather than a call for enthusiasm and active participation. The form sends a signal: there is no call for worry; nothing extraordinary is going on. The meeting expresses risk-minimization: a grand-scale effort to create enthusiasm would involve invoking the expectation that something really significant is to take place, with the risk of also stirring up negative emotions associated with a fear of losing jobs and boredom with organizational redesigns.

3.2.2   The reinforcement of the managerial ideology – or the position as subordinate?

As the reader has perhaps observed, Martin is keen to emphasize that those present are managers. This is why they have been invited. No doubt they understood this anyway, but a reminder of this aspect of their status does no harm. The idea is to reinforce the sense of responsibility associated with the role and perhaps to give them some small confirmation of their identities. The opportunity to participate in the meeting, to "meet" (listen to and observe) the head of their sector, could also be seen as a kind of symbolic reward. Those present belong to "the chosen few". They are being informed about the change one day before "the troops". But the agenda and content were roughly the same on both occasions.

It is not particularly obvious that people are "managers". It is not just a question of appointing somebody to a particular formal position, since the identity and the ideology (discourse) which characterise the person in question are also crucial factors. It is not obvious that people who are given such positions regard themselves primarily as managers (even at second or third hand), or that they are regarded as managers by their environment. The crucial factor, in this context, is the capacity in which they have been "called" – we have only to think of all the possible identities and ideologies which are available (cf. Deetz, 1992a; Therborn, 1980). A particular person, for example somebody who has the title of department manager, is (or may be viewed as) a manager, a professional (e.g. an engineer or a marketer), a subordinate and a colleague – as well as a friend, a member of a family, a female, middle-aged, perhaps a "green", a union member, and so on. People are subject to a variety of other people´s expectations and attempts to put them into categories.

> The meanings of and membership within the categories of discursive practice will be constant sites of struggle over power, as identity is posited, resisted and fought over in its attachment to the subjectivity by which individuality is constructed. (Clegg, 1989a: 151)

Corporate management competes with other groups and categories for the individual´s time, self-perception, attention and loyalty. Ideally, from top management´s point of view, "managers" should regard themselves primarily as company people. It is therefore important to maintain and reinforce this identity of theirs. Appealing to them as "managers", also means that certain ideas and values about the job are being accentuated: it is a question of responsibility, loyalty, work morale, result orientation, etc. Thus, it is an important task for top management to continually constitute people who take "managership" very seriously, and who give priority to values, ideas, feelings and actions associated with being a "manager". At the present meeting this is what is taking place (on a small scale). The basic idea of the meeting could be to remind people that they should perceive the reorganization through pro-managerial spectacles.

The meeting also clearly expresses the fact that (most) managers are also – and in many cases primarily – subordinates. If this feeling becomes too explicit, then other ideas and an identity not associated with "managership" might come to dominate. Subordinates belong to a different category from superiors.

Some may identify themselves perhaps with another group apart from management, for example the department, the profession or the union. The self-image is projected in different ways, depending on how the different identifications and identities assert themselves. The risk here, from top management´s perspective, is that the identity as a "company person" no longer predominates. At the same time it is crucial to establish the "subordinate" image in the self-connection of the "manager" in order to secure top management in its role. Discipline and obedience are vital qualities in "managers", at least in the vast majority who are to be found at the lower and middle levels. As Galbraith (1983) has pointed out, managers are more strictly controlled in many respects than other employees; for instance they have to be more careful about what they think and, in particular say. (See Jackall, 1988, for an excellent study on this matter.) Top management´s task is to ensure that the subordinate and superior persons are yoked together to constitute the optimal managerial identity.

Clearly, however, top management rarely feels that systematic efforts or rhetoric are needed to reinforce the subordinate identity of the manager: people are sent on management courses, but not on "subordinate courses".

There is generally an instinctive understanding of the subordinate position, even in the absence of explicit messages reinforcing it. On the other hand, people are constantly being reminded of this subordinate identity in their everyday lives and in implicit ways. Top management seldom exploits any explicit ideology of subordination (although trade unions and workers´ collectives do). This aspect of our central issue will be discussed in the following chapter, where I will examine the way in which the subordinate attitude is created, referring at the same time to Foucault´s conception of power. In the present section we are concerned with the way that people at the meeting were made to feel their membership of the managerial category, and to absorb values and ways of thinking associated with this class. Thus, in this particular case, the subordinate identity was not explicitly emphasized – on the contrary. For instance, Martin did not tell his listeners, "You are here because you are subordinates", although this would have been at least as true as to tell them they were there because they were managers; in fact they were at the meeting because they had not previously been made party to the discussions about the reorganization or been informed about it. In the more obvious ideological contexts in companies, the important and indeed crucial aspect to emphasize is just the manager (superior) role. If people can command that role, then they are also likely to be able to cope with their subordinate position – which for some reason is often seen as a function of the managerial or leadership role. This, anyway, is how people often seem to argue in discussing leadership – and not subordinateship. And so top managements generally seek to reinforce the manager identity and the ideology associated with it – all of which, it is felt, will yield most in the way of hard work, loyalty, etc. We have an interesting paradox here: the more strongly people see themselves as managers, the more willingly will they submit themselves, subordinate-wise, to imperatives from above. I shall return to the theme of this paradox in Chapter 6.

To an observer it was difficult to tell whether, or how strongly, the meeting generated feelings of subordination amongst the employees. However, it did appear that the meeting evidenced a sense of subordination and passivity amongst the "managers" who were there. They were quite clearly being addressed as subordinates – and not as individuals, but as a collective or flock. As many as could be fitted into the hall were invited and they were then given a two-hour presentation. There was a rather limited direct opportunity for activity or dialogue, or anything else of that kind. The managers were given the role of listeners and observers, as regards both the overall changes and their own current situation. Their passivity is emphasized by the fact that they hardly asked any questions. (More about this later.)

Thus the meeting helped to establish the character of "the managers", both as managers (important, responsible, forceful) and, even more so, as subordinates (not so important, passive, followers). It might be thought that the "objective" impact would be heavily in favour of the latter. Some studies have indicated, however, that people show a strong tendency to minimize their "subordination" and to emphasize "managership" in their conscious thinking, supported by societal values and management ideologies which tend to glorify management and leadership (Laurent, 1978).

Naturally the situation is not always so clear-cut. Borgert (1994), for example, reports a case in which people (mainly women) who had been defined by top management as "managers" (of small groups), were unwilling to adopt such an identity. They were not prepared to attend management courses, as they did not see themselves as engaged in management. Thus managership is by no means unambiguous as a source of identity, and people may reject it by one means or another. (See also Watson, 1994, for a study in which managers express nyanced self-understandings of themselves and their work situations.) Normally, however, cultural values probably push people, perhaps especially men, towards accepting managership as a source of identity in ambivalent situations.

The reinforcement of subordination may perhaps be hidden from those involved, or at any rate not fully recognized by them (also no doubt it is still a powerful factor). For existential reasons people prefer the more attractive offers of identity confirmation, and ignore the less desirable alternatives. They like to see themselves as members of a high-status group (Ashforth and Mael, 1989). It is therefore not inconceivable that "the managers" at Multi may have left the meeting with their commitment to managerial ideology still intact or even reinforced. However, there is also the possibility (or the risk, if we look at it with top management's eyes), that the contradiction between the management ideology as signalled by

Martin in his introductory address, and what the meeting communicated overall may have been too obvious, and that participants will tend to react more like "subordinates" or cynics than "managers" or company people.

3.2.3   The historical description: making the present rational

Invoking history in a pragmatic context such as managerial work is seldom "neutral" or innocent matter. The purpose is rarely to seek or uncover the "truth", but to accomplish certain effects. Historical description can be used to throw a particular light on the present. In our case, the review of the company´s past history was preceded by the question, "How should we be organized in the best possible way?" and it was flavoured by top management´s interest in making the current changes seem sensible and rational. The historical background was naturally given in a highly simplified form, this may have been unavoidable because time was limited, but there is no reason why a historical survey had to be included at all. Apparently for thirty years or so after the war everything was simple, but then came stagnation and a "buyer´s market", and, recently, "we conducted a strategic review". The main point seems to be that whereas in the past external forces were in control, it is now a question of will-power, ability and acting – all qualities it is easy to identify with. It is "we" who decide (whoever "we" are, presumably Multi´s top management). A strategic review, and the resulting decision to go for aggressive growth, are what count.

It is thus being suggested that while Multi´s history has hitherto been steered by external conditions, it is now the rational, forceful actor who sets the tone, in the shape of a strategically competent top management. This sounds like a definite improvement, and something which can pave the way for acceptance of whatever top management may propose in the way of new approaches. The little foray into history writing thus legitimizes top management and suggests that the current changes are in some manner supported by clear lines of development in the company´s history.

The extensive historical review may also have something to do with the fact that Martin had only been with the company for a limited period of time. The history talk, and in particular the use of "we" in a historical sense, can be seen as a legitimizing tactic to counteract the scepticism that some of the staff felt about him as an outsider.

3.2.4   To be No. 1

Two almost obligatory themes at meetings of this kind are quantitative growth and market shares. Martin asked why DMT should be "first" in every single business segment. This was the only time that a "why" question was heard. The answers were two: inspirational effect and quality: "We can be as good or better than our competitors, as we have more money to invest." The second factor seems to have been regarded as the most important, but the coupling of quantitative market leadership (volume) with quality, is naturally not as simple as Martin implied. Volume and profit (a surplus to invest in improving quality) do not necessarily go together. The definition, or at least the indicator, of being "best" in business is after all largely a question of profit and growth, in which case the reason for being first is that the company then has a large market share which can be retained as a means of maximizing profits. It is not perhaps very likely that a possible surplus will be invested in improvements in a more general sense; after all, the money goes to the shareholders and to such investments as will pay best, e.g. to buying up competitors. That these acquisitions – a central component in growth strategies – will make a company "better" cannot of course be guaranteed (cf. Perrow, 1986, Ch. 7).

But the idea of improving things in a broader sense than simply achieving a certain percentage of the market, probably went down well with much of this partly technically minded audience of engineers. To "do well" or to "improve" represents a indisputable ideal, so long as it is not examined too closely. The terms are open to different projections. And the close connection implied between volume and quality – quantitative results as a measure as well as a guarantee of quality – lends further legitimacy to the ideal of an increase in volume.

On a more general plane expressions such as "good", "best" or "first" can, although abstract, serve to create or reinforce an emotional link with the organization and to generate a sense of corporate pride. Identification with the company is encouraged by the prospect of "excellence" or market leadership and the inclination to object to changes claimed to be necessary to its realization may be mitigated.

3.2.5   We and you

Martin´s next point partly contradicted his previous one. Being better was regarded in connection with the first point as a question of having "more money to invest", while the answers to the questions about how the company could improve were largely directed at non-financial factors, such as inertia, blurred lines of responsibility and a lack of long-term thinking. Of course, these organizational problems may have financial consequences, but bigger investments and changes in the organization represent essentially different means for improving the company.

It is interesting to see how the current organizational changes were legitimized on a basis of the idea that the staff had been asked and were regarded as having responded, in a certain manner. A kind of pseudo-involvement was being built up; the impression was given that the opinions of those now present had been the basis for the reorganization. (It is not clear how far this had been so. Since the EDB staff seem to have counted on EDB becoming a separate division, a solution which they preferred but which did not happen, the reorganization cannot be seen as a direct consequence of all the employees´ opinions.) Although Martin normally spoke of "we" during the meeting, and thus in an undefined way appeared to be referring to DMT (or those present, or Multi´s top management), a distinction was made here between "we" meaning DMT´s top management (i.e. Martin himself and a few others) and "you" meaning everyone else in the room.

Martin´s question-answer monologue may be regarded as a social drama reflecting a "reality" of specific social relationships, although only one actor was involved. This "reality" was manipulated by the "we" and "you" terminology. "We did as you said" counteracts the idea that power is directed from the top downwards; it suggests that the decisions are anchored in the staff and that top management is only carrying out the wishes of the collective. This obviates the possibility of resistance to the decisions, since the staff have apparently been able to influence them. Instead, "we" and "you" become simply "we". It is worth noting that the only time top management was distinguished from the rest of the population was when it was claimed that top management was falling in with this population´s standpoint. It was thus being implied that the only reason for separating management from the rest of the organization (the low-level managers) was to indicate its role as the executive instrument of the majority. In a more reflective context, few people would have accepted such a description as accurate. But in the specific situation this use of "we" may have considerable rhetorical appeal. At least the MD appears to think that this is the case.

The constant references to "we" are part of an attempt to integrate activities, to constitute a common identity amongst those present and to make them feel that they belong to the same unit, with the same interests and objectives. "We" is presented as a natural category, but it could just as easily, or perhaps more easily, be seen as an artificial element, a questionable way of representing social relations. The interesting point is that the "we" group is encouraged to take matters for granted. In a study of a management conference in a British company, Knights and Willmott (1987) noted that:

> Through the use of the terms our and we all, the conference agenda asserted that a common purpose could be taken for granted: the ends were agreed upon and unproblematical, and the legitimate objective of the conference was to identify and acquire the relevant and effective means (techniques) for their attainment. (p. 52)

An interesting idea suggested by Young (1989: 191), is that the inclination to adopt a "we" approach may be most powerful in the context of threatening conflicts or the absence of community feeling. Neither Knights and Willmott´s case nor the one presented here contradicts this claim.

In a purely imaginary way the audience were involved as active participants. "How are we to organize ourselves to face the future?" Martin asked rhetorically on behalf of them all. The question implies consensus, unity, involvement, near equality and decision sharing. An alternative question "How has top management (Martin) chosen to organize us?" may thus be staved off. And the same applies to the idea that differing interests may be at stake, which could allow other responses to the question.

The fact that the reorganization is very much a matter of top-down control is at least to some extent concealed with the help of symbolic techniques and language use. The presence of "we" blurs the verticality of the focal situation.

3.2.6   Symbolic denotation of the wishes and interests of the personnel

By referring to the fact that the employees have been asked how they can do better and by interpreting what they want, the impression is communicated that the reorganization is a result of these views and wishes – or is fully in tune with them. However, the link is distinctly weak, and the implied consequences far from certain: it is not obvious that the re-organization will mean increased responsibility, interesting jobs, more influence and better development opportunities for the present audience, nor is it at all certain that Martin´s representation of the employees´ ideas and wishes is particularly accurate. (Many seem to feel strongly about being able to go on working in Northtown, but this was not brought up at the meeting.) However, the point is that by putting the employees´ opinions and needs on the agenda, albeit briefly, an interest in and concern for the situation faced by employees are being suggested. This appears to have a positive and calming effect, even though it does not in fact have much to do with the reorganization. But even such a symbolic denotation may have an effect on feelings and attitudes (Pfeffer, 1981a). When it comes to employee wishes and interests, these were touched on selectively and the spotlight was directed at points which appeared to be in line with the reorganization, while aspects not fully in harmony with it were de-emphasized. To some extent this technique helps to create ideas about needs and wishes, and expectations as to how these are being met (Salancik and Pfeffer, 1978).

Positively charged words constantly recurred during the information meeting: decentralization, speed, flexibility, development. Possible negative aspects such as stress, sub-optimisation, lack of coordination, fragmentation, and the confusion and disorder that repeated reorganization normally involves, were not mentioned. Ambiguous conditions were projected selectively, and the wording was chosen so as to conjure up positive associations. As Czarniawska-Joerges (1993) points out, "decentralization" is at the present time as good as "centralization" was in the 1960s; it creates a context of positive expectations, thereby blocking potential protests.

In events of this kind it is not only the exact content of what is said that is important however; what also matters is that top management is ritually confirming the importance of the staff, emphasizing that its interests, wishes and ideas are being considered. This can suffice to make people feel acknowledged and thus to keep them happy. In the post-autocratic society people are unwilling to submit themselves entirely and uncritically to authority. Sennett (1980) emphasizes the typical ambivalence of the modern individual´s attitude in this respect. Previously, obedience and subordination were taken for granted attitudes in relation to authority; today such qualities arouse a certain antipathy and uneasiness. The patriarchal boss´s attitude – "Do what the boss says, he knows what´s the best for you" – is no longer really acceptable. Social forms that allow visible respect for the ideas of subordinates can help to moderate the relationship, to soften the abstract conception of authority. At our meeting the ritualised expression of respect for the subordinate ranks – the meeting itself, the reference to the earlier responses of the subordinates to the question "How can we improve?" – was perhaps as important as the exact content of what was said. In this light we can say that it was the ritual reference to the wishes of the staff that was important, not how well those wishes had actually been captured.

3.2.7   Tension and anxiety

Despite every attempt to emphasize the sensible and positive aspects of the changes, it is clear that top management anticipated certain negative reactions. In the company as a whole, it was clear that people were far from enthusiastic about the frequent reorganizations. The answers to two of the three minor questions which were asked suggest this. In response to the question as to whether all units were to advertise the posts available, the answer was that the unit to which the questioner belonged was not included, and he "need not worry". The questioner denied that he had felt any anxiety, and the question can indeed be understood as emotionally quite neutral. The interpretation was steered more by the personnel manager´s expectations than by the question itself.

An interesting but purely speculative thought comes to mind regarding this very brief exchange about "anxiety". Perhaps it is significant that the female personnel manager responded and tried to counteract some anticipated "anxiety". Perhaps this made the questioner react; maybe he did not want to be regarded as an "anxious" type, needing to be calmed down (by a woman), and so he emphasized his positive approach: he saw it as "an opportunity and not as a cause for anxiety".

When someone asked where one of the divisional head offices was to be located, Martin broke in with the remark that everything has "both good and bad sides". Since strictly speaking the question did not contain any value judgements, Martin´s comment can also be seen as an expression of the expectation that the change might arouse negative feelings.

3.2.8   Passive resistance

There were thus elements of tension in the air. In other contexts some of those now present had expressed frustration over the proposed changes. Perhaps it is possible to discern some passive resistance in the audience, in the shape of an almost demonstrative silence. The careful planning, the precision and the order of the meeting also had an effect. The opportunity for spontaneity, encouraged by the form of the meeting and the openings for activity, were not utilized – although, despite everything, they did exist. But notwithstanding a zealous attempt on the part of the head of the business sector to encourage questions, only three were asked, and they seemed to be basically factual and neutral. This could be seen as a lack of interest, enthusiasm and involvement in the organizational change on the part of the staff present. Knights and Willmott (1987: 57) also noted passive resistance in their study of a management conference in a British company.

It is perhaps equally possible, however, to regard the information meeting as a reproduction of a more general pattern of communication between different levels in the company hierarchy. On this particular occasion the expression of this pattern may have been rather inconvenient and frustrating to Martin, who would obviously have liked to see more interest on the part of the audience and more questions asked.

As my brief account of reactions to the meeting has shown, people apparently judged it in a fairly positive light, which does not necessarily mean that there was not a certain amount of resistance to the reorganization – resistance which the meeting may have helped undermine.

3.2.9 Symbols of security

The meeting can also be seen as an expression of opposition to experiences of vagueness and indecision, uncertainty and organizational chaos, where nobody knows what unit they belong to, who they are working with, where the organizational frontiers lie, who is in charge of whom, and so on. The meeting and the behaviour of the heads of the business sectors appear to represent well-thought-out, carefully considered decisions, rationality, order and security.

The overhead pictures reflected, amongst other things, a structured reality. They suggested the opposite of arbitrariness, insecurity or disorder. They were not carelessly thrown together but were professionally designed, thus reflecting the new "reality" in a structured manner. This may appear as a trivial observation, as it only confirms what could be expected. Nevertheless, the persuasive power of well-prepared overheads and other kinds of visual representations of organizations is worth taking seriously. These modes of representation often form effective rhetoric, often spontaneously perceived as good or at least informative tools for the mirroring of actual or future reality, even though they perhaps are better understood as mystifications – given the messiness and ambiguities of complex organizations.

The carefully planned agenda of the meeting and the inclusion of all the important points – history, the market, customers, staff and strategy, and the emphasis on modern organizational principles – were also part of an attempt to counteract uncertainty and the risk of people seeing the change as confusing, arbitrary or involving insecurity. The fact that there had been a continual series of reorganizations in the history of the company, and that the boss had abandoned an idea presented only a couple of months earlier – whereby EDB, for example, would have become an independent division –

might have led to feelings of insecurity and arbitrariness, but there was nothing at the information meeting to remind anyone of this background. Thus, top management was signalling that they knew what they were doing. The phrasing of the question: "How should we organize ourselves in the best possible way?" suggests that the answer had in fact been worked out, and this may have had a calming effect.

As several authors have pointed out, an important task for leaders is to serve as symbols representing the personal causation of social events (Czarniawska-Joerges, 1993; Pfeffer, 1978). The leaders thus confirm that corporate life and outcomes are controllable. Such is presumably seldom the case, but it is important to maintain the appearance of simplicity and controllability in order to maintain faith and confidence.

> the leaders´ role is to provide the rest of the cast and the audience with the illusion of controllability. They are paid vast sums and granted so many privileges not only because they may have to play the scapegoat some day; no, we reward them because, thanks to them, we can stop fearing disorder. ... The arbitrariness of life – especially organizational life – is too frightful to envisage. A leader who fails to provide the illusion, not by a poor performance (which is only human) but by showing us the illusion for what it is, cannot expect to be applauded. The illusion must be supported at whatever the cost. (Czarniawska-Joerges, 1993: 42)

This does not necessarily mean that subordinates ascribe omnipotent capacities to corporate leaders, but that their importance to performance and the possibility of control are overemphasized – by leaders and others (including business journalists and many management researchers). In the present case, the key actor sent strong signals that he was in control – and that the organizational world of Multi was controllable. Let us take a closer look at how the MD performed his role.

3.2.10 The boss: tension-regulator, commander, capitalist, judge of character

Martin, the head of the business sector, dominated the entire meeting. His behaviour embraced a mixture of seriousness and of playing-down the situation. Business aspects and attempts to influence ideas and attitudes dominated, but there were also several examples of using jokes and colloquialisms to defuse the tension. Martin said, for example, "It must have been wonderful to be an executive in those days", and "Your turnover is a billion kronor at the moment, and you´ve promised two billion, Gunnar. So now I´m going to sit back, smoke a cigar, and see how things go." These comments are examples of the way Martin toned down the gravity and the drama, by joking about his own role. This expresses self-confidence: he is relaxed about of the situation and in control of it. It is also a typical way of concealing the exercise of power by defusing a situation. A symbolic action was used here to counteract any disquieting aspects of the reorganization and to blur people´s perceptions of the social and power structures. Humour is important in such contexts; it is usually easy to charm people by joking.

At the same time some elements were intended to increase the tension, e.g. when Martin raised his voice and reminded them all that Northtown was no longer a world manufacturing centre. However, an interest in defusing the atmosphere seems to have weighed more heavily with this main actor at the meeting. He does not appear to have conceived the meeting mainly as an active instrument for change. This would have called for a different framework altogether, for the employment of threatening images, new rhetorical tricks or other gimmicks which would have had a powerful effect on the audience and would have involved them more. It would probably also have involved stronger participation on the part of significant groups of subordinate managers, not so much during the meeting, but in discussing and rethinking organizational issues in other contexts (e.g. project teams, workshops) over a longer time period. But Martin seems to have been mainly interested in reducing uncertainty, frustration and opposition, in achieving a reasonable level of understanding and acceptance for the new organization. There was also a certain attempt to arouse enthusiasm and new thinking, but this seems to have been less crucial to him.

In this respect the boss seems to have acted as a tension regulator. But other meanings can also be attributed to his behaviour. I have referred above to the participant who described the MD as a sergeant-major. In this role Martin´s influence was exercised by varying his vocal pitch. By (sometimes) raising his voice, he got the audience to pay attention.

Loudness signifies leadership. By varying the power of his voice, some of Martin´s words had a dramatic effect. That he was the top boss was emphasized not only by the fact that he spoke more than all the others, but also that he talked loudest. His forcefulness was emphasized. The image of the big boss puffing away at his cigar and waiting for the millions to roll in, arouses images of the capitalist. (It also has a strongly masculine flavour.) In large divisionalized companies, with a multiplicity of different business lines and products, the management function often generates a capitalist or banker type of leadership. The prime example is the pure holding company, which owns and administers but does not directly run or control a number of independently operating subsidiary companies. Many other companies, including Multi at the group level, come close to this way of working, and in connection with the reorganization even DMT´s business area management will come a little nearer to it. Control is primarily a question of measuring profits, without any great involvement in productive operations (cf. Lindkvist, 1989). Thus, despite all the jokes, the image Martin conjured up reveals something important. The business area manager will become something of a capitalist in the divisionalized structure. What is interesting to a capitalist is to measure profits and to keep a check on anyone who does not achieve satisfactory results. So Martin was indicating that others are to do the job, and they will also be held responsible.

However, the boss also emerged as someone who is, or lays claim to be, a judge of human character (a psychologist), one who knows that men and women live not by market shares alone, or by the acquisition of competitors or by increasing turnover. He knows, he told them, what his staff need and want. It is worth pointing out here that for once, according to one of my interviewees, Martin actually emphasized the importance of the staff, and he swore far less than he usually did. Obviously he felt that the occasion called for a more human approach than was customary with him.

The boss as tension-regulator, commander, capitalist and psychologist all rolled into one, provides a set of metaphors signifying the "cold" or "hard" and the "warm" or "soft" elements in the leadership of organizations. Linguistic usage and the projection of certain aspects can direct the subordinates´ attention to different images of both the boss (in our case Martin) and the company, creating a multifaceted impression. A careful juggling with these elements is needed to get people to do what they are expected to do with reasonably good cheer. Harmony apparently prevails between "what people want" and what the capitalist or boss requires. Need and profit become allies. The psychologist and the capitalist agree, and support one another. This is the regular thing in managerial rhetoric, when the two sets of values/considerations are addressed (Alvesson, 1987). In the context of our meeting it was mainly a question of subtle indications: by including certain *items* on the agenda and using suitable phrases, it was possible to influence ideas and to sway people´s attitudes.

3.2.11 Hierarchy

Meetings of this type generally reinforce the established hierarchy, and our case is no exception. Naturally, hierarchy is not just a question of organizational charts, job descriptions and other formalized elements of authority relationships. The vertical differentiation of social relationships is perhaps even more a question of entrenching authority patterns in collective frames of reference and in ideas associated with and defining formal positions, classification boundaries, etc. In other words, hierarchy is a question of culture: the social structure must be entrenched in the common frames of reference and shared meanings "behind" visible behaviour and interaction patterns (Alvesson, 1995a; Ranson et al., 1980; Silverman, 1975).

In the course of the meeting, the existence of four differentiated categories was stressed. The first category consists of Martin, who is obviously DMT´s leading actor. Martin himself took up more than half the total time, and made his position clear by commenting on other people´s contributions. If anything was to be communicated with particular clarity and force at the meeting, it was that Martin is the top leader. At the same time, of course, the message also came across, perhaps unintentionally, that the divisional heads are not quite as important as some of the talk about decentralization might suggest.

A second category, which is the next most important, comprises the three divisional heads. They were clearly visible and were allowed to talk for fifteen minutes each. The third category consists of people who belong to DMT´s staff function. Their relatively minor importance was denoted when their names were mentioned and they were encouraged to stand up. They were soon dealt with. But for a few seconds they had been allowed to stand out from the anonymous crowd. As a result of this visibility their identity and social position was marginally acknowledged. The other ninety-odd people at the meeting constitute the fourth category. The fact that they are considered to possess a certain importance was symbolized by their being invited to attend the meeting. But as we have seen, the meeting mainly served to reinforce their relatively subordinate position. They appeared as a part of the crowd.

Thus, hierarchy was communicated and reinforced in a clear and unambiguous manner.[3] Those assembled learned or were reminded that they were working in a hierarchical organization. We can assume that this had a motivational effect on the lower-ranking managers, who hope to get promotion, and that it helped to encourage a sense of responsibility amongst those who were most clearly singled out from the crowd. (This also applies to the heads of the business sector and the divisions.)

At the same time it should be pointed out that the situation studied here hardly provides a simple reflection of general hierarchical patterns in the company, nor that it contributed in anything but a very limited way to producing asymmetrical social relations as these can reveal themselves in other situations. Attempts to establish stable, general, hierarchical patterns are problematic, since they can easily lead to the reification of social processes and relationships. Any attempt at understanding hierarchies must also allow for variations in social context. Formal hierarchies and the behaviour of key actors involved in symbollically significant situations represent important "resources" and may encourage expectations that affect the negotiation of the exact nature of situation-dependent asymmetrical social relations in a variety of micro-contexts. But the fact that hierarchies are limited in time and space, that they are temporarily established and re-

---

3 The close correlation between position in the hierarchy and the amount of time spent talking in social situations, has been documented by Moxnes (1981) in connection with a study of a psychiatric hospital; Moxnes found that a person's salary grade correlated perfectly with how much they spoke at a meeting. The most inexperienced houseman, for instance, would speak at much greater length than the staff nurse. Moxnes comments tersely that people talked as if this was what they were paid for. Maybe he has a point.

established and must be understood also in situational terms, does not prevent the situation described here from throwing some light on the production and demonstration of hierarchies in corporate contexts.

3.2.12 Contradictions

There were thus certain contradictions in what was said and done in the course of the meeting. The main idea of the new organization is to emphasize the independence of the divisions and the profit responsibility of the business lines. This does not really harmonize with the fact that managers from the whole DMT organization were assembled at this information meeting. The meeting was still signalling the greater importance of the larger unit, and it forcefully emphasized the pervasive role of the head of the business sector. While the big boss was continually talking about decentralization, and the overhead pictures showed the organization structure in horizontal rather than the traditionally vertical terms, the implicit communication was saying the opposite. The statement that "the individual should decide as much as possible" is contradicted by the impression that it is the top manager who will decide most things. (Perhaps he is "the individual" referred to.) We thus have an explicit message pointing in one direction and a "meta message" pointing in the other.

One possible interpretation is that the organizational culture, or a more general management ideology, is speaking to the participants without any control on the part of top management. That is to say, "non-manipulative" symbolism is not an expression of rational, conscious considerations and decisions; rather, a hierarchically inclined organization culture generates communications which contradict what top management says it wants to achieve. (To put it in Argyris and Schön´s terms, this is a good example of the difference between "espoused values" and "values-in-use" (Argyris, 1982).) Values-in-use can be understood in psychological and cultural-theoretical terms.

However, it could be claimed that at a more detailed level the meeting met certain rational requirements and was not a psychological or cultural expression in the sense that it was determined by taken for granted ideas and functions, to some extent independently of will-power and conscious choice. Perhaps it can be explained in terms of top management (Martin) wanting to embrace both options: a clear, taken for granted hierarchy and beliefs about decentralization. The divisions are to be permitted to operate fairly "independently", provided they realize who is boss and the rules of control. There may also be a certain ambivalence on this issue. Or perhaps it is felt that the possibility of considerable structural space for independence does exist at lower levels, and that the importance given to the head of the business sector during the event described here is more a question of providing a sort of symbolic counterweight to this space for autonomy. It could then be said that decentralization was achieved by way of structural types of control (e.g. extensive decision "space" for the division), while hierarchy is (re)created at higher levels in the form of symbolism. In other words, disciplined people can be left to their own devices and relative freedom. (This is discussed further in the next section, inspired by Foucault´s views on power and discipline.) All these interpretations – and many others too – may be correct, or at any rate useful. My impression is that the unplanned aspects ("culture") help to make the contradictions comprehensible; at the same time, and this is not unrelated, it is possible to discern considerable ambivalence *vis-à-vis* the concept of decentralization and a more or less conscious attempt to produce "subordinate-cum-independent" people. It might be added that the decentralization idea is ambiguous in itself. The word can have the most shifting connotations. In the present case, seven units are being transformed into three divisions, which can hardly be described unambiguously as "decentralization". As Czarniawska-Joerges (1993) notes, "almost identical organizational or political changes may be described as centralization or decentralization, depending on the intentions of the label-producers and on current fashion" (p. 20). Perhaps the word decentralization has no meaning beyond the local context – a particular conversation, speech or written text – in which it is invoked. But within particular contexts such as our information meeting, it can affect ideas and meanings. In this sense the term may have temporary and spatially limited meaning and significance for those involved.[4]

---

4 Cf. Silverman (1975: 297) where, with reference to another comparable concept, the absence of any intrinsic meaning is stressed:

3.2.13 Summing up

The information meeting can be regarded as a good example of cultural organizing, that is to say, a process whereby the organization is created and recreated for those belonging to its world of ideas and (inter-) subjectivity. The organization´s fundamental elements in the shape of hierarchy, cohesion, social order, and the rationale of objectives and means, are communicated to and established in those who are present. Social differentiation and social integration are interwoven, as their subordinate-and-manager identity is established. They have to obey orders and instructions, but they are also respected and listened to, and they are included in an overall concept of "we". As Czarniawska-Joerges (1993: 71) notes, "meetings, presentations and conferences can generally reconcile conflicting rationalities; a meeting is considered successful if a single rational account of previous happenings or planned actions emerges as its result". Change is legitimated by reference to various important and apparently relevant circumstances, and is presented as contingent upon the company´s history, its strategy, the needs of the market and the staff and so on – in fact, almost as a logical result of these things. The meeting symbolizes a high degree of rationality. We do not know much about its specific impact on the audience, but as was mentioned in Chapter 2 the impression is that it worked – and that it is an instructive example of efficient management.

At the meeting the social order is constituted/reproduced by symbolic means, and the risk or possibility that the change might disrupt the social order as a result of doubts, negative feelings, resistance to change etc., is counteracted. As Rosen (1985: 47) has said:

In itself, then, bureaucracy has neither an intrinsic meaning nor is it the determinant of actions – it does not have this kind of ontological status. Rather the concept of bureaucracy exists in and through the socially sanctioned occasions of its use.

Decentralization, like bureaucracy, does not refer to any unambiguous external circumstance, and can only be understood in terms of the context in which the word is used. In fact this probably applies to a number of words, concepts and expressions, i.e. that they should be understood in light of their dependence on the narrow local context to which they are restricted.

> Precisely because ritualized social drama serves to postulate social convention as unquestionable, it is frequently used to objectify that which is most in doubt.[5]

This is as far as we can go in our attempt to read something interesting from the general frame of reference outlined above, with its focus on the general culture, ideology and power. In the next chapter an attempt will be made to extend this framework by linking it to Foucault's and Habermas's approaches. Some interpretations will be suggested which emanate more clearly from a reading of the work of these two scholars and their interpreters in the field of organization theory.

---

[5] The appropriateness of the drama metaphor receives some empirical support from one of our interviewees, who referred in positive terms to Martin's acting skills.

4 The meeting as an expression of power and an occasion for discipline: a Foucault-inspired interpretation

In this chapter I start from Foucault´s concept of power, which has led me to some further interpretations of the information meeting. It is with some hesitation that I invoke Foucault, who is after all an historian (although hardly of a conventional type) and philosopher; it is not altogether certain that the present empirical material really allows for interpretations in this light. Furthermore, Foucault was not primarily concerned to develop an integrated theory or a coherent frame of reference. Rather, much of his uniqueness lies in his way of ordering and analysing historical material. However, my intention here is not to offer a strict interpretation of the meeting based on Foucault's overall approach or on any of the diverse and sometimes contradictory ideas that he expressed over the years (Dews, 1987; Hoy, 1986).[1] My intention is simply to provide some relatively free interpretations that start from a certain familiarity with Foucault´s concept of power and his ideas about the individual (the subject). I am thus taking him as a source of inspiration, but the way I make use of his ideas will be coloured to some extent by my own affiliation with the world of organizational culture research. Nonetheless, since this chapter is clearly influenced by my reading of some of Foucault´s writings on power and the production of the individual (the subject), I will begin by saying something

---

[1] It is usual to divide Foucault's work into three periods (even though this exaggerates certain differences), namely the archeological, the genealogical and the ethical. In the first period he explored the rules and procedures that made it historically possible for people to get their statements in various fields recognized as "truth" or "science". It was a question of examining how certain practices and conceptual frameworks came to be accepted in particular historical periods as natural, self-evident and irrefutable. In the genealogical period Foucault sought to show how social practices and discursive formation exist independently of subjects and how they constitute the individual as a describable, analysable object. In the ethical phase he was primarily concerned with the way individuals constitute themselves as ethical subjects, "those ways in which individuals objectify themselves so as to recognise, and become committed to, a particular sense of their own subjectivity" (Knights, 1992: 518). In the present study I refer essentially to Foucault's work during the genealogical period.

about his power concept before returning, with this in mind, to the information meeting. (On Foucault, see, for example, Burrell, 1988; Clegg, 1994; Daudi, 1986; Dews, 1987; Hoy, 1986; Townley, 1994)

4.1 Foucault´s concept of power

Foucault (1974, 1976, 1980, 1982) has developed a discourse of power that differs markedly from the traditional view. He does not employ the usual sociological categories and concepts such as individuals, structures, interests and ideologies, nor does he delimit or define power as such. He refuses to embrace such conventional approaches. Nor does his work relate specifically to the positions and debates within the field of power studies. Clegg (1989a: 3) notes that in contrast to the mainstream of cautious debate, "Foucault´s influence seemed to be promiscuously metaphorical where one had been schooled to anticipate more clinical precision." Power is not for him an abstract concept that can be isolated and studied on its own. Power has no essence and cannot be measured; it exists only in relational terms or when expressed in action. Foucault understands power as

> the multiplicity of force relations immanent in the sphere in which they operate and which constitute their own organization; as the process which, through ceaseless struggles and confrontations, transforms, strengthens, or reverses them, as the support which these force relations find in one another, thus forming a chain or a system, or on the contrary, the disjunctions and contradictions which isolate them from one another; and lastly, as the strategies in which they take effect. (Foucault, 1976: 92-3)

Foucault is thus not concerned with who *has* power, whatever the source of that power may be – rank, charisma, knowledge, legal rights or anything else. He rejects the view of power as a commodity, tied to a sovereign agent (king, ruling elite). This view implies that power is clearcut and centralized, a view that trivializes it and tempts us to disregard its multifaceted character. Power cannot be localized or tied down. For Foucault power is a "machine in which everybody is caught, those who exercise power just as much as those over whom power is exercised" (1980: 156).

Foucault´s ideas of power must be understood in a particular, although broad historical context – that of modern society. The feudal society called for fairly loose control at the level of everyday life. People´s lives did not have to be regulated in detail. Repressive political interventions were dramatic but occasional, in the shape of brutal physical punishments. In this context the traditional idea of sovereign power made good sense as a way of understanding what was going on. But in recent centuries and in contemporary society, economy and society both call for a much more sophisticated control of individual behaviour. No single centre – king, feudal lord, state or capitalist – exercising control over subordinates from above can master it. Hence, Foucault´s network theory of power.

Power relations can best be understood in terms of the forms and techniques in which they are expressed, in particular in terms of the constraints that people impose on their own bodies and these of others. It is the *exercise* of power that is of crucial importance; it is the practices, techniques and procedures which give effect to power that should interest us. Only then, says Foucault, can we talk about power in a meaningful way. This means that laws and formal rights tell us very little about power. In fact, Foucault´s whole project can be seen as an attempt to "reveal the micro-techniques and the subjugations that underwrite such formal rights" (Knights and Vurdubakis, 1994: 190).

Thus, essentially, power is all around us. It is omnipresent, expressed in various microcontexts and cannot be restricted to any particular entity or dimension such as the state, corporate management, capitalism and so on. Institutions – schools, factories, hospitals – form a fine-meshed network of discipline exerting influences. The study of the "micro-physics" of power requires us to attribute effects of domination,

> not to "appropriation", but to dispositions, manoeuvres, tactics, techniques, functionings; that one should decipher in a network of relations, constantly in tension, in activity, rather than a privilege that one might possess; that one should take as its model a perpetual battle rather than a contract regulating a transaction or the conquest of a territory. In short this power is exercised rather than possessed; it is not the "privilege", acquired or preserved, of the dominant class, but the overall effect of its strategy positions – an effect that is manifested and sometimes extended by the position of those who are dominated. Furthermore, this power is not exercised simply as an obligation or a prohibition

on those who "do not have it"; it invests them, is transmitted by them and through them; it exerts pressure upon them, just as they themselves, in their struggle against it, resist the grip it has on them. (Foucault, 1974: 26-27)

Foucault has neither defined power nor formulated any clear theory about it, as is natural in view of his particular ideas on the subject. This is contingent upon his interest in the diversity of power – an interest that prevents universal statements about it. He regards power as the visible arrangement of practices, or open structures which are applied in a variety of forms and different social fields. Foucault presents no theory of power to restrict this field of analysis, no theoretical ordering to stake out the boundaries within which "power" is supposed to "be". Power "is" not, but the practices within which and by means of which it exists – they, potentially, are everywhere (Beronius, 1986: 32).

According to Foucault, the most significant form of power in the present context is disciplinary power. This power, which originated at the beginning of the eighteenth century in prisons and clinics in the name of behavioural reform, aided by the emerging human sciences, revolved around systems of surveillance and normalizing judgements. Through systems of observation and careful prescriptions as to what is appropriate (normal, therapeutic), the regulation of conduct was and is accomplished. As Clegg (1989a: 156) points out, Foucault focuses on discourses which increasingly limit, define and normalize the motives and meanings which are "available in specific sites for making sensible and accountable that which people should do, can do and thus do". Originating in institution-alized contexts, the systems of observation and classification and the normalizing judgements associated with these are taken over by our own reflexive gaze, as we evaluate ourselves and make ourselves objects of discipline according to these prescribed patterns of meanings and standards of conduct. Foucault´s work is primarily concerned with the production of bodies, and sometimes he almost gives the impression that the drilling of bodies is the means, and docile bodies are the desired end, while the underlying mental processes are a matter of indifference. However, his basic position was that behavioural change is achieved through "a general recipe for the exercise of power over men: the ´mind´ as a surface of inscription of power, with semiology as its tool; the submission of bodies through control of ideas" (Foucault, 1974: 102).

In any attempt to understand power, it is important to consider the potential for resistance. Control of the purely physical kind – violence – can be immediately comprehended for what it is. But power is relational, and in this it differs from sheer dominance (violence, force, etc.). Power can be seen as struggle rather than direct repression. Foucault's favourite metaphor is power as war. He paraphrases Clausewitz and says that power is war continued by other means (Foucault, 1980: 90). Power always presupposes the possibility of resistance to power. By definition the relationships of power can not then be too asymmetrical; it then ceases to be a matter of power and turns into something else. Resistance is not clear-cut, any more than power is, nor does it generate a coherent force. Resistance to power can assume many forms, but always within a network of power relations. Resistance and evasive action lead in turn to new forms of power (reading Foucault's work rarely inspires optimism!). Power is ubiquitous and cannot be evaded. Ideas on resistance are by no means prominent or well developed. Commenting on Foucault's perhaps most important book, *Discipline and Punish*, Geertz says that Foucault seems to turn the conventional progressive descriptions of history upside-down, seeing it "as the rise of unfreedom" (quoted in Hoy, 1986: 143). In most of Foucault's texts subjects tends to react as "determined" by prescriptive forces, rather than showing much success in resisting the operations of power. (For another opinion on this matter see Knights and Vurdubakis, 1994.)

Perhaps the "essence" of Foucault's conception of power is its quality as a crucial aspect of relations in which subjectivity, defined as complex, contradictory and shifting experience is transmuted or reproduced by way of social practices expressing power (Knights and Willmott, 1989: 541). This leads to that self-consciousness "becomes a constraining force tying subjects to their (our) own identities" (p. 551).

Whereas the conventional view is that the subjects – the actors – lie behind the social practices (prevalent modes of action), Foucault maintains the opposite. In his analysis discourses precede and shape the subjects. This is not achieved in a mechanical way. Rather the form of the subject and its way of relating to itself and its world is discursively constituted. Thus phenomena such as "reason", "madness", "criminality", "morality", "sexuality", "needs" and "motives" appear not as natural objects that are part of part of (wo)man´s way of being, but as artificial objects which it has been possible to constitute so that they appear at one and the same time as the object for certain forms of knowing and as the target of historically specific reform and regulation projects (Beronius, 1991). "Madness" is thus not just something that exists "out there" in the minds of particular individuals; rather, it is something that has been brought to the fore during a particular period and with the help of various techniques and procedures as a special object of knowledge and attention (incarceration, treatment). The "raw material" is there, in the shape of behaviour, gestures, biochemical processes and so on, but what is perceived as obsession, immorality, the wrath of God or mental illness is the result of a process of differentiation, classification and positioning on a material and an epistemological dimension. Likewise, such things as motivation and strategy are not merely phenomena existing "out there", but are things created discursively and materially in the shape of various practices. Any attempts to chart the nature of human motivation or to generate ideas resembling "natural laws" on the subject of, for example, strategy, leadership, job satisfaction or motivation, are thus doomed to failure (see Knights, 1992; Townley, 1994).

Knowledge and knowing are thus central concepts in Foucault´s thinking. He argues that "power and knowledge directly imply one another, that there is no power relation without the correlative constitution of a field of knowledge, nor any knowledge that does not presuppose and constitute at the same time power relations" (Foucault, 1980: 27). Various forms of knowledge are in the service of power and function as instruments of discipline, among other things by indicating what is normal and what is deviant. Accepted ideas in science and other societal institutions about what is normal and reasonable, thus help to regulate the individual´s self-perception and behaviour. As Foucault sees it, knowledge and knowing cannot be separated from power and cannot indicate neutral insights. Power and knowing are parallel concepts, but not of course identical. His interest is in how "games of truth" (a game is an ensemble of rules for the production of the truth) "can put themselves in place and be linked to relationships of power" (Foucault, 1984: 16). However, sometimes one gets the impression from Foucault´s writing that the exercise of power and the advancement or application of knowledge are very intimately related. By creating normal curves, by classifying, codifying, calibrating and subdividing phenomena, it is possible both to handle these phenomena and to acquire (additional) knowledge about them. Knowledge and institutional control go hand in hand – at school, in psychiatry, correctional treatment, sex therapy, childcare, working life, etc. Power refers to a certain coherence in social relations contingent upon, as well as making possible, the construction of a grid of intelligibility.

Foucault´s project does not aim to separate truth (science, knowledge) from ideology (which is then roughly equated with something false or misleading, e.g. prejudice, distortions), but to reveal the mechanisms whereby the "politics of truth" are constituted in a power-knowledge relation. "Truth" to Foucault is always a social construction, which constitutes and is constituted by discursive practices in a particular historical period. Foucault is inspired by Nietzsche who claimed that the will to know is intimately connected with the will to power. Knowledge lies at the root of the exercise of power, while the exercise of power also produces knowledge. To put it another way, power becomes a central dimension not only of knowledge supported by institutional practices, but also of institutional practices based on knowledge. Not only repressive knowledge but also "supportive" and "progressive" forms of knowledge are associated with power, and operate in a discipline-imposing manner. Discipline in the sense of a branch of knowledge, makes possible discipline meaning a system of correction and control, and vice versa. (Walzer, 1986, remarks that Foucault sometimes appears to be committed to nothing more than an elaborate pun on the word "discipline".) Examples discussed by Foucault include medicine, psychiatry and psychology. "Management" could appropriately be added to this list (Deetz, 1992a; Knights, 1992; Townley, 1993, 1994). Management methods, even the apparently most humane or technical, would according to this view be regarded not as "neutral" control and coordination, but as instruments of power, whereby individuals´ field of action can be circumscribed and restricted in various ways, by shaping them – the individuals – as subjects.

In Foucault´s view the most interesting aspect of power in modern society is the power that is directed against subjectivity and its constitution. In one of his later works he even declares, "it is not power, but the subject, which is the general theme of my research" (Foucault, 1982: 778).[2] Due to the close coupling between power and the creation of the subject, however, this shift in emphasis is of slight importance only. In the creation of subjectivity, the individual is made into an object for subordination as well as developing (being provided with) a particular identity. As in the case of the concept of discipline, Foucault exploits the ambiguity of language and says: "There are two meanings of the word ´subject´: subject to someone else by control and dependence; and tied to his own identity by a conscience or self-knowledge" (Foucault, 1982: 781). Power is thus exercised by binding the subject to a particular identity or form. It is not any autonomous or genuine identity that is meant; rather, Foucault rejects an essentialist view of man: we cannot say anything about man as such; all we can study are the discourses and practices which shape the individual and through which he or she emerges as an object of knowledge and influence. "The individual is the effect of power" (Foucault, 1980: 98).

The constituted identity limits but also enables some action. The individual´s self-perception is controlled and regulated through the effects of power:

> Subjection is accomplished through the development of modern organization´l practices and institutions – such as the clocking-in system, the open plan office or the appraisal system – that promote an accountability of the self. Through their operations, modern subjects are constituted whose sense of self-identity is invested in the reproduction of these practices – not simply to achieve material rewards or avoid punishment but to gain and confirm a (self-disciplining) sense of their own normality as sovereign subjects. (Willmott, 1994: 106)

Power has a positive or productive side, even though Foucault seems to pay more attention to its "negative" or restrictive aspects, at least in the works referred to in this book and of greatest relevance in our present context.[3] At any rate optimism is hardly a spontaneous reaction to a

---

2   In an interview he states that the knowledge/power problem was not the fundamental theme, but an instrument allowing the analysis "of the problem of relationships between subject and games of truth" (Foucault, 1984: 10).

3   Particularly in some of his late writings, Foucault's formulations on power were more "positive" in character, depending on a change of orientation, including an interest in non-coercive practices involving the self-formation of the subject (e.g. Foucault, 1984). Here it

confrontation with Foucault´s texts; nor is it his intention to make his readers feel happy about what may appear "reasonable". In so far as it is not simply a question of repression and restrictiveness – something which partly falls outside Foucault´s focus – but also of showing that certain potentials are developed, then we can talk about the economics of power. This is concerned with disciplining individuals so that they become self-disciplined and productive beings, ready and willing to learn. These positive attributes can generate a benevolent attitude towards the forms of power (which may not even be perceived as power), since they are associated not only with constraints and fixations of subjects but also with productive functions such as capacity and constructive attitudes as well as with identity and the affirmation of identity. My empirical case illustrates this.

There are certain elements of functionalism in Foucault´s work (Dews, 1987; Walzer, 1986). No subjects are responsible, but mechanisms producing "positive" (productive) effects for the social order are still in force. At the same time Foucault´s critical undertone and occasional calls for struggle alert us to contradictions in this position. In addition to his in certain respects (almost) functionalist account of power and social development, the persistent imposition of order in the development and use of knowledge is conceived as being triggered by a basic fear of uncertainty and disorder, of the chaotic and unclassifiable. Here the figure of thought (or root metaphor) seems to be one of obsessive neurosis or ontological anxiety, which is quite far removed from functionalist thinking. If Foucault´s consideration of resistance and the accompanying restrictions on the smoothness of the power mechanisms in force are also taken into account, the limited elements of functionalism could be described as a partial and critical version of the functionalist approach.

If the potential accomplished by the operations of power does not develop freely, nor as determined by particular actors, what then accounts for the shape of these operations? The crucial element, Foucault tells us, is certain dominating and historically generated ideas, so-called discourses. A discourse is a theoretically based line of thought, regulated and inspired by

---

is a question of being able, with the help of aesthetics, to develop a positive type of self-control which is not constrained by a repressive structure (Coles, 1991). This orientation differs greatly from his earlier work and will not be addressed other than marginally here.

power relations and social practices, but also constituting and regulating these practices; it is thus both socially and economically determined and determining. It provides frames for thinking and is associated with the development of knowledge during a particular period, and contributes to the determination of practices. Discourse enables and orders statements and endows them with a uniform pattern. It also indicates what is not "sayable" and how objects are spoken of in a certain manner. Discourses exist over and beyond the individual subjects. They produce forms to which subjectivities are linked and adapted. As we have seen, Foucault wants to break with the Western notion of the central role of the independent subject. He denies the existence of an autonomous subject, and claims instead that the discourses define and control the individuals. (There has been much debate on this issue see, for example, Hoy, 1986.) Not only subordinates but even those "in power" are subordinate to these discourses and their related structures. In our case it may appear as though the managing director, Martin, has full control over the situation, but appearances can be deceptive.

Finally, any review of Foucault´s work must emphasize that he does not believe in the idea of progress. At least, he provides no criteria or other forms of assistance about how knowledge (games of truth) or social institutions and practices should be evaluated, but encourages a deep universal suspicion of them all. New forms of knowledge and new practices in social life or in management and control – apparently more rational or humane – deserve just as much scepticism and criticism as earlier authoritarian and obviously repressive conditions. For power lurks everywhere – not least behind euphemism and seemingly happy circumstance. These last in particular must be subject to a power analysis.

4.2   Critique of Foucault

Despite or rather because of Foucault´s international popularity since the late 1970s, a good deal of sometimes quite harsh criticism has been levelled against him. As well as reviewing this, I will also note some further critical points or themes that the power analysts following in his footsteps would do well to be wary of. Not all the comments that follow are meant to lay any specific blame at Foucault´s door. I simply want to comment on some problems that could arise from the uncritical application of a Foucauldian perspective in research.

One danger is that a Foucault-inspired approach becomes something of a "rubber theory". To scrutinize apparently neutral or "good" situations and practices for their power implications is naturally laudable, but the idea risks taking over the empirical material. It is hard to imagine any observation that could be immune to Foucault´s interpretation of power. How, for example, could one express doubt about the idea that the individual is an effect of power? Everything can be brought under the yoke of Foucault´s theory; and the inherent danger when any potent theory or conceptual apparatus is turned upon the non-obvious, is that it embraces not only "everything" but – by the same token – also "nothing". If power is everywhere, it is also nowhere. If it explains everything, there is a fair risk that it explains nothing or, to put it a little less strongly, that it pushes imagination and the interpretive bias too hard in too narrow a direction and along a tightly prestructured line of thinking. (This could, of course, be said of others besides Foucault.)

There is a totalizing element in Foucault´s work – or in the kind of thinking that he encourages. Sometimes he defines power in such general terms that it is hard to disagree on its overall significance and persistence. In a late interview, for example, he claimed that "in human relations, whatever they are – whether it be a question of communicating verbally or a question of a love relationship, an institutional or economic relationship – power is always present: I mean the relationship in which one wishes to direct the behaviour of another" (Foucault, 1984: 11). These words make quite a different impression from most of Foucault´s writings on power, but are hardly incompatible with them. I will not embark on sorting out the differences and inconsistencies in Foucault´s position(s) here, but have simply quoted this passage to illustrate his tendency to view power so broadly that it lacks precision, depth and communicatibility. The use of the term power and the insistence on privileging an understanding revolving around it, conflates quite different phenomena – despite his interest in diversity. Knights and Vurdubakis (1994) defend Foucault by arguing that his claim that power is in all social relationships does not mean that power is exhaustive of such relationships: "it is not the case that all social relationships are *nothing but* power relations" (p. 182). The above quotation from Foucault does not indicate that a person in a relationship wishes all the time to direct the behaviour of the other. But from a Foucauldian position it is difficult to say anything about the non-power aspects of social relations. The coherent research agenda allows only relationships of power to appear. Other aspects or qualities are lost.

In Foucault´s historical studies his theoretical approach is naturally used in a more specific way and with a considerable analytical bite, but the general problem still remains for his followers – unless they are very careful – of avoiding a totalizing approach. The guru himself sometimes tended to see the same mechanisms of power in quite diverse contexts (Calhoun, 1992), but the problem is more noticeable in some followers. According to some critics, his work "has been shamelessly appropriated by his universalizing disciplines who ... are prone to overtheorization" (Aronowitz, 1992: 315) and have neglected the fundamental idea of conducting detailed empirical studies producing local knowledge.

A related issue is the tendency to determinism and the view of the individual as oversocialized (Wrong, 1961). The scope for human agency is extremely limited in the world of Foucault´s texts. Subjects resist in terms of mobilizing a counterforce to the powers operating on the individual. Other kinds of action are directly contingent upon the effects of power and control. But as will be discussed below, Foucault has little to say on the matter of resistance. Given that discourses do not form themselves, there seems to be a case for an appreciation of an active, creative human subject not solely produced by power, but able to be active in relation to – and not only as an result of or within – discourses. Foucault himself would be an example. (For another view, see Knights and Vurdubakis, 1994.)

Another problem concerns the limitations inherent in the micro-focus that Foucault applies. The idea that power has no centre or essence is forcefully argued, but it means that some apparently vital phenomena fall outside the Foucauldian spotlight, for instance power relations associated with economic conditions. Foucault rejects the importance of ideology but, as Clegg (1989a) contends, it is hard to understand the role of a Thatcher or a Reagan without taking ideological considerations into account. Walzer (1986) is critical of Foucault for failing to recognize the significant role of the (central) agencies, such as the state that establishes the general framework which shapes the character of disciplinary institutions and practices. Legislation, for example, constrains the micro practices adopted in prisons. He argues that every act of local resistance is an appeal for political or legal intervention from the centre. This is perhaps a slight exaggeration, but the point makes sense. Perhaps one could argue for a reduction in the importance of some forms of sovereign power, but there are certainly centres in the contemporary world not directly operating on subjects through disciplinary power but still forming material life conditions in various ways, including those that indirectly affect subjectivities, e.g. the economically and legally based power to make people unemployed. Walby (1992) claims that Foucault's concept of power is too dispersed and that economic conditions, relations between social classes and certain fundamental aspects of relations between the sexes, disappear from view. Of course, one could hardly expect any scholar to take all kinds of power into account. The problem in a Foucauldian approach is partly that it overstates its case for the micro-physics of power in the battle with other conceptions of power, and partly that the popularity of this approach may lead to other forms of power being lost to sight or trivialized. A warning against an uncritical privileging of a Foucauldian understanding of power is called for. What scholars could do is to maintain a Foucault-inspired focus but to write in such a way that they as well as their readers are reminded of other power and control issues which could be considered but which are not being pursued in the study in question. This may be accomplished, for example, in comments, in notes, or in self-reflexive passages in the main text (Alvesson and Sköldberg, 1996; Law, 1994).

A third problem, according to critics of Foucault's position, springs from his comprehensively pessimistic view of new forms of knowledge and technology. Everything tends to be a question of power and normalization. At any rate there are no guidelines for identifying things that may lie beyond the range of these two, or things which may represent less "negative" forms of power. Foucault may be said to exaggerate the use of prison as a model for understanding contemporary social life in general (Walzer, 1986). His position indicates the irrelevance of institutional purpose and his concepts tend to flatten out institutional differences such as those between total and non-total institutions (Armstrong, 1994). This is not to deny the point in looking for and emphasizing the ways in which schools, hospitals and factories resemble prisons on the level of practice or the technologies of control, but a micro-focus on power may miss some important aspects. Appreciating the meaning and effects of various technologies of control may call for a consideration of the wider context in which they are employed. The prison as a model may discourage any positive evaluation of the functioning and outcomes of other institutions.[4] Foucault´s stance leaves him unable to discern the positive aspects of advances in technology, law and medicine, for example (Dreyfus and Rabinow, 1986). Everything becomes "problematic", and no clues are given as to what may be regarded as particularly so. This means that an analysis which is at least usually regarded as political and critical, risks turning into the opposite, i.e. the analysis loses its critical thrust and becomes apolitical. Without some form of normative position against which the "problematical" can be seen, then the "problematical" easily emerges as a universal quality which could equally well be described as its own opposite. Something becomes "problematic" (worthy of criticism) only in light of (the possible existence of) something "unproblematic" (cf. Dews, 1987).[5]

---

4   This problem is very noticeable not only in the works of Foucault and his followers, but in critical management and organization studies in general. Positive outcomes such as products and services that meet socially legitimate demands tend, for example, to be neglected.

5   There is a peculiar co-existence between the pessimistic-negative understanding of power in many of Foucault's works, and passages indicating a more positive and functional view of the subject matter found in some of the texts. In a late interview he even seems to see "normal" power, as opposed to abuses of power, as something good (Foucault, 1984: 10, 18). Against Foucault's often hypercritical opinion of social institutions, discourses and practices in terms of power, the view expressed here verges on the uncritical, with negative features seen almost as deviations from the normal operations of power, e.g. "the effects of domination which will make a child subject to the arbitrary and useless authority of a teacher" (p. 18). Power is to be seen as "the relationship of power as strategic games between liberties" rather than as states of domination (p. 19). A certain degree of balance seems to be regarded as a characteristic of power relationships. Thus a pluralistic view of power is expressed. Most typical of Foucault's approach, however, is its pessimistic undertone – even when he is emphasizing the productive capacities of power mechanisms – and this is clearly the most salient theme in the Foucauldian work which is referred to here and which most authors in management, organization and accounting studies have followed. Here the strongly asymmetrical – as opposed to the pluralistic – nature of power relationships is emphasized, and Foucault is explicit in his sympathy for the unpriviledged.

A way of countering this critique, or rather of softening it, could be to recall the purpose of critical work, namely to refrain from encouraging an uncritical view of the presumed good or unproblematic. Caution in authorizing certain social institutions or practices is of course motivated. But there is a middle ground between providing moral blueprints to guide people in their lives, and treating everything as dangerous. Here we find, for example, Habermas´s idea of communicative action.

Despite Foucault´s frequent talk of resistance and his encouragement of local struggles, he has little of substance to say on this issue. Fraser (cited in Hoy, 1986: 8) poses the question: "Why is struggle preferable to submission? Why ought domination to be resisted? Only with the introduction of normative notions of some kind could Foucault begin to answer this question. Only with the introduction of normative notions could he begin to tell us what is wrong with the modern power/knowledge regime and why we ought to oppose it." In addition, Foucault has hardly anything to say on successful local resistance. As Sarup (1988) remarks, for Foucault resistance is simply a residual category. An important question here concerns where the resistance come from. The fluidity of the effects of power and resistance against the mechanisms of power, hardly appear in Foucault´s theory:

> If resistances and subjugated knowledges are fashioned from intellectual materials extrinsic to prevailing regimes of truth, the manner of co-existence of these "truths" needed to be explored. If, on the other hand, they are fashioned from the materials of the regime itself ... this appears to require an ambiguity in regimes of truth which was not allowed for in Foucault´s power-knowledge identification. (Armstrong, 1994: 33)

According to some Foucauldians, e.g. Knights and Vurdubakis (1994), the stability achieved by power relations is precarious and contingent upon discourses working in complex and unstable ways. Technologies of power operate on subjects who already bear the imprint of forms of subjectivity constituted in sites encountered earlier in the life trajectory. The plurality of discourses working in historical sequence, or simultanously, may thus fuel ambiguity and resistance. There are also uncertainties and in-consistencies within a specific discursive relation constitutive of a particular institutional site.

Another critique of Foucault concerns his relativism. He is convincing in his treatment of different forms of knowledge as discursively constituted and implicated in power. But what about his own position? Are Foucault´s own knowledge products also "truths" implicated in power relations? When he says that "truth is a thing of this world; it is produced only by virtue of multiple forms of constraints" (Foucault, 1980: 73), this presumably also has some relevance for the evaluation of his own work. One can hardly escape the dilemma by arguing that his knowledge products are not truths. After all, Foucault is a highly respected academic and his validity claims are not radically different from others in the human sciences, even though his interest, focus and style differ from those of conventional approaches. Like other relativists, who run into the paradox of stating as a sort of truth that there are no truths (at least not independently of power), he has difficulty in escaping altogether from being caught by his own assumptions about the general nature of knowledge. Having said this, it must be acknowledged that the problem of relativism is complicated, involving many different levels. As Brown (1994: 22) remarks, "the fact that a truth is socially constructed does not make it untrue". The problem is, however, that the idea of something being true or untrue tends to be irrelevant or impossible to investigate, if social construction and/or the power aspects of knowledge are being emphasized. Not only "truths" but also the power effects of a "truth", i.e. claims about the truth of the consequences of the truth produced, must be understood in the context of power. Perhaps a stronger response to the relativism problem is to suggest that Foucault is "focusing on the *how* rather than the *what* of truth or virtue and he implies a form of knowledge/power that may be more open and democratic than existing ones" (Brown, 1994: 30). But even the "how" of Foucault´s work could be focused upon, rather than just being reproduced or applied in new areas.

A final point of criticism concerns Foucault as an empirical researcher. Several critics have pointed out that his work is based mainly on sources such as written projects and proposals for arrangements, plans for architectural sites, handbooks for rules and regulations, but rarely on actual accounts of practices and experiences (Walzer, 1986). Silverman (1985: 91) sees this as the most fundamental weakness in Foucault´s work, and says that Foucault occasionally fails to follow his own methodological injunctions. To some extent these critics forget that historical studies cannot include direct observations by the researcher. The critique is more valid when it comes to researchers interested in contemporary phenomena. Many of Foucault´s followers in organization and management studies, for example, can be rightly criticized for being more interested in general theoretical discussions, and for drawing empirically oriented conclusions based on texts with an uncertain relationship to social practice. Knights and Morgan (1991), for example, tend to treat corporate strategy as a social practice, as if academic textbooks told us much about micro practices in corporations and how the subjects are actually produced. Even in more empirically oriented studies, for example in the accounting field, where interest in Foucault has been fairly strong among critical scholars, the preoccupation has been more with managerial intent than with actual operations and effects (Armstrong, 1994: 74).

The absence of detailed empirical studies of "real" situations and practices in management and organization research may be read as a warning of the difficulties involved in such projects. Perhaps the reader should not expect too much of what follows below. Nevertheless, the shortage of studies of real encounters in corporate life makes the present one even more important. However, although my study moves beyond plans and formal regulations and investigates a "real" encounter, the specific effects of power are noted only marginally.

Some of the critiques reviewed above are – like so much criticism – somewhat unfair, in that they turn less on the foci of Foucault´s own interest and more on the borderline between what he treats and the things he chooses not to explore. In order to make an original and significant contribution – something which Foucault definitely has done – delimitation and concentration in the theoretical project are of course absolutely necessary. And naturally none of the criticisms can alter the fact that Foucault is a crucial source of inspiration for critical social science on a broad front. However, there are problems and weaknesses in his work, not perhaps so much in his less historically specific works as in his more general, theoretical texts and statements (which, however, has the considerable advantage of making his work relevant also beyond the particular historical contexts, such as prisons in the seventeenth and eighteenth centuries). It is important to remember that disregarded areas do exist, if we are to understand a thinker´s position without becoming blind to everything beyond the spotlight of his or her theory. A theory sharpens our attention in certain directions, but can in so doing weaken it in others. As Armstrong (1994) shows, authors in accounting who follow Foucault sometimes run into obvious difficulties when they try to press all their observations into a Foucauldian framework. They miss obvious candidates for explanation, or use commonsensical – and plausible – explanations without noticing that they fall outside Foucault's approach or are even inconsistent with it. On the basis of his review of a number of case studies and of various theoretical considerations, Armstrong (1994) argues that when confronted with resistance – and corporate life quite often exhibits less compliance than the victims of the "rise of unfreedom" in Foucault's texts – the systematic surveillance and behavioural norms of disciplinary power can only work "within a matrix of physical coercion, economic power, negotiated order or some combination of these" (p. 41). I will maintain a focus on Foucault-inspired ideas and concepts, however, and will only exceptionally extend the interpretations clearly beyond that in the next section.

There is one general implication associated with several of the critical points raised above, which I should like the reader to bear in mind. This concerns the element of hyperscepticism and paranoia in a (typical) Foucauldian position – at least as expressed in his most influential writings. In Foucault's world, where "everything is dangerous" (cited in Knights and Vurdubakis, 1994: 187) alien elements (power) take over human bodies like the body snatchers from outer space in the fifties movie: "power reaches into the very grain of individuals, touches their bodies and inserts itself into their actions and lives" (Foucault, 1980: 39). Bearing this metaphor in mind might encourage a slightly ironic distance to Foucauldian ideas, an attitude which I believe is important in general in academic work, but perhaps especially so in the case of Foucault because of the seductiveness of his theory and the limited possibilities of letting empirical observations kick against it. The contemporary popularity of Foucault's work – and the absence of self-reflection, in most of the apologists' writings, on the historical context of the discursive formation of these subjects as Foucauldians – provides a rationale for exploring at some length some of the difficulties of his writings, especially if they are seen as a general theoretical perspective and not only or primarily as a series of restricted historical studies of doubtful relevance to the understanding of other contexts.

Now, however, it is time to make constructive use of his work, which after all is so fascinating in so many ways.

4.3   The information meeting and the activation of power techniques

In Foucault´s terms the whole meeting can be described as an exercise in discipline rather than an information meeting. With Foucault-like suspiciousness – a strong sensitivity to the micro-physics of power – we can interpret "informing" as the "forming" of the subjects, and the meeting as the activation of a whole set of power techniques. One perhaps trivial example is the strict control over attendance before the meeting even started, and the way the personnel manager – as the boss´s obedient handmaiden – kept a watchful eye on who was there: the number called and the number present had to tally; there were not even any extra chairs. The meeting was mandatory. It is thus absolutely clear who controls these people´s movements and decides where they should be at what time – it is of course top management. The fact that the meeting had nothing secret to reveal, and nothing that had to be passed on in just that particular way, suggests that power was involved rather than any expression of the practical or "natural" – a distinction that is in fact alien to Foucault, since ideas about what is "natural" are bearers of power rather than separate from it. Thus the control over attendance, in our case, was an expression of arbitrariness/variability that characterizes all social relations.

On the whole, however, this situation exhibits hardly anything in terms of the "drilling of bodies", which is otherwise Foucault´s key example of disciplinary power. The creation of docile bodies is not significant in the operation of technologies of control over subjects doing "intellectual" rather than "behavioural" work, such as those present in the meeting.

4.3.1 Sovereign power as a "truth" and element in disciplinary power

Just after the audience had been told that they were at the meeting "because they were managers", it was announced that production was now located in eighteen different countries and that Northtown was not the centre of the world. The way this was put tends to identify the members of the audience as people with narrow horizons, incapable of understanding the broader view. It was clearly implied that what was "the centre of the world" to them was a very tiny part of the great big world beyond. They were thus defined as "locals" in an international concern. It was also being clearly demonstrated that the "power-knowledge" coupling put them at a disadvantage in the present situation. The framing of the situation made experience-based knowledge appear irrelevant in the current context. Just this consistent but subtle underlining of the knowledge gap between corporate management and "the rest", helps to soften up "the rest" and make them receptive to management´s messages. It may be added that the current reorganization affected only a part of the company, and the present audience was better placed to evaluate this change than to judge various other issues touching on the whole company and its market.

Conventionally, this could be understood as the straightforward operation of sovereign power. A centrally located agency possessing legal authority, a surplus of information, a certain body of skills and experiences, and control over material sanctions, enables the troops to follow. Whether and to what extent centralized decisions and plans are implemented is, of course, always an open question.[6] From the theoretical position adopted here, however, the "sovereign power" of top management is better understood in terms of various elements in the network of power that establish the "truth" of this central agency. It has power effects on the subjects to the extent that they are produced as subordinates in relationship to practices defined as emerging from the "sovereign power" of top

---

6 To what extent resistance may be said to account for the discrepancies between decisions/managerial intentions and outcomes is open to debate. Even when the discrepancy is obvious, it may sometimes be understood as a matter of ambiguities, uncertainties, complexities and changes in circumstances rather than resistance. To make a strict distinction between ambiguities and other problems of complex dynamic social situations on the one hand and issues of resistance on the other, however, is not easy, as the first may fuel the second and represent a crucial element in it.

management. In other worlds, "sovereign power" does not function as such. It is not best understood as an objective, well-integrated agency causing certain outcomes through its power base, but should be seen as elements in particular discursive operations. Such is the case, for example, in situations where top managers appear as representatives of sovereign power, and their "leadership", e.g. exercise of discipline regimes, is backed up by beliefs about this power (discourse on the sovereign nature of management). Let me try to formulate this point in yet another way. The knowledge or game of truth that definites top management as a sovereign power, produces subjects placed at some distance from this sovereign centre and as subordinates relative to that knowledge or power. In simpler (and less Foucauldian) terms: it is the defining of top management as a sovereign power, i.e. the incorporation of a conventional/commonsensical view of power, and the definition of oneself as a responsive object in relation to this power, that result in the power-induced effect. Whether or not Foucault is "correct" when he says that sovereign power is out of fashion (not significant) is not the point here; what matters is that it is a firm standard cultural belief (established management discourse) that sovereign power exists and is vital. This belief has power-induced effects on individuals, even in a Foucauldian sense.[7]

The information meeting is a good example of sovereign power as an element in – or a resource used in – the operation of control technologies in the exercise of disciplinary power. When top managers meet or address newcomers or junior managers, the symbolic element in their ritual activities can often be interpreted as the utilization of beliefs in sovereign

---

[7] We have an interesting paradox here *vis-à-vis.* Foucault's position. The prevailing discursive formations in business and management – well supported by mainstream academic research and teaching – assume that sovereign power rather than disciplinary power is central. See for example the mainstream literature on strategic management. The "truth" of top management as a central agency is well established (although there are also other "truths" on this point, which play down the importance of top management). The truth about management as being crucial to corporate performance, like other institutionalized knowledges, generates its own effects. Ideas on sovereign power should thus be treated not only as theoretical ideas of solely academic interest, inferior to Foucault's insights, but also as a discourse "out there", i.e. constituting a form of knowledge that produces a certain kind of subjects with a pre-formed responsiveness in relation to the central agency. As such the discourse on sovereign power cannot be neglected. But it can be interpreted in – as I interpret it here – accordance with Foucault's position, i.e. as knowledge incorporating the notion of sovereign power as an element in disciplinary power.

power to reinforce the exercise of their socializing and disciplinary power. Unless the people involved accept the meaning of sovereign power, there would not be such strong effects.

I will return to this general issue later in the chapter, in the section on strategy.

4.3.2 The meeting as a technology for producing organizational distinctions

Power plays its part in organizations, as in social life in general, by inscribing and naturalizing a variety of distinctions. Social order is created by making distinctions, for example between managers and workers, top management and the rest of the staff (including middle managers), etc. The distinctions are realized in various physical forms, as in the distribution of geographical space and the presence or absence of various kinds of social status symbols, but perhaps they possess their most powerful expression in language.

Essential to power in Foucault´s sense is concealment. Power creates its effects not through arbitrary arrangements and operations but through what is (defined as) natural, self-evident, practical, rational, true and logical. These features do not simply exist; they must be discursively constructed. Meetings and other social events are significant markers of distinctions. They operate according to a logic of inclusion/exclusion. It is well known that meetings function as political rituals, whereby a particular set of ideas and understandings are being transferred (Knights and Willmott, 1987; Kunda, 1992). Content and form have been emphasized in cultural studies. As we noted in the previous chapter, the hierarchical structure of the company is made visible and thereby reinforced during the meeting. More important in a Foucauldian perspective, however, are the distinctions created by absence or presence at the meeting. What is a manager? One answer is that a manager is somebody who meets other managers, especially those occupying top positions. A manager, in one perspective, is somebody who is not a worker. In another, we could say that all employees in both these categories work, and thus are "workers", and all control certain activities, and thus are "managers". What "managers" actually do may well be too vague and diverse to generate any coherent idea about the management category, which could be used in dividing up the organization, linguistically and physically, in such a way as to create order and to enable the management discourse – from which management should emerge as a specialism and managers as a particular category. And given the vagueness and diversity of managerial work mentioned above, this is obviously no easy task. As will be discussed in greater detail below, the strategy discourse is one helpful vehicle for the constitution of managers, but it functions primarily for the high-level managers, and as in Multi is sometimes reserved for this group. In this case "strategy" is actually being defined and practised in a way that excludes rather than constitutes the audience of managers. A middle manager in this company, at least in the context focused on in the present text, is amongst other things a "non-strategist", a mere implementer of corporate strategies. The absence of strategic work as a discursive practice which could constitute the middle managers in the company may account for the means used here whereby a managerial identity is visibly confirmed at the information meeting, e.g. the initial opening words addressed to the audience as managerial persons in the company and the exclusion of non-managers from this specific situation.

The division of labour (prescribing work behaviour) is of course a result of various technologies of power: the formalization of tasks, instructions, induction and teaching programmes, etc., but everyday work behaviour may not be sufficient to produce or support powerful language distinctions. Because of the ambiguities involved, people may be able to avoid regimentation, not having been sufficiently "formed" by the distinctions and associated identities. Moreover, divisions of labour are to some extent accomplished through the effects of a distinction between managers and workers (as well as other linguistic separations). By utilizing a particular combination of time and space (= meetings) in which managers can interact and demonstrate their "manager-ness", the visibility and credibility of this category, and thus its productivity in terms of identity-creation, may be reinforced.[8]

---

8   In one of the units in Multi which we studied in some detail, EDB, the unit manager arranged regular meetings for those who were regarded as key personnel, i.e. employees important to the integration of the organization. Some uncertainty accompanied decisions on this point. One suggestion was to include all white-collar workers. This idea was rejected,

Meetings of this kind illustrate the way in which the self-evident nature of the distinction between managers and workers often accounts for the composition of the assembly at particular meetings. But such compositions also make the distinction self-evident. Distinctions are routinely produced by the way in which all wage-earners are categorized in various ways: from the structure of pay rolls and membership in various unions to their presence or absence in different situations. The significance and meaning of these situations are a result of the composition of the participants, while at the same time the significance and identities of the actors are an outcome of the various situations in which they do or do not participate. A meeting is important because important people are there. People are important – in their own eyes or in the eyes of others, and thus distinguished from the others – because they participate in important social situations. Meetings may therefore be seen as technologies of power in themselves, operating through the logic of inclusion/exclusion. They thus help to produce hierarchical social order and to constitute subjects and relations in particular ways. Seen as an example of how networks of social situations function in a distinction-making and identity-forming fashion, a

---

partly because it was felt that the blue-collar workers might take it badly. It was further believed that to take white versus blue-collar status as a basis for inclusion or exclusion might go against corporate interests and provoke resistance. Swedish expectations about equality did matter. It was decided that all "managers" were to be invited. This group included anyone with some kind of responsibility for subordinates, with the addition of some people from the marketing group to whom this did not in fact apply. Despite this, and despite the fact that many of the invited "managers" could not really be said to work mainly on supervisory or other management duties, this meeting was referred to as a manager meeting. At first by no means everybody turned up, which triggered a signal from the unit manager to the effect that they were expected to participate; those invited were asked to say in advance if they could not come. The idea of the meeting was to integrate the organization and create some community within it, especially among significant personnel. The meeting was run in a soft, anti-hierarchical manner (Alvesson and Björkman, 1992, Ch. 10). The unit manager was every inch the host: standing at the door and welcoming the participants, serving them with coffee together with a secretary during the break, and keeping a fairly low profile during the meeting. This did not of course prevent the event from producing certain distinctions concerning who are key employees and who are not, or from affecting those included in a particular way. On the contrary, the (contradictory) combination of the obligatory nature of the meeting and its relatively pronounced non-hierarchical symbolism, established the significance of a group membership associated with participation in the meeting. This example underscores the assumption of the tactical importance of inclusion (and thus exclusion) in significant events in corporate life.

close reading of the meeting can give us some ideas about these particular aspects of the subtext of organizational life.

4.3.3   The strategy discourse as discipline

A reminder about the central role of strategy during the initial part of the meeting has the same effect as the framing of the reorganization in the context of world-wide business: the playing down of the relevance of the participants´ local knowledge in the specific situation. Strategy – evoking the idea of a fieldmarshal (corporate management) surveying a complicated situation and then deploying his troops (the combined assets of the organization) accordingly – conjures up the idea of decisions that demand top-level handling. By introducing the concept of strategy, management (which "represents" corporate strategy) is endowed with an even greater – possibly monopolistic – capacity for interpreting or "knowing" what the organization should look like. The strategy, as a special component in the informing process, is preceded by remarks about the size of the organization, its international spread and the importance of its history. These elements evoke a sweeping view and the ability to match the resources of the organization (including its structure) with the demands of the environment, that together constitute the idea of corporate strategy as a special area of knowledge and practice (Knights and Morgan, 1991).[9]

Thus it is top management – personified by Martin (although his importance is limited to providing a focus for the discourse) – which emerges as the (only) actor to have the answer to the problems. The top manager´s domination of the meeting follows almost logically from the

---

[9] Two types of knowledge are involved here: (a) knowledge associated with the discipline of strategic management and related forms of formalized knowledge (on organizational design, leadership, etc.) and (b) local management knowledge contingent upon the overview enjoyed by a top manager, and the information that flows through the structural positioning of such a person. Compared with the "real" professions and the knowledge system of which they are a part, managers cannot rely so heavily on abstract, generalized forms of knowledge, but must operate more with the practical knowledge of the specific industry and their own company's "strategic" situation. This knowledge is a result of the manager's structural location in combination with his/her professional knowledge, which has arguably brought them to their present location and provided them with the appropriate abilities to exploit it.

nature of the problem. And the audience – or so I imagine – responds with
subordination and acceptance; their tendency to docility is stimulated. The
strategy idea thus speaks with the voice of power. It implies a managerial
professionalism and a position of superiority, which by definition excludes
anyone but corporate management from the really weighty activities.
Defining an issue as "strategic" is the equivalent of the silencing voices
from structural locations other than the "strategic core".[10]

To be able to understand this more fully we should briefly consider the
general importance that discourses on corporate strategy have acquired
over the last twenty-five years or so. (Previously, top managers were
concerned with "production", "distribution", and "planning", but not with
"strategy" as a distinct area of knowledge and activity.) Strategy has
become established as a more or less distinct discourse about knowledge
and practices of which corporate management has – or can claim to have –
a monopoly in practical life, and it has also become established as a special
academic field (Knights, 1992; Knights and Morgan, 1991). The strategy
discourse has certain implications as regards power, among other things in
that it sustains and enhances the prerogatives of management and negates
alternative perspectives on organizations, and that it demonstrates
managerial rationality to colleagues, customers and subordinates. Moreover it constitutes the subjectivity of top managers. As strategists involved
in strategic practices based on special knowledge of corporate strategy,
members of top management develop and reinforce a special, masculine
identity (Knights and Morgan, 1991).

Because the reorganization becomes framed in strategic terms, the top
manager becomes a bearer of this discourse, the crucial interpreter of what
is rational. The subjectivity and arbitrariness which inevitably marks

---

10 What may be regarded as the strategic core or which actors may be considered significant
and active in strategic processes, will vary from one type of company to another. The use
made of the strategy idea during the information meeting – and by extension, the points
made here – must be understood in terms of the relatively centralized nature of corporate
strategies which seem to have characterized the studied company (which perhaps most
resembled Mintzberg's "machine bureacracy"). In a different kind of company the discourses
on strategy would probably take on a different meaning. In an adhocracy, for example, a
strategy discourse would constitute a broader swat of managers and possibly even non-
managers as "strategists" (cf. the idea of "grass root strategies" in Mintzberg and McHugh,
1985).

decisions and actions – not least in such ambiguous situations as our present one – is partially obscured by the strategy discourse. Two points suggest that the discussion of strategy at our meeting and the brief historical review can be regarded as power techniques rather than as "neutral" representations of obviously relevant circumstances or as necessary control factors.[11] First, from the point of view of general representation, the word "strategy" could have been replaced with advantage by some term such as "goals" or "ambition", which seem less mystifying, more accessible and easier for everyone to relate to, in the present context, at least. Secondly, the organizational change has no essential or direct link with what were referred to throughout the meeting as strategies. The reorganization could have been motivated on general grounds of efficiency and control, without bringing in the idea of "being number 1" or the company´s history at all. Uncertainty, arbitrariness and other factors indicating the limits of rationality and the importance of guesses, judgements and other subjective factors could also have been mentioned, if a "true" account of the decision situation was to have been provided.

My point is not to emphasize or to doubt that the head of the business area could attain a better overview and had more time for thinking about the reorganization than the others, or that his references to the organization´s international character, its history and its strategy had no meaning or no concrete basis. Rather, I am suggesting that in this situation he was activating various "resources" in the shape of history, strategy, etc., and in so doing was not just neutrally reflecting the asymmetry that exists between himself (i.e. top management) and his present audience, but was actually strongly emphasizing, producing and legitimizing it. Asymmetric power relations are certainly to a great extent a question of differences in the basis for the relations concerned, in terms of "objective" differences in knowledge, formal rank, structural location, access to material and symbolic resources etc.; but they are perhaps even more a question of making it clear and probable that these differences do exist. It is not enough to "have" more knowledge than other people; this advantage and

---

[11] As already noted, a Foucauldian perspective would not see anything as neutral or technically necessary (or rational). This should not prevent a researcher drawing upon Foucault from using such terms, albeit handled with caution and awareness of the possible inconsistencies in relation to the main framework.

the inequality it implies must also be made clear to others. The knowledge must be exposed to the subjects, who must then be convinced of its truth value. Ignorance and doubt would not lead to docile subjects. Knowledge is closely related to power, but others must recognize the significance of this knowledge and must know who possesses it, i.e. the representative or medium of a particular game of truth. In terms of power the distribution and acknowledgement of "knowledge" are crucial, primarily as an input into the self-definition of the subjects as subordinates in relation to this knowledge. The choice of representations – i.e. describing a reorganization as an element in corporate strategy – for creating and reinforcing an impression of legitimate and unavoidable asymmetry is therefore of critical importance to the establishment and maintenance of power relations. The information meeting can thus be regarded as an example of making this point. Of particular importance here was the explicit and implicit introduction of the strategy discourse.

The interweaving of (the mechanisms of) power and (claims to) knowledge is obvious in the run-up to this reorganization, quite apart from the specific power techniques employed. Admittedly it is the head of the business sector, who "has" both the knowledge – such as competence in "strategic management" – and the authority to handle this kind of question, who is centrally located in the discursive space of strategy and can regulate the application of this discourse (cf. the comments on sovereign power above). But such a supposition is neither neutral nor apolitical, as it would be easy to envisage other conditions and solutions, e.g. more participative forms of organization whereby knowledge could be distributed – or simply defined – in other ways. Some modern conceptions of strategy as process would go in that direction. I will return to this point later. It should be noted, however, that Foucault would not be prepared to accept these as being "free" from elements of power either. We cannot reduce power to a simple function of knowing, or knowing to a concomitant of power. Foucault (1974: 27-28) emphasizes that

> power and knowledge directly imply one another; that there is no power relation without the correlative constitution of a field of knowledge, nor any knowledge that does not presuppose and constitute at the same time power relations. These "power-knowledge relations" are to be analysed, therefore, not on the basis of a subject of knowledge who is or is not free in relation to the power system, but,

on the contrary, the subject who knows, the objects to be known and the modalities of knowledge must be regarded as so many effects of these fundamental implications of power-knowledge and their historical transformations.

Transferred direct to our case this means that the power relation which controls the reorganization and – more immediately – the information meeting about the reorganization, is based on an asymmetry in the knowledge possessed by the parties concerned. At the same time this asymmetry is the product of another one, namely, the sharply asymmetric power relation, which was emphasized at the meeting for instance by reminding everyone "that production is located in eighteen different countries". Strategy as a discursive practice implies a concrete embeddedness in particular ways of acting and organizing operations, which has certain consequences in the shape of knowledge; at the same time this knowledge, and the asymmetrical power relations associated with it, produce particular forms of subjectivity and subordination that are taken for granted. For instance, a top manager "is" by definition a strategist, while employees at lower levels see themselves in relation to "strategic management", and are "reduced" to being the people who follow the strategy.

It should be added here that the top manager is not, according to Foucauldian thinking, a sovereign agent freely drawing upon strategic management as a resource for the disciplining of his subordinates. The top manager is also caught and constituted by this game of truth.

4.3.4 Normalization

As we have seen, the attempts to encapsulate and shape the subjectivity of those present at the meeting – their emotions, ideas and self-perceptions – comprised several dimensions. For instance, the meeting illustrates a way of reproducing the subjects as subordinates and managers at one and the same time. On this point the analysis in Chapter 3 above coincides with a Foucault-inspired interpretation. I will therefore limit myself here to a few additional comments, concerned less with ideology (as in Chapter 3) and more with some other aspects of the reproduction of subjectivity, associated with managerial subordinancy. In the ranks of the lower- or middle-level managers a variety of social identities emerge, associated with hierarchical positions. Hence we are talking about two different forms of subjectivity – manager (superior) and subordinate – which like other forms of subjectivity are constantly being exposed to different practices which constitute and reconstitute them "...through a myriad of practices of talk, writing, cognition, argumentation, and representation generally" (Clegg, 1989a: 151). The individual, according to Foucault and other poststructuralists, is not a harmonious synthesis of different ideologies and forms of subjectivity which together produce a consistent subject (the Middle Manager); rather, all individuals are swept up in – and are formed by – a continual flow of practices, techniques and procedures which recreate them, often in inconsistent and contradictory ways. One could say that the middle manager is rarely a Middle Manager, but in organizational life experiences him- or herself and relates to others in a rich variety of often contradictory ways, e.g. as a superior, subordinate, professional, man or woman, middle aged, etc. The term Middle Manager may have great relevance in illuminating certain experiences, relations and episodes, and less in others.

As the information meeting demonstrates, the flow can rapidly switch from one element to another. The roles (structural positions) of manager and subordinate can be seen as the most prominent themes of identity at the meeting, although affiliation to the business area, the division, or the areas of responsibility at lower levels was also touched upon. The role of manager, as we have seen, was indicated by the very fact of being called to attend and take part in the meeting, by the emphasis on the particular importance of the members of this audience, by highlighting ideals, values, views etc. that denote "the normal" for the manager category. Subordination was ensured among other things by the way the meeting was set up, whereby the marginal position and lack of knowledge of those attending was established with varying degrees of subtlety, by introducing the strategy discourse which underlines top management's prerogatives and middle management's simultaneous exclusion (at least in this company, and in the particular context). The point is thus not merely that people "are" superiors or subordinates (or any combination of the two), or that they become fixed in these roles more or less permanently during a period of socialization, but that these forms of subjectivity are being constantly constituted and reconstituted even within the same local setting.

As a result of practices that in various ways shape the subjects, different types of competence emerge. These in turn can be emphasized in different kinds of context, e.g. a person switches from being a productive superior to being a productive subordinate, or from decision-making and control to the consumption of other people´s decisions and submission to control. Thus, in the Foucault view, paradoxes and contradictions need not necessarily appear as such, as they would if we perceived the subject as an entity, a whole. This does not mean that all subjectivity production is successful or goes uncontradicted. Rather, there are a great many practices and much resistance to the effects of normalization and other techniques of power, and lots of ways of escaping from them. Against the norm of the "company person", for instance, modern society offers a discourse emphasizing individuality and independence. The idea of "individualism" is then normalized in such a way as to make it difficult for other forms of normalization, e.g. a docile attitude in bureaucracies, to have their full effect. At the same time, normalization in a corporate/bureaucratic context severely constrains the power effects of individualism in our late (modern) society. In an organizational society the mechanisms and techniques of power and control also tend to give individualism a shape which contradicts too varied and unpredictable a form of the self.

An interesting example of the way discipline is exercized by way of normalization occurred at the meeting, when one participant ventured to ask about the advertising of vacancies, and got a reply insinuating that he was being "anxious". In this context the desire for information on a certain point was perceived as uncertainty, which in turn was defined as anxiety. A simple, neutral question possibly indicating the tiniest sign of a non-positive attitude towards the reorganization was understood and explained as the expression of an anxious nature. "The normal" was being defined, and it consisted of a positive or at least emotionally neutral attitude to the organizational change. The implication was that a manager in a modern company is not "anxious" or "inflexible" but "change-oriented" and "dynamic". More or less voluntarily the questioner then corroborated the norm, as he assured the assembly that he regarded the advertising of the new posts as an "opportunity". The laughter that greeted this remark can be seen as a way of defusing the slight tension introduced by this exchange on the subject of the anxious versus the normal and desirable, but it also acted as a collective confirmation that the swings of this particular pendulum had their comic side. The episode, like the meeting as a whole, encouraged identification with "opportunity" rather than "anxiety", with a denial of doubt and uncertainty and a positive attitude to "change" and the "will to change".

In the ethnography of a division within the company of which the present study is an offspring (see Chapter 2), a set of interviews with various (managerial) people about their stance as regards "organizational change", indicated some variation in attitudes expressed in relation to specific reorganizations. Some, in particular the not-so-old managers, embraced the positive and necessity of the changes. Comments such as "It is creative, you develop yourself" and "Change means something positive for everybody" were heard. Those critical of the reorganizations in the company during recent years, declared that changes took place "too often". One, for example, said that it was the fashion "to have change for the sake of change", and indicated that "people were not tired of the changes as such, but of the fact that they went on all the time, and things did not improve as a result". Another expressed some ambivalence towards the reorganizations in the company ("even if you make large-scale changes, you don´t need to do it in departments that are functioning well"), but ended by saying "It is actually healthy to have changes, but it´s stressful. Sometimes change is needed for the sake of change. Despite all, I look at it positively."

All these statements can be seen, in line with Foucault´s theory, as examples of the way people become normalized. Those who feel negative towards the (frequent) reorganizations in the company, are not against change, they say, but focus on what they see as the excessive and thoughtlessness behind the changes in recent years. In particular the last quotation, where the respondent associates himself with the norm of being change-oriented despite some scepticism about the value of changes in some parts of the organization, brings the effects of the discursive production of normality close to the surface. It is difficult to trace particular opinions to the operations of power, however, and to make a strong case for this specific connection. A conventional researcher, explaining the attitudes as a result of life history (e.g. the effects of age) or of the specific experiences and evaluations of those concerned, has an equally strong (or weak) case as regards normalization as an interpretive device. The absence of "proof" does not of course prevent us from recognizing the potential insights that a Foucauldian focus and interpretation can yield.

4.3.5   Surveillance and the constitution of the subject

Another good example of how "the normal" was defined, and how the subjectivity of those attending the meeting was determined, concerns the principles for evaluation and control. These were formulated most clearly by Martin when he declared: "it´s responsibility and being able to measure results that makes things fun". Indirectly this talk of responsibility was a way of getting people not only to accept the necessity of (a certain form of) control but also to feel positive about it. At the information meeting the point was made that individuals (units) were (or would soon become) "decentralised", responsible, motivated and controlled. The overall message was thus that these four are inextricably intertwined. As a result of partial independence and decentralization, the individual can be made responsible for results. Once again this can be regarded as the creation of a particular form of subjectivity and the (productive) potential for action that ensues. The information meeting can be seen as one ingredient in the myriad of micro-impulses – inside and outside the workplace – which help in the creation and maintenance of result-orientated organizational man, the person who synthesizes "motivation" and "control".

It is important to note here that the delegation of formal responsibility and authority does not necessarily give the subordinates a stronger power base. Cf. Clegg (1989b: 108) who writes that:

> delegated authorities cannot be guaranteed to be loci of wholly predictable and controlled agency, other than if they are dutiful servants. Thus the problematic of "power in organizations" centres not on the legitimacy or otherwise of subordinates, capacities, as in the conventional view, but on the myriad practices which *incapacitate* authorities from becoming powers by restricting action to that which is "obedient", not only prohibitively but also creatively, productively.

Because results can be measured (it is claimed), people are subject to a more refined and total form of control: instead of being made responsible for seeing that orders and rules are obeyed, and being evaluated for concrete actions, subjects are now being linked to results. The idea that measures and figures can "objectively" evaluate an individual´s entire performance, means that the control is extended to include the totality of all actions. As Miller and O´Leary (1987: 261) put it, accounting is "concerned with the active engineering of the organizationally useful person".[12]

As a power technique "decentralization" thus implies the strengthening of a particular type of control. (Obviously it means a lot of other things as well, but we will concentrate here, perhaps a little negatively, on power and control.) The scope of the control will vary according to the extent to which the word "decentralization" is followed by actions and statements that express the local (situationally specific) meaning of decentralization, in ways which fasten on to and reinforce or contradict and weaken the various manifestations of it. (The dependence of this term on a local and unstable meaning – that is, its sensitivity to the context in which it is uttered – must be carefully considered in order to evaluate its impact.) By "control" is meant the possibility of following up and imposing sanctions on behaviour and/or results, or – and this is probably more significant – the subordinates´ perception or anticipation of such a possibility. By establishing norms and recording deviations from them, a basis for control and discipline is created (Miller and O´Leary, 1987). But – as the definition implies – this control is neither objective nor given. The interaction between control as external form and as internalized concept is generally crucial. The internalized conception includes ideas about the possibility of control (a belief in one´s own actions and the controllable nature of the particular operation), and a belief in the legitimacy of the control itself. Control works insofar as individuals assume that they are responsible for results and that these can be measured.

A number of things undermine this "ideal". There are obvious problems connected with quantifying and measuring results in a complex reality, and there are always circumstances which affect the outcome but which are

---

12 As Armstrong (1994) points out, a problem that arises in the extensive and rapidly growing Foucault-inspired accounting research, is that the master's interest was mainly in the regulation of behavioural details, while modern accounting deals with economical outcomes. Nonetheless, Foucault's work has an obvious relevance also in the context of accounting.

outside the individual´s control (internal contingencies in the company, natural disasters, state regulations, the situation on the labour market, the state of competition, changes in foreign currency exchange rates and so on). Some scholars claim that top managements have little control over results, due to external dependency relations (Pfeffer and Salancik, 1978). This is a controversial view, but we can say with a clear conscience that the question of the influence of managers or results remains an open one. (For an overview of positions and debates, see Whittington, 1993.) Lower management levels generally have even less chance of influencing their own sections. Furthermore it is not at all sure how well such influence could be measured in the final results. Thus the relation between personal input and results as measured is probably rather a vague one. The interesting point, however, is how the element of discipline inherent in the very *notion* of responsibility and the measurability of results can help to develop an awareness of the link between personal and social identity and worth on the one hand, and economic results on the other – results which the individual believes can be influenced and (possibly) measured.[13] In other words, this exercise of power, which involves the transmission and creation of receptiveness to experienced responsibility for results, is of the utmost importance to the successful entrenchment of control in the subjects (in their identity and desire for the confirmation of identity).[14]

---

[13] It is important to understand the unstable identity of the modern individual (compared, for example, to the identities of people in stable, socially integrated societies of a tribal nature), in order to understand the willingness to accept various forms of control that offer identity-endorsement:

> ...the identity of the typical modern worker is (socially) underdetermined. S/he is constituted as an individual who is obliged to strive continously to validate him/herself as a person who has ability and value. Unlike the peasant, s/he has no fixed identity, nor is s/he valued irrespective of the status s/he achieves. S/he is subjugated by individualizing pressures to make something of him/herself as a sovereign, free agent. As Sennett and Cobb have remarked, virtually everyone in modern society "subject to a scheme of values that tells him he must validate the self in order to win others' respect and his own". (Willmott, 1994: 102-3)

[14] Miller and O'Leary (1987: 239) define accounting as "the development of a range of calculative programmes and techniques which come to regulate the lives of individuals at work".

With the help of rhetoric ("decentralization", "it is people who decide") and material and legal indications (e.g. financial control systems, corporatization or formation of subsidiaries), the connection between responsibility, the measurement of results and subjective commitment to the way of working, is reinforced. By stressing that things are (or should be seen as) fun, interesting and in accord with what people want, it is easier to create a positive acceptance of this sort of control; people are also more likely to submit themselves to it cheerfully, to see results as intimately linked to their subjectivity and as a crucial source of confirmation. It is just this coupling between the three elements – "objective" control (structural and administrative arrangements), ideas about the possibility of supervision and a positive subordinate attitude to this – that works most efficiently as an instrument of power. These elements, taken together, discipline the individual, and open a possible path for productive input. In other words, what is central in this context is the constituting of the individual as a person whose actions as a whole are accessible to measurement (that is to say, it is believed that they can be measured), rather than the measuring of results as such. Another important aspect, too, is the creation of a will to be measured and controlled. Motivation, wishes and control are all interwoven. The whole point of measuring results and of trying to establish ideas about the normality of such measurements is thus that they operate as power techniques which help to create the "right" form of subjectivity (values, norms and self-image). An emphasis on the result-defining and result-controlling subject – the head of the business section and his/her team – as an important subject of control ("visual superego") completes the picture and indicates yet more elements in the exercise of discipline.[15]

There are actually two elements involved in this kind of power. One is that the subject believes in and accepts the control system. The other is that he or she may be sceptical or uncertain about it, but expects that others may be taking it seriously. Even if you are doubtful whether your own (unit´s) performance can be measured and evaluated fairly, you may suspect that other significant people do perhaps take the logic seriously, and then it is

---

[15] Even though it falls outside Foucault's framework, it is worth pointing out that there may also be material sanctions contingent upon results, which have an effect on people's behaviour, on top of the exercise of distinct forms of disciplinary power (Armstrong, 1994).

probably wise to behave as though the logic of control definitely functions and to demonstrate that you too take it seriously. Such behaviour is likely to affect the beliefs and behaviour of others, i.e. producing subjects in a particular way.

In this sense we can say that the whole point of the information meeting was to help to create the "subordinate-independent manager", someone who voluntarily uses his scope for action in a subordinate way, with a proper faith in hierarchy and (objective) control, and a positive attitude towards these things. But the affected individual is naturally not only disciplined in a limiting way; he or she also possesses developed productive capacities. The subjectivity that the information meeting – as one element among myriad expressions of micropower in the organization – helps to form, embraces the economy of power and enables productive action adapted to the modern bureaucracy´s need for "decentralizing" and "result-orientated" forms of action. The meeting thus helped to qualify those who attended. In this context the coupling between identity and results is the crucial factor.

4.3.6   Motivation

As noted in the previous section, Martin´s talk contains a number of references to human motivation in a work organizational context. In particular, it is said that the staff want responsibility, interesting jobs, influence, seeing results and the opportunity to develop. On other occasions during his talk mention is made of the importance for those present – and for individuals in general – of these and similar features of their work. There is an emphasis on the need for feedback. Feedback is here equated with financial results, expressed in the management accounting systems. The "need" for "feedback" is thus linked to a highly specific form of feedback.

Leaving aside the question of whether the reorganization has any direct bearing on these qualities, and of the links between motivation and (financial) control discussed in the previous section, it could also be interesting to consider the model of the man- (or woman-) at-work which Martin invokes in his talk.

The concept of the individual at work and his or her motivations features prominently in contemporary North American inspired work on motivation and job satisfaction. It is very similar, for example, to the model suggested by Hackman et al. (1975), according to which intrinsic motivation, job satisfaction, low personnel turnover and high work quality are said to be the result of a work situation involving variation, task identity (identifiable and holistic work), job significance (work leading to identifiable results), autonomy and feedback on work performance. As an intermediate variable – between work characteristics and outcomes – the authors propose "decisive psychological experiences" in the form of experienced meaningfulness, experienced responsibility and knowledge of actual results produced. But if the model is to work, it is also necessary that the individual has "a need for growth". This model summarizes an entire body of motivation and leadership literature since the 1950s (Maslow, Herzberg, Argyris, McGregor, Alderfer, etc.). It reflects a form of knowledge claiming to represent the nature of the individual and his or her motivational structure.

Scientific knowledge is not referred to directly during the meeting, but the "truth" of this kind of discourse on human beings at work has been widely established as a result of university teaching, management development programmes and popular management books, all of which have long been disseminating this and similar models. In modern companies many managers and personnel specialists learn and spread this knowledge. And the presence of such knowledge brings an element of psychological truth into a context (here the meeting), indicating that the analysis is anchored in knowledge about people (personnel psychology). At the same time, this kind of knowledge becomes reinforced.

This "truth" about the individual is not, of course, acceptable from a Foucauldian perspective. The truth of the model must be established through the location of the person in a particular arrangement in which the qualities mentioned can emerge, i.e. be separated and measured. In many historical contexts ideas such as task significance, job satisfaction or feedback do not make sense. The essential material and discursive conditions are simply not there. As Sievers (1986) says, the notions of job enrichment and motivation emerge as surrogates for meaning in bureaucratic work organizations. Structuring work tasks in such a way that feedback can be sorted out as a particular function or form of input, and that can be regulated by a particular agency (management), is thus a precondition for the development – and not just the application – of this knowledge. The knowledge in force may then confirm the truth of the model. A precondition here, of course, is that feedback is operating as a mode of power, e.g. the use of a technology of power through which the experiences of the subject can be produced.

The openness and undecidability of the subject is thus counteracted by the operation of the knowledge-power combination. The person is frozen in a set of articulations, naturalized and neutralized, "as spontanously there" (Deetz, 1992a: 276). Through this frozen image of the person and his or her work motivation, he or she can interpret needs, wants and behaviour and adjust these to the model. Others can be controlled through the normalizing and disciplinary options of the model: "we all need feedback" and "give a man autonomy and he will feel responsible and accomplish high quality work". At least for the normal healthy person, the one with "a need for growth", this knowledge is valid, according to this discourse.[16] Arguably, truth-induced effects arise. A managerial person who feels or communicates an urge for stability, repetitiveness and concentration may feel inadequate. Others may perceive him or her as an obstacle to change. The notion of "resistance to change" is a crucial element in the discourse that disciplines subjects in a modern, "dynamic", "change-oriented" business life and society which has little sympathy for "rigidity" and "conservatism".

Naturally, invoking knowledge of motivations during the meeting does not in itself produce anything. This is just an element in a chain of management knowledges inscribing and prescribing the normal, motivated person on the corporate stage. It is the steady stream of this motivation-producing discourse – in written texts, everyday talk, expressions of

---

[16] The idea of a need for growth represents an interesting trap. In most (US-based) motivation theory "growth" is portrayed as a "normal" need or psychological orientation. If somebody is not functioning according to the model this indicates a deviation from normality. Given the establishment of the regime of the truth of the model people may be wise to comply. In most real situations, the disciplinary success of this knowledge is limited, as it often encounters various kinds of resistance. For example, workers sometimes respond to "job enrichment" by claiming even more influence or demanding even higher pay, thus invoking a new discourse, which changes the nature of the struggle.

"leadership" (managers "motivating" their teams with talk of "vision" etc.), management seminars and programmes and so on – that accounts for its effect. In this sense the information meeting is but one instance of the continuous production of motivation and of the subject receptive to "motivation". By the repeated use of knowledge, the subject in "need of" task significance, feedback, etc. is produced. Naturally feedback receptiveness does not take over the subject altogether – there may be resistance to that receptiveness and there are other corporate and extra-corporate discourses which construct the subjects in other ways – but the power-knowledge interplay puts an imprint on them, at least according to Foucauldian thinking.

4.3.7   Leadership as self-discipline

This form of disciplining is not concerned only – or even mainly – with the lower managers. In fact it strongly affects the divisional managers, who in turn (it is presumed) pass it on in other contexts. (This is an important aspect of organizational change.) Even Martin, the big white chief, is "subordinated". The other side of all this talk about responsibility and so on, and his very high profile during the information meeting, is that he too is being "captured", i.e. the self is being defined according to a particular form. The strong emphasis on himself and his own central position puts him straight in the firing line. The prominent position he assumes during the meeting has the double-edged effect of emphasizing not only his superior position, but also his personal responsibility. As the prime architect of the reorganization, he can only up to a point pass on the delegation of responsibility which is claimed to be the idea behind the whole thing. The spotlight thus falls not only on the disciplining of the others, but also on the disciplining of the boss himself. He can hardly remain unconcerned about results in the business area: he is trapped by his own statements and his own visibility; he becomes highly dependent on his own subordinates. This dependence – and the attendant possibility of countervailing power and even mutuality – can easily remain concealed, among other things as a result of the kind of social situation we have been discussing here (cf. Knights and Willmott, 1985). The image of Martin smoking his cigar while checking the financial results accomplished by the divisions, may invoke feelings of fear and subordination among the managers and marginalize the insight about the vulnerability of the position and career of the boss and its dependence on what people in lower positions actually do.

The corporate strategy discourse in particular falls into this category. When a top manager sees himself as a strategist and conveys this image to others, it is not only a question of defending or expanding a prerogative. By claiming – not only to others but also to himself – to have at least some control over relations between the organization and its environment (not simply being at the mercy of the buyers´ or sellers´ markets), his vulnerability is being greatly increased. Paying for poor results by losing his job becomes a definite possibility.[17] More interesting in our present context is that identity becomes clearly linked to positive financial results, and is thus also highly dependent upon them. The results may become a reflection of the self, and the risk of social and psychological reverses is thus considerable.

4.3.8   Final comments

Among other things power prevents subjects from developing standards of their own. Standards are discursively produced. Discursive formations – sets of discourses that support each other – regulate social relations and the functioning of the subjects. The discourses of competition and growth, of strategy, of change and flexibility as being the norm, of the measurement of results and feedback as a key to human motivation – all these support each other in the context of the contemporary business culture.

The functional quality of the discourses that are prominent in corporations leads to the enablement of subjects. These subjects are not repressed; rather, they are produced and become capable of acting. Productive here are the representation of corporate reality in a particular way, the underscoring of the central role of strategy and the priority of strategic

---

[17] Here, on two counts, I go beyond a focus closely linked to Foucault's ideas. Decisions about firings and other material sanctions are (a) coupled to sovereign power (legal rights), and b) also operate outside the limits of disciplinary power. Nevertheless, the threat against an identity related to a particular job position which is associated with this sanction, may be one crucial element in disciplinary power. Thus, according to the framework used in this chapter, it would not be the economic consequences of losing one's job, but the threat to self-identity that would be the important thing.

knowledge, the regulation of the distinction between strategists and other managers as well as that between (all) managers and other employees, the provision of standards for the psychology of the motivated and willing-to-change employee – as a result of all this the abilities of those present at our meeting are developed and/or reinforced. A degree of certainty, direction, identity and confirmation is created, in an otherwise notoriously complex and potentially chaotic world.

A single situation like the information meeting has of course a limited impact. The stabilizing effects of power are not accomplished by means of single episodes, but must be understood as outcomes of a network of micro-practices. However, the information meeting does exhibit discourses and technologies of power which are in operation in myriads of settings in everyday corporate life. The meeting is a good example of a setting in which power in corporations is in action in a dense and rich way.

Hardly anything has been said above about resistance, largely because there are no direct signs of it in the account of the situation. However, I will return to this theme in Chapter 6.

5 The information meeting as communicative distortion: a Habermas-inspired interpretation

In many respects Habermas is Foucault´s opposite. He emphasizes the possibility of evading power and speaks of evaluations and decisions based on reason. Thus according to Habermas power does not necessarily infiltrate knowledge, but at least some forms of knowledge can counteract the relations of domination and allow for emancipation based on freedom from restrictions and limitations. This can be achieved as a result of critical reflection and independent thought, and the clarification of man´s desires and ideals by way of the thoughtful evaluation of various viewpoints and arguments in an open dialogue. Knowledge, and the validation of the truth of various assertions, is seen as being intimately connected with freedom from power relations. Habermas recognizes legitimate power, which "arises only among those who form common convictions in unconstrained communication" (Habermas, 1977: 18). This form of power is based on true consensus, emerging without the interference of (illegitimate) power. Of course, Foucault´s and Habermas´s ways of talking about power are in some respects different. It is less a question of different views on a specific subject than of different outlooks on the social world and different basic ways of reasoning, which up to a point are addressing different themes.

Habermas is a rationalist and humanist, and as such believes in the possibility of common sense and reason, despite all the threats and distortions which these have been – and still are – exposed to. He is the most prominent representative of what is known as "critical modernism" which takes the ideal of enlightenment very seriously but which sharply criticizes tendencies towards technocracy and the rule of the experts which follow in its wake, as well as the circumscribing of the knowledge concept (positivism and empiricism) to which the enlightenment view can sometimes lead. Foucault, as we have seen, is sceptical of rationalism and humanism (the emphasis on the active role of the subject), and indeed of the system-building aspirations which Habermas represents, i.e. seeking to develop a comprehensive and coherent theory. Foucault sees any attempt to give privileged status to one particular view as just another expression of the knowledge/power connection, which locks the subject into a specific position by using a particular norm for human self-understanding and conduct.

Thus to a great extent Habermas and Foucault are each other´s opposite poles, at least within the context in which many contemporary debates are framed. But, as was mentioned in the introduction above, many philosophers and social scientists have sought to relate them to one another. Many feel that both can provide fruitful inspiration for the kind of social science research which aims at a critical understanding of social phenomena (Alvesson and Willmott, 1992, 1996; Alvesson and Deetz, 1996; Deetz, 1992a; Hoy, 1986; Mumby, 1991). Common to both men is a critical and suspicious attitude towards certain societal conditions and to dominating forms of knowledge. Both feel sympathy for social groups which are particularly disfavoured by asymmetrical power relations and dominating ideas, passed on in the guise of neutral knowledge and rationality. It is seldom possible to arrive at straightforward or self-evident judgements concerning the similarities or differences between various authors and schools. Foucault and Habermas can both be used in a critique of mainstream functionalist and objectivist ideas, but they can also be mobilized in attacks on each other and on the intellectual styles and convictions they each represent. On the whole, however, Foucault and Habermas maintain positions which have interesting and inspiring differences, and the idea of the present book is to allow these to give rise to distinctive interpretations of the empirical material on which the study is based.

5.1   Habermas´s theory of communicative action

5.1.1   Communication as the road to rationality

Jürgen Habermas (1971, 1984) has sometimes been called "the last rationalist". His overall project can be described as an attempt to explore and underpin the role of critical reason in a world in which, paradoxically enough, the dominant views on rationality are themselves among the greatest threat to reason. He seeks, at one and the same time, to extend and to specify more exactly, a position which conceives of reason as a critical, reflective and dialogue stimulating form of rationality, which neither capitulates in face of positivist, technocratic, bureaucratic and economic concepts of rationality, nor regards rationality and reason as concepts not worth salvaging so that other ideals and opportunities for avoiding dominance relations are called for (e.g. play, pleasure, pluralism, nihilism).

Unlike earlier advocates of the intellectual tradition to which he is considered to belong (the Frankfurt school of Critical Theory), Habermas has refrained from functioning primarily as a "nitpicking cultural critic" (a role that with some fairness may be ascribed to some of his predecessors, such as Horkheimer and Adorno, 1947 and Marcuse, 1964) and has concentrated instead on building a systematic philosophy in which language theory and communicative action are of pivotal importance. A crucial element here is that evaluation and critique are transferred or "decentralized" to society´s citizens, instead of being regarded as the primary concern of all free-thinking, intellectual critics (Bubner, 1982). The task of critical philosophy in its Habermasian version is not in the first instance to reveal specific relations of domination and ideologies directly or investigate substantive threats to autonomy and self-clarification. Rather, it is to indicate the possibilities (opportunities and obstacles) that people encounter in communication in everyday life and political life, for exploring these relations of domination and for reaching well-founded views on ethical and political issues. The focus of the critical project is thus on procedure and process rather than on specific subject matter.

The underlying notion in Habermas´s project is that people are – or given favourable circumstances may become – the supreme judges of their own best interests, which are formed and discovered in free dialogue between all those involved. The idea is thus to open up public, democratic processes, based on dialogue between citizens. His approach shuns technocratic ideologies on politics and administration (including business management).

Habermas (1971, 1984) is thus critical of the dominating concept of rationality, instrumental rationality, which emphasizes the development of suitable means with a view to achieving a specific goal. This is too narrow an approach, reflecting a society in which political and ethical dialogue has been lifted off the agenda and subordinated to goal-related technocratic action. By relating the "rational" to acts that can be critically examined, defended and grounded in arguments, the idea of rationality is extended in a communicative direction that goes beyond the notion of cognitive-instrumental rationality that is associated with science and knowledge about the objective world. A downplaying of the differences between different statements – whether these concern objective nature or social affairs – then ensues, as elements in all speech are highlighted. The centrality of validity claims, dispute and justification is universal in human action, Habermas claims, and this motivates a general, communicative notion of rationality.

Habermas´s project has shifted away from its initial focus on cognitive interests, i.e. on different forms of knowledge and on establishing these in various spheres of human interest and forms of consciousness, and towards a focus on language and the nature and potential of communication. In his conception of the different cognitive interests (Habermas, 1972) – where he distinguishes between the technical, practical-hermeneutic and eman-cipatory interest (springing from the desire to control nature, the desire to operate linguistically-culturally and to understand the ways whereby this control is achieved through language-mediated understanding, and the desire to overcome repression and constraints – in that order), he strongly emphasized human consciousness and cognition as the basis for critical research. A yearning for liberation, which is entrenched in human nature and institutionalized in different kinds of science, legitimized the emancipatory cognitive interest which he wanted to help develop. Since the beginning of the 1970s, however, Habermas has turned to language and communication as the absolutely crucial ally of critical social science. This has become known as "the linguistic turn" in Habermas´s development (Wellmer, 1976). This move from consciousness to communication is part of a general trend in social science and philosophy, in which language rather than human subjects is seen as the central site for meaning. The move may be seen as a fusion between Habermas´s practical-hermeneutic and emancipatory interests, to some extent at the expense of the latter, as the emphasis on the operations and potentials of language receive more attention than the social constraints of communication in real life settings.

Language use is nevertheless the principle resource in reducing irrationality in human affairs, according to Habermas. He talks about two kinds of rationalization processes in society. The first is that which is commonly recognized as involving farreaching development in terms of rationality, and which is often perceived as successful and progressive, i.e. the spheres of science, technology and economics. The productive forces have been so transformed that purposive rational action systems function very much more efficiently in modern technological-capitalist societies than used to be the case. What Habermas calls the system has thus become radically rationalized over time, especially during the last century or so. According to his predecessors in the Critical Theory of the Frankfurt School, this has occurred partly at the expense of the opportunity for individual autonomy and the preconditions for independent ethical and political judgement. As mentioned above, Habermas also sees the domination of technocracy as a force that erodes the quality of the political sphere of society (Habermas, 1971).

In the development of modern society he finds, however, that, despite its many drawbacks, it has involved a letting-up of those strong ideological ties with religion and other repressive modes of thought which characterized authoritarian social relations. As a result of political democracy, more education and information, and the economic development that has virtually abolished the necessity to fight for survival in modern technological-capitalist societies, a "modern conciousness" has emerged to embrace a growing number of people. This in turn has made people more receptive to the possibilities that language and communication provide for testing (in the sense of critically examining) ideas and evaluating various social institutions associated with them. We thus have here the potential for a more comprehensive rationalization of human existence. In other words we do not simply allow outselves to be steered by traditional ideas and values; instead we can explore and test them, and the ideas that emerge from such a process will have a better chance of being well grounded. Habermas argues for the systematic improvement of the lifeworld, for an experience-based way of relating to reality and the creation and recreation of patterns of meaning. The lifeworld can be regarded as rationalized to the extent that it permits interactions that are guided not by imperatives from the system – contingent upon the money code or formal power – nor by the unreflective reproduction of traditional cultural values, but by communicatively achieved understanding (Habermas, 1984). Habermas thus separates two historical learning processes, the technological-scientific-strategic associated with the system, and the communicative-political-ethical associated with the lifeworld, and tries to contribute to the latter, thus counteracting the colonizing effects of the powerful media and the logic associated with the system.

A key element in Habermas´s theory is the idea of undistorted communication, i.e. free discussion based on good will, argumentation and dialogue. On a basis of such rational discussion he assumes that consensus can be reached, regarding both present and desirable states. He maintains that in language itself and the way it is used there are certain conditions for achieving this ideal: the expectation and the wish to be understood and believed, and the hope that others will accept our arguments and other statements, in combination with the general anticipation that statements can be supported by arguments and that arguments are open to questioning and exploration. Without such expectations and ambitions there is little point in either statements or discussions.

Undistorted communication provides the basis for the "highest" (or perhaps the widest, most reflective or basic) form of rationality, namely communicative rationality. Here it is not power, social status, prestige, ideology, manipulation, the rule of experts, fear, insecurity, misunderstanding or any other form of mischief that furnishes a base for the ideas. Really only one thing counts – the strength of the good, well-grounded argument.

People no longer obey the priest because only he can interpret the word of god, or the prince because he has inherited a title and other privileges. Instead they examine the legitimacy of various imperatives, and demand reasonable arguments (or rely on institutions which are perceived as having a rational basis). Arguments and other statements claiming to have a rational basis can be examined and discussed, in principle until consensus is achieved that one of the approaches or ideas is the correct or best one, either in the sense of being "true" or appropriate in terms of certain well-tried and tested needs and preferences.

> This concept of communicative rationality carries with it connotations based
> ultimately on the central experience of the unconstrained, unifying, consensus-
> bringing force of argumentative speech, in which different participants
> overcome their merely subjective views and, owing to the mutuality of
> rationality motivated conviction, assure themselves of both the unity of the
> objective world and the intersubjectivity of their lifeworld. (Habermas, 1984:
> 10)

Communicative rationality thus denotes a way of responding to
(questioning, testing and, possibly, accepting) a statement´s claims to
validity. Communicative action thus allows for the exploration of every
statement on a basis of the following (universal) validity criteria:
comprehensibility, sincerity, truthfulness and legitimacy. Thus if the level
of communicative rationality is high, the ideas emerging from the
discussions will be based on comprehensible statements; the people making
the statements will have done so with honesty and sincerity; the various
utterances will have been true or correct and will conform prevailing
norms.[1] In normal linguistic interaction it is expected that anyone making a
statement should be able to substantiate it and to satisfy the validity claims
inherent in their words, or be prepared to modify their position. The
important point is that these four elements can be adequately explored in a
free dialogue. It is thus vital that the social situation allows for the
exploration of these validity claims, and that there are fundamental and
equal opportunities for breaking off or exiting an ongoing interaction (e.g.
a practical-instrumental, problem-solving interaction), for testing the
statements (communicatively exploring these), and for reaching a common
understanding in open dialogue. The competence of the individual, i.e. his
or her reflective ability, is also crucial here. Communicative action is
therefore an important aspect of social interaction in society, in social
institutions and in daily life. The ideal speech situation, which allows
communicative rationality and is in turn pervaded by it, exists under the
following conditions:

---

[1] When Habermas speaks of "truth" he does so in a special sense which lies a long way from
the "positivistic-objectivist" approach, in which truth is identical with a scientifically
verifiable hypothesis. A statement is true when the validity of the speech act with which it is
asserted is justified by the agreement of each and everyone who under optimal conditions

...the structure of communication itself produces no constraints if and only if, for all possible participants, there is a symmetrical distribution of chances to choose and to apply speech-acts. (Habermas, cited by Thompson, 1982: 123)

This means that all potential participants have the same opportunity to initiate and maintain a dialogue by asking and answering questions and making claims and counterclaims. No preconceptions are excluded from scrutiny. Equal opportunities exist to express attitudes, feelings and intentions with a view to clarifying the questions under discussion. Of course, the ideal speech situation is not a quality of ordinary communication, but a counterfactual anticipation that we make when we seek mutual understanding, trying to achieve the form of argumentation we presuppose we are able to step into when we try to step aside from the flow of everyday action and check a problematic claim.

The opposite of undistorted communication is the type of communication that is systematically distorted. Here various circumstances frustrate the achievement of consensus in open dialogue. Power relations, ideological domination etc. infiltrate the communication process, making it difficult if not impossible to question statements or to promote comprehensibility, honesty, correctness, and legitimacy to the utmost. Instead the proceedings are dominated by ambiguity, mystification, dishonesty, manipulation, rhetoric, distorted descriptions, inaccurate information and so on. The main question that should be asked is the following: "are social norms which claim legitimacy genuinely accepted by those who follow and internalize them, or do they merely stabilize relations of power?" (Lukes, 1982: 137). Habermas distinguishes between "normatively secured consensus" and "communicatively grounded consensus". The first of these represents unity resulting from the uncritical adoption of common ideas, either because of manipulation by an elite or because cultural tradition uncritically mediates taken for granted norms and ideas. "Communicatively grounded consensus", on the other hand, is the result of open discussion which involves critical exploration and reflection leading to valid agreement. Consensual ideas about what exists and what is good can then be seen as an outcome of a reasonably rational procedure.

---

can partake in the discussion. "Truth means the promise to attain a rational consensus" says Habermas (quoted in Thompson, 1981: 99).

A major source of distorted communication is the dominance of the "goal-rational systems of action", according to which imperatives arising from given ends-means relationships consistently enjoy priority and dominate the agenda (Habermas, 1971). Or, to put it another way: efficiency considerations determine what is regarded as relevant, important, and legitimate, leaving hardly any leeway for questioning the more fundamental connections. Attention turns chiefly on the best way of achieving goals which are largely taken for granted, while little scope is left for testing or reflecting on the values, interests, or lines of reasoning that lie behind the goals.

5.1.2   Critique of Habermas

As is the case of Foucault and all other scholars of real significance, there has been a lot of criticism of Habermas´s work. His theory of communicative action is said to be intellectualist and unrealistic; it overestimates people´s functioning in relation to valid arguments, neglects the ambiguities and uncertainties in language use and is of limited empirical relevance. I will briefly review here some of the critique (see also Bernstein, 1985).

Of course disturbances in communicative processes are unavoidable for a number of reasons. No more than any other social attributes or ideals can communicative capacity in this sense really be optimized. Even sympathetic critics have admitted this. A typical stance is that Habermas´s ideas are intellectualist, and that the contradictory and irrational character of fundamental social structures must be countered by social action rather than by endless argument and discussion (Bubner, 1982). Moreover, in many cases rationally grounded consensus has no prospect of success, since real differences in preferences and interests cannot be resolved by the force of a widely acknowledged "better" argument – it is unlikely that an argument recognized as valid by disputing parties can be produced, or that it would have sufficient force to counteract perceived interest differences if it could (Giddens, 1982; Lukes, 1982, etc.). Perhaps it is simply that Habermas presupposes a degree of critical flexibility well beyond the reach of most people and most situations. Desires, norms, and thoughts are not as immediately responsive to good arguments and the twists and turns of discussion as Habermas supposes. Because Habermas´s conception of truth – i.e. communicatively reached conceptions of what is true – is separated from will, politics, and compassion, it bears no clear relation to practice (Brown, 1994: 22).

Habermas to some extent acknowledges the problem of subjects which are not fully flexible in relation to argumentation, maintaining that outside the ideal situation of genuine consensus, it may often be more realistic and rewarding to speak of compromise. Communicatively grounded compromise is not the same as the negotiated compromises of the pluralist view, based largely on the relative strength of various self-interests. Habermas distinguishes between legitimate and illegitimate compromises, depending on whether or not the basic guidelines for compromise-construction are themselves justified in communicatively rational terms (White, 1988). The problem of the ability and willingness of participants in discussions to modify their positions in response to valid arguments still remains. If there are genuine differences of interests and asymmetrical relations of power, it may be difficult to separate legitimate compromises from those that are contingent upon power. Nevertheless, the idea of communicatively grounded compromises does go some way towards reducing the "realism problem".

Another critique is associated with Kuhn´s discovery that most discussions in the scientific community concern disagreement on questions of detail within a broad framework of fundamental shared assumptions, of which the participants are unaware (Dreyfus and Rabinow, 1986). Because of these last, it is sometimes possible to reach agreement – but only on condition that people do not start investigating the non-conscious shared assumptions. The problem is thus that the dialogue-based consensus does not directly touch on the "paradigmatic" basis of the discussion, which is in fact one of the prerequisites for reaching consensus. Postmodernists such as Lyotard (1984) have launched a similar critique, arguing that legitimate truth only emerges within particular language games and that these have no bearing outside a highly localized setting and the rules that govern it. However, as counter-critics have pointed out, Habermas´s idea is to develop a procedure that cuts across various language games. This procedure, and the common structure that all language uses, can in principle make it possible to avoid being locked into the constraints of a specific language game (Brown, 1994; Dews, 1987). At the same time, however, communicative rationality requires that the extremely inaccessible paradigmatic base – including taken for granted assumptions and ideas – upon which all discussion is founded, should be subject to critical exploration and testing. There is thus a certain conflict between exploring the conditions underlying a particular shared view and the achievement of a consensual view through discussion. By incorporating the ideal of dissensus as a constructive principle for transcending premature or "closed" formations of consensus, some of the problems may be counteracted (Deetz, 1992a). However, his ideal does clash with Habermas´s somewhat rigid preference for valid arguments leading to consensus.

Also in other respects Habermas´s efforts to balance between a philosophical and a social science orientation, with its consideration of empirical issues and "real life problems", creates problems. One may, for example, discuss whether the distinction between lifeworld and system is defensible.

> To suggest that the former can be conceived independently of domination and power whilst the latter is constructed independently of consensus is to engage naive dichotomization which falls at the first empirical hurdle. In straddling the distinction between the transcendental and the empirical here, it is the empirical which all too easily escapes Habermas. (Burrell, 1994: 10)

One could argue that Habermas does not rule out forms of domination affecting the lifeworld. His approach can be regarded as an effort to counter domination by promoting the rationalization of the lifeworld, i.e. the critical-communicative exploration of ideas and assumptions reproduced by tradition. As Habermas sees it, domination of lifeworld contexts is, in certain vital aspects at least, contingent upon the media of the system colonizing the lifeworld. Nonetheless, his conceptualization is not very sensitive to lifeworld forms of power. With Habermas, one could also say that in many contexts the operation of money functions without any deeper involvement in a consensus-formation process leading to valid agreement. Even if we have to accept that the use of money is based on and governed by social norms, and that economic life is culturally embedded, the operation of money often works "beside" processes of meaning-creation. Nevertheless, as Burrell and other authors have argued, the transference of Habermas´s concepts to empirical settings is by no means unproblematic.

Much of the criticism that has been levelled against Habermas is connected with his system-building aspirations, and is concerned with the limitations of the theory of social or dialogue-based reason. The fact that there are certain aspects that cannot be captured by the theory, and that the theory itself cannot solve all the problems or avoid contradictions, does not mean that it cannot throw light on some important aspects of social conditions and relations. The theory functions as an ideal and an interpretive framework which can help us to understand the degree of communicative rationality in various social contexts, and thus indicate some crucial dimensions of both emancipatory and repressive conditions. As Wellmer (1985: 62) suggests, the interesting point is not really whether ideal communicative situations are historically possible; what is important is how "the grammatical depth structure of our historical projects may be understood". Or as Ottmann (1982: 96) has put it, the idea of repression-free communication can operate as a thought experiment and thus a basis for questioning the legitimacy of institutions.

Even though there are difficulties in using Habermas in empirical work and in relation to the "realistic" functioning of human actors and social institutions, he is also relevant, or can be made to be relevant, in contexts less philosophical and abstract than those which are the main focus of his interest. Some important objections to such a "pragmatic-empirical" turn in the Habermasian project should be noted. Even pro-Habermasian scholars have argued that:

> The critiques of his work, focusing on intellectual elitism and hence problems with the universality of his universal pragmatics and his restrictive negative account of power, have to be taken seriously. And his emphasis on consensus formation leaves out the equally important task of reclaiming dissent and conflict as a necessary first, as well as continual move to keep any consensus (no matter how legitimate in formation) from becoming dominant and suppressing emerging conflict. (Deetz, 1992a: 8).

The study of companies and other organizations in terms of the ideal speech situation can be combined with the (partially poststructuralist) idea of spotlighting fruitful differences and conflicts, rather than the prospects of lasting consensus. A different mix of consensus and dissensus as ideals could be pursued, in which discussions aiming at consensus are vital, but the exploration of diversity and clarification of differences are also legitimate and important ingredients in dialogues. (This would differ not only from Habermas´s position, but would be at odds also with the post-structuralists´ privileging of diversity and dissensus as principles.) In more empirical contexts, we could for instance play down Habermas´s more universalist ideas about the almost infinite possibilities of language and communication, and limit ourselves to studying communicative pathologies on a local level and providing inspiration for pragmatic thinking and communicating that might reduce such manifestations or their consequences.[2]

5.1.3   Forester´s contribution

When it comes to using Habermas´s ideas in an applied organization theory with empirical ambitions, the work of John Forester (1983, 1989, 1992, 1993), is of particular significance. Forester has related Habermas´s theory to organization studies and planning practice and has helped to increase our awareness of situations of dominance. He has also suggested ideas for a more pragmatic use of the Habermasian communicative framework. In his view the communicative turn in Habermas´s work opens up possibilities for a more applied and empirical development in the use of Critical Theory. His approach, referred to as critical pragmatism, means, among other things, "putting ideal speech aside" and the exploration of "the actual social and political conditions of ´checking´, of political voice, and thus too of possible autonomy" (Forester, 1993: 3). An empirically oriented Critical Theory should be "(1) empirically sound and descriptively meaningful; (2) interpretively plausible and phenomenologically meaningful; and yet (3) critically pitched, ethically insightful, as well" (p. 2).

---

[2]   In more practical contexts we could envisage a reworking of Habermas' philosophical position in the direction of the pragmatic position suggested by Rorty (1992). Here tolerance, conversation and persuasion are seen as possible expressions of a soft version of "rationality" and as a counterweight to "irrationality" in the sense of "invoking force".

Forester distinguishes between unavoidable and socially unnecessary disturbances, between socially *ad hoc* problems and more socially systematic structure-related sources of distortions. There is not much one can do about unavoidable disturbances. (It is of course often difficult to distinguish between what is avoidable, what is difficult and/or costly but still possible to overcome, and what is unavoidable.) They are associated with various more or less inevitable limitations, with random problems and asymmetries arising from the fact that people possess different amounts of knowledge on certain issues and that the transmission of information does not always work perfectly (even if the will is there). Unnecessary disturbances, on the other hand, can be avoided as they are the result of easily adjustable social arrangements and the actions of individuals. *Ad hoc* problems are of a more temporary nature and are associated with individuals or circumstances rather than more stable social conditions, whilst structure-related disturbances are, as it were, built into a particular social order. If the two dimensions are combined, we get four types of communicative distortions (types of misinformation). See Figure 1 below.

Phenomena that can be clarified on a basis of Box 4 are thus the most interesting to explore and to act practically to change, whilst Box 1 indicates a social constant. Boxes 2 and 3 represent phenomena that may be worth attending to. Obviously it is difficult to translate the model directly to empirical phenomena, but it possesses considerable heuristic value and does indicate the aspects that can and should be looked at in a Habermasian perspective. In this view organizations can be understood as structures of systematically (non-accidently and possibly avoidably) distorted communications or as social/communicative infrastructures mediating between structural relations and social actions in economic and working life contexts. Irrespective of the extent to which distortions can be avoided in practice, knowledge and insight of these distorted communications are certainly of value.

Autonomy of the Source of Distortion

Contingency of Distortion	*Socially Ad-Hoc*	*Socially Systematic/Structural*
	I	II
	• idiosyncratic personal traits affecting communication	• information inequalities due to legitimated division of labor
Inevitable Distortions	• random noise	• transmission/content losses across organizational boundaries
	(cognitive limits)	(division of labor)
	III	IV
	• willful unresponsiveness	• monopolistic distortions of exchange
Socially Unnecessary Distortions	• interpersonal deception	• monopolistic creation of needs
	• interpersonal bargaining behavior (e.g. bluffing)	• ideological rationalization of class or power structure
	(interpersonal manipulation)	(structural legitimation)

Source: Forester (1983)

Figure 1: Types of Misinformation or Communicative Distortion

Forester (1993) views the organizing of attention as a crucial feature of administrative and organizational processes of social reproduction. He draws upon Habermas´s model of reproduction, which includes (1) cultural reproduction of world views (ideas, knowledge, beliefs); (2) social integration, in which norms, obligations and patterns of social membership are reproduced; and (3) socialization, in which social identities, motives, and expressions of the self are altered and developed. At stake in specific communicative/organizational acts (and struggles) are thus the reproduction/challenging/reformulation of beliefs, consent and identity. Crucial research as well as practical questions include "what makes possible or impedes a worker´s finding out information at the workplace, challenging rules or norms, or expressing needs, feelings, his or her identity, way of being?" (ibid., p. 131). The problem here, Forester notes, is to link control structures to daily experience, voice and action. Such an account becomes a structural phenomenology: it is structural because it maps "the systematic staging and framing of social action; it is phenomenology because it explores the concrete social interactions (promises, threats, agreements, deals, conflicts) that are so staged" (p. 140).

5.2   The information meeting in terms of communicative rationality

Inspired by Habermas and other writers who have related his theory to organizational research (in particular Forester, 1989, 1993), we can therefore look at the information meeting not primarily as an instrumental, goal-oriented activity intended to produce certain results, such as acceptance of the change and a willingness to work according to new directives aimed at improving economic results, but as a set of communicative actions by no means free from distorting elements. This means that:

> By attending to the character of communicative action, we can explore a four-layered practical structure of social and political interactions shaping (more or less true) beliefs, (more or less appropriate) consent, (more or less deserved) trust, and (more or less aptly focused) attention. In so doing, we can identify subtle, yet powerfully pragmatic moves of social actors who both seek ends

> instrumentally and yet continually reproduce social and political relations too. (Forester, 1992: 61-62)

I have already discussed some of these aspects in earlier chapters. I shall therefore limit myself here to some additional comments, the only difference being that these are now linked more clearly to Habermas´s theory of communication.

I shall adopt three angles of a Habermasian approach to the information meeting, which is regarded here as an expression of the organization as a communicative action structure. The first is concerned with what is said at the meeting in terms of comprehensibility, honesty, correctness (truth), and legitimacy. I will illustrate how a Habermasian framework can be used to interpret specific distortions of communicative acts. The second concerns the communicative situation that the meeting represents, touching among other things on what is not said, on the passivity of the audience, on what lies behind this in light of the way the meeting was planned, etc. The third addresses the wider communicative context, i.e. the organization as a communicative infrastructure which both frames the meeting and is constituted in communicative situations such as this one. (On a basis of the present empirical material it is of course only possible to take up certain limited aspects of this third theme.)

5.2.1   A critical reading in terms of validity claims

Looking at the statements made at the meeting we can see that on several occasions some scepticism, triggering a questioning of validity claims, would certainly have been justified. This applies particularly to the truth or correctness and the legitimacy of the norms and values that were presented as self-evidently the right ones (the production of beliefs and consent, to use Forester´s terms). But let us look at the meeting, with reference to four of the layers of communication indicated by Habermas.

Most of what was said was comprehensible and easy to grasp; impenetrable statements by experts, a battering of surplus information and similar mystifications were certainly not typical of this meeting. And yet the reorganization of the company was not exactly made clear by the information provided. Very little concrete information was given, and nothing was said about the more specific motives and ideas that determined the chosen design of the new organization. Interviews with a couple of people from one of the sections affected some time after the meeting, indicated that at least some people either failed to see any obvious reason for the changes, or perceived them as a (legitimate) step in generally cutting down the organization (a reason not mentioned during the meeting). Thus, in terms of comprehensibility, the information meeting can be seen – at least if we stretch Habermas´s ideas a little – as including elements of obfuscation. Primarily it seems to have been concerned less with "information" and more with the creation of trust and confidence. The claim to inform is thus only fulfilled to a limited degree during the meeting. The fact that more space is used to reduce anxiety by signalling that all reasonable considerations have been taken into account and that management knows what it is doing, rather than providing a lot of information about the specific reasoning behind the new structure and its exact character, is not so much a problem in itself, as a problem in terms of the promise that the topic of the meeting was to be information. By framing the situation in this way it is mystified. People appear to develop positive attitudes, even though – or perhaps because – only limited time and energy is devoted to actual information. On the agenda are "pseudo-reasons", i.e. vague, positive-sounding accounts ambiguously related to the change, rather than more substantive arguments for the specific new structure or information about its precise character.

It is often difficult to judge the sincerity behind an assertion. In our present case there are several instances when Martin´s, or top management´s, sincerity could be called in question: Martin refers frequently to the change as something that is clearly in line with the wishes and views of the staff; and yet on other occasions he seems to be expecting reactions of anxiety or worry about possible negative consequences. This is clearly indicated by his response to the questions asked. The discrepancy between promises of "information" and the actual character of the subsequent meeting may also raise doubts about sincerity. Another question concerns the certainty that is expressed at the meeting about the "best" organization. The audience hears nothing about the uncertainties involved in choosing the "best" organizational design. Different messages regarding the new organization structure had been sent out, and changes in the intentions announced earlier regarding the structure were made shortly before the information meeting. The self-assurance of the top manager, and his claim to have found the best way, are a poor reflection of the difficulties and uncertainties of the decision process. Of course, during a meeting such as this it is arguable whether those present would find it interesting to hear much about such things, but it would not be unreasonable for the top manager to indicate that matters of organizational redesign are tricky and plagued by uncertainties, rather than claiming to have found the self-evidently best structure, logically contingent upon history, corporate size, strategy and the wishes of the staff.

It is often difficult to make reliable evaluations of the sincerity behind a set of statements. The idea of a Habermasian critical reading is not to arrive at a verdict, but to indicate the possible need or the chance to question validity claims and thus possibly to modify the communicative situation. A practical intervention on the part of of a participant at the information meeting, if conceived as motivated, could have sounded as follows: Given that this is (advertised as) an information meeting, could you tell us ...

Statements about the wishes of the staff and what accords with their interests, for example, or the assertion that striving to be number 1 leads to excelling or being best, all call for checking against the truth or correctness criterion. There could be different opinions here: what is said need not necessarily be untrue, but could well be worth testing (critically scrutinizing and debating), modulating, or qualifying. Nor can we assume that the idea of a completely harmonious relationship between the profit and growth requirement on the one hand and personal needs and wishes on the other is necessarily correct, in the sense that other connections could equally well be invoked. There is a tendency throughout to suggest strong links between various phenomena, when in fact any connection between them could perhaps more justifiably be described as weak or at least questionable. In particular, claims regarding connections and causalities between different means and goals are oversimplified. Positive outcomes are consistently linked to each other. In a world where Habermasian ideals were more seriously accepted, one would expect such oversimplified and consequently potentially misleading pictures to be subjected to discussion and argument, so that a more balanced and "better" set of beliefs could emerge.

The legitimacy criterion could also have been invoked in several instances, if only the audience had been more prone to question the presenter´s claims to validity, or to enter into a dialogue with him. This applies for example to the choice of the "information" presented and the criteria quoted for evaluating the organization. The obvious priority given to two particular values, namely growth (in practice largely through acquisitions, which can mean less investment in existing units) and profit, was not necessarily an expression of the will of the present audience. Many statements assumed that it was so and that consensus reigned on this point. The problem from a Habermasian position was not so much that the present assembly had not been able to determine or influence the goals and guidelines for operations in a democratic way, but that these goals and guidelines were presented as though they were indisputably in accord with the employees´ values and norms – indeed as though they had been based on the views of the present audience. Habermasian objections would not thus have been concerned primarily with the democracy problem, which is important but more of indirect than immediate relevance here; rather, the objection would have been that the boss supplied a description of the audience´s values and norms and pre-empted their chances of determining these things freely and without pressure for themselves. Something that was conspicuous by its absence was any kind of collective discussion context, in which employees could express and explore their own ideas and values and norms, and the relations between these and the organizational principles and arrangements. Thus the following criterion for illegitimate attempts to create consensus seems to to have been fulfilled here:

> Decisions reached without legitimate representation of public interests but appealing to public consent as if this were not the case. (Forester, 1983: 241)

What we have seen has been the fictitious involvement of the employees. Their views were frequently referred to, the meeting was designed with apparent scope for questions and answers, and there was constant repetition of the all-embracing "we", meaning the category of people who consensually control things. The boss assumed the role of spokesman for the common will.

Perhaps the audience at the meeting really did represent the needs and wishes ascribed to them, and perhaps they really did acknowledge the ideology whereby profit and growth constitute the self-evident guiding rule for a company´s operations, in relation to which other values are subordinate or of instrumental interest only. Would this mean that there was no need to question the legitimacy of the picture of norms and values that was presented? In fact, the problem remains, since there was really only very limited possibilities for communicative rationality in this case, even in the weak version of being able to speak out freely, e.g. without being located in a strongly subordinate position. (I will refrain for the moment from introducing more substantive criteria of communicative rationality, which involve not only the free exchange of opinions but also critical reflection about the grounds for particular views, including "the formation of knowledge, experience and identity, not merely their expression" (Deetz, 1992a: 47).) The boss´s articulation of central values and norms was not based on any previous opportunities for the people attending the meeting to give their own opinions on these matters (so far as I know); nor were they given more than marginal opportunity during the meeting either. Thus any agreement (due to chance or some other non-communicative factor), between alleged and actual collective norms cannot be described as adequate in terms of Habermas´s view of communicative action. What is decisive is that the employees are subjected to the decisions and rhetoric of an administrative elite. Whether or not this elite is enlightened is of secondary importance.

Obviously every time a notion is presented as consensus-based, it does not have to be subjected to a special "public" discussion, nor need its alleged communicative grounds be scrutinized. This would make unreasonable demands on people´s time and energy. But it would be reasonable to ask that statements should not claim too much in the way of representing consensus, that there should be formal or informal opportunities to discuss values, ideals and important goals, and finally that these opportunities should have been realized to the extent that statements about consensus do enjoy support in the shape of communicative action. Otherwise references to "us" and "the needs of the staff" etc. would be illegitimate. Either the speaker is guessing how things are, or it is more or less a question of intentional manipulation. If the statements do correspond to consensual values and norms, then it is a matter of normatively grounded values and norms, and it is perhaps even more accurate to say that the representations (re)produce that kind of consent.

On a basis of the empirical material we can tentatively add another criterion of communicative rationality to the four which Habermas introduced. Some of the deficiencies revealed by the meeting in relation to the ideal do not seem to be fully captured under the headings of the comprehensibility, sincerity, legitimacy and truth criteria. These include such things as were depicted either partially or selectively (albeit not strictly speaking illegitimately or incorrectly), as well as things that were never included in the agenda at all. In order to throw some light on these problems a criterion is proposed which could be called focusing, or possibly selectivity. (In many ways it resembles what Forester calls regulating attention.) It is concerned with what is included and what is not included in the agenda. Communicative rationality presupposes that not only statements but also a set of speech acts will avoid the demarcation or reproduction of taken for granted conditions, when it comes to what is addressed. The focusing problem refers not so much to individual statements, which can be tested in terms of Habermas's criteria, as to a series of statements and the relation between them; it also refers to what is not said. Among other things, the problem touches on the associations that attach to the ordering of different statements. For instance, by taking up the company's history first, before talking about the reorganization, it was implied at the meeting that the second of these was somehow a natural sequel to the first. This was not an explicit claim, but the order of the accounts produces this impression. Communicative distortion can thus arise as a result of the (selective) arrangement of utterances, each of which can be validated separately. It is thus important to scrutinize the structuring of the agenda. Our case provides a good illustration of this. Habermas's criterion of saying yes or no to various statements, and of engaging in communicative action aiming at exploring validity only when confronted with a statement one thinks is wrong or doubtful (and believes is significant enough to warrant questioning), does not fully address this issue. The claim to validity enters upon a higher level than individual statements. Thus it is important to monitor the way the organization of a collection of statements relates to the criteria of comprehensibility, credibility, truth and normative legitimacy and how it accomplishes certain kinds of attention, trust, beliefs and consent.

Referring to Deetz (1992a, b), we can note that a social situation such as our meeting contains many openings for fruitful tensions and conflicts between different ideals and interests (see also earlier chapters). Many of these are impossible or at any rate difficult to solve, at least in a given situation. There may even be good reasons not to raise doubts about them, e.g. practical constraints. But developing a capacity for spotting and paying heed to these tensions and conflicts can help to counter the kind of dominance that the more widely held views and representations of a taken for granted social reality otherwise easily acquire. The point is thus not that readings of the present sort necessarily inspire direct, immediate action to "improve" a situation by stepping out of a flow of statements and calling for justification and/or modification of the claims involved. Improvements of the general quality of organizational life – in terms of communicative criteria – can be achieved as well, or even better, if it is possible to develop a critical-reflective attitude towards (sets of) statements expressing validity claims in situations and modes of action such as the one interpreted here. The level of consciousness (the kind of identity developed) is crucial to the capacity to question validity claims – to say "no" to questionable statements – and to engage in critical/explorative dialogue. Through critical consciousness the effects of the illegitimate exercise of power can be partly nullified. The critical reading functions as a counterforce to normatively grounded consensus, and represents a promise that consensus formation will be realized through communicative action. By this I do not mean that greater insight is the only consequence to be expected of a Habermasian reading. It can also motivate changes in the functioning of social institutions and the actions of the people in these institutions. But the really important point is that Habermas-inspired interpretations can be valuable insofar as they help to sustain and reinforce people´s capacity for communicative action – even if this capacity cannot and should not be exploited in all public situations.

The primary value of a Habermasian framework may thus lie in its capacity to sensitize human subjects to communicatively mediated or expressed opportunities for fruitful tension, and to facilitate the articulation of such tension. It thereby does more to encourage the reorganizing of attention than is accomplished by the operations of corporate power. When and in what form such a capacity to say "no" to claims and to call for a process of checking is brought into action, will depend on other conditions, for example, practical constraints and evaluations of the significance of what is at stake. I will return to this issue.

5.2.2   The character of the situation

Thus far a few ideas about the content of the statements made at the meeting have been presented. The fact that no-one actively questioned the claims to validity that were obviously problematic, in the sense that they could very well have been challenged, questioned, modified, etc., suggests a low degree of communicative rationality in the social situation. Rather, the situation was dominated by an instrumental or strategic rationality: on the one hand, there was a desire to tell people what they needed to know in preparation for the work to come, and on the other, a wish to reduce potential resistance towards the changes and to create the "right" approach and attitude to the new organization.[3]

That an instrumental or strategic rationality characterized this situation *may be seen as* up to a point perfectly legitimate, bearing in mind the purpose of

---

[3] Apart from action governed by instrumental rationality in the sense of the optimal use of the means for achieving the company's goals, the situation in question could probably also be seen in terms of political action. (If any reader prefers to see attempts at implementing instrumental rationality as political action, which is a perfectly reasonable view, then my point must be reformulated. We could then perhaps suggest that other forms of political action, apart from those included in or integrated with instrumental rationality, were also being expressed during the information meeting.) It is hard to imagine that people are guided solely by considerations of efficiency (or the profit motive). Other motives – improving his power base, status, prestige, the appreciation of others, etc. – may very well have influenced Martin's behaviour. I shall not speculate on this here, however, but will concentrate instead on the relation between communicative and instrumental rationality.

Habermas makes a distinction between instrumental and strategic action. Both are examples of goal-directed action, i.e. oriented towards success rather than understanding. Instrumental action refers to the manipulation of thing- or thing-like objects and is thus basically non-social (even though it may involve social relations). In strategic action other subjects are central and are seen as rational players whose counteractions must be considered. My concept of political action illuminates aspects slightly different from strategic action, as the it draws attention to motives and goals outside those of a strict business rationality.

the information meeting and – more generally – the task of top managements and corporations. The disturbances that we have described can be regarded primarily as the result of aspirations associated with this form of rationality, and with the structuring and managing of the social world to which it leads. All that matters, essentially, is that profits should be maximized, and everything else is subordinated to this logic. The meeting emanates from the world of the goal-rational action system, with its one-dimensional emphasis on the use of the means for optimizing results. It is the aspects of this rationality that are problematic in communicative terms which deserve our attention, besides the attempts at manipulation and the other expressions of distorted communication that exist alongside the rather narrow legitimacy that goal-rational action can provide – a legitimacy that according to Habermas and the present author is often also inadequate.

Some might object, of course, that companies are not academic seminars or arenas of political debate, and that a Habermasian view is irrelevant in contexts such as our present one. It could be argued that the corporate management had a strong case for installing a new organizational structure, and surely the only relevant criteria were those that were related to this type of situation and to its (legitimate) purpose of securing organizational efficiency and corporate profit and survival? But the objection assumes that only goal-rational action can really be seen as relevant in a business company. In a critical-theoretical perspective this is too narrow a view; it leads to the erosion of the basis for democracy, autonomy, critical thinking and responsibility – not only inside but also outside the company, since companies and other organizations are modern society´s most important institutions, with a whole host of direct or indirect implications for everything from identity-formation to ecology (Alvesson and Willmott, 1996; Deetz, 1992a). In an age of "corporate colonization" it is important to balance goal-rational action with other kinds of logic, not only in the diminishing sectors of social life still to be found outside formal organizations and institutions, but also inside them.

It is clear that the situation is not only or even primarily of a productive character, i.e. instrumental in accomplishing an economic outcome (even though the organizational change is aimed at achieving such a result), but involves the reproductive organizing of social relations. The situation is thus clearly different from that facing a fire brigade fighting a fire or a group of engineers trying to solve a technical problem. In the latter situation there is normally no reason to invoke a Habermasian ideal of minimizing distortions (although even communication in strictly pragmatic or technical situations demands that statements are comprehensible, sincere, true and normatively correct. Even when understanding is not the objective, it is still a precondition for instrumental action).

An interesting issue concerns the relationship between instrumental/ strategic and communicative rationality in terms of the relative importance of the former in corporate practice. In a Habermasian perspective the legitimacy of the dominance of the former is contingent upon the extent to which it is communicatively grounded. If a group of people reach a communicatively achieved mutual understanding that instrumental/ strategic criteria should be the major or the sole consideration in (large parts of) corporate practice, then this must be seen as legitimate. But if these criteria are taken for granted, i.e. normatively secured without any critical exploration of, for example, the appropriate place of the money code or formally based authority, then the definition of instrumental/ strategic action as providing the only relevant criterion for contexts such as the one discussed in this book is not acceptable.

It should perhaps be emphasized once again that a Habermasian position does not entail consistent action in accordance with the notion of the ideal speech situation. A reasonable demand in companies and working life would be to counteract any extreme deviations from the ideal, and to develop and maintain – on the social, cultural and personality levels – conditions favouring such action. This calls for maturity and good judgement, in that people not only leave ongoing interactions when necessary and promote critical reflection and dialogue, but that they also show restraint and good judgement when such is called for. It is a question of striking a balance between instrumental and communicative rationality, between getting institutions to function in a practical, goal-directed sense and opening them up to actions aimed at securing a broader sense of rationality, and keeping a critical eye on instrumental action.

This ideal could be described in terms of sensitivity to communicative action and a willingness to promote it, while also tolerating deviations from the ideal speech situations. Although the lack of political or ethical sensitivity to communicative distortions is the biggest problem facing contemporary organizations according to Critical Theory, this does not mean that oversensitivity to deviations is not also a potential problem, that could in principle result in endless meetings and discussions – and thus frustrations. Ideally there should be personal, cultural and structural conditions allowing for a flexible and fruitful oscillation between instrumental/strategic and communicative action. The values and forms of understanding that enable such a situation must then enjoy support in the shape of institutionalized social forms, which allow for crossovers and switches between different speech forms.

Here there is a need for flexible structures in corporate contexts – including situations encouraging horizontal communication – as well as cultural conditions and identities of organizational members which make free and open speech possible. The absence of arenas encouraging this last possibility – as well as the above-mentioned values and subjective orientations – will limit this kind of action to informal situations inside the corporation. It may also possibly limit it in a general way, i.e. outside working life, since people learn from corporate experience. They form passive identities and subordinate themselves to experts, and other authorities, and to the abstract media in politics and public life outside formal work organizations. Just creating arenas without the necessary competences – linguistic and cultural – in the participants, will lead to failure and an unwillingness to participate. A crucial precondition for such competences are probably (re)education and socialization inside and outside the corporate context, with a view to stimulating critical reflection (Alvesson and Willmott, 1996).

Apart from acknowledging the contradictions and consequent need for a trade-off between instrumental and communicative action, relations between the two forms of action can also vary considerably. For instance, the conflict between instrumental and communicative rationality need not necessarily be as extreme as it was in our example. Organizations exhibit considerable variety when it comes to communications and workplace democracy. To varying degrees communicative infrastructures facilitate or prevent processes for checking validity claims and the achievement of mutual understanding. Many authors recommend participative management and organizational forms which tally more happily with Habermas´s views on rationality (see for instance, Aktouf, 1992; Alvesson and Willmott, 1995; Gustavsen, 1985; Payne, 1991; Weisbord, 1987). Westley (1990) has documented and discussed the extent to which middle managers – the group concerned in our case – are included or excluded in strategic conversations, and demonstrates the negative effect on motivation and the reinforcement of bureaucracy when managers are treated simply as "suppliers of information and consumers of decisions by the top-level managers" (p. 338). That decisions about reorganizations, for example, are made by top management with little or no involvement at lower levels – which seems to have been the case in our example – is as much an expression of arbitrariness, power and tradition, as of "the best way of managing". Thus the character of the information meeting and the processes preceding it was not determined by any natural law, nor by any obvious practical requirements or limitations. On the contrary, it was determined to a very high degree by social and political considerations, and is thus open to – and well fitted for – a scrutiny in Habermasian terms.

The low level of communicative rationality was actively engineered by the top manager in the case, reflecting the company´s hierarchical structure and the (absence of) action on the part of those attending the meeting. The power techniques employed undermined the conditions for a high level of such rationality, by reducing the audience to passivity. Indeed, the entire arrangement of the meeting contributed to this: the 100 participants who had been told to set aside exactly two hours for the meeting, the carefully planned structure and the absence of opportunity for anything but asking questions – none of this exactly encouraged dialogue. Equally important is the fact that people arrived completely unprepared. To a certain extent the communicative distortion had occurred even before the meeting started. By failing to provide an opportunity for the participants to familiarize themselves with the issues, to raise their voices in earlier discussions, and by putting them in the position of a (mass) audience, such a powerful sense of "communicative subordination" was created that it was able in part to determine the outcome. The agenda reinforced this. By posing questions in a particular manner, only certain answers become possible, and to produce them you need the answer book in your hand. The manner in which Martin chaired the meeting consistently underlined the prevailing asymmetry as regards opportunities to speak.

One example of distortion at the meeting concerned the way strategic action was expressed in a deceptive form. "In situations of concealed strategic action, at least one of the parties behaves with an orientation to success, but leaves others to believe that all the presuppositions of communicative action are satisfied" (Habermas, 1984: 332). One may argue that no pretence was made that what was expressed at the meeting was grounded in communicative procedures leading to valid agreement. But in various ways the meeting was framed so that consensus-formation processes were made to appear to have been involved. The reference to the participants´ response to a survey on the problems of the organization, the imaginary dialogue with questions and answers, the frequent use of the pronoun "we", all this smooths over the lack of participation and thus functions as a communicative distortion. If the strategic action had been open, and the lack of participation had for example, been legitimated with reference to time constraints and practical difficulties etc., the situation have would seemed less communicatively distorted.

However, not only the manager and the orchestration of the event from above, but even the audience contributed in some degree to the high level of distortion. It was not impossible to ask questions, deliver opinions, or make comments. There was certainly some room for demanding clarification or raising objections without incurring any harsh sanctions. But this was not exploited. The audience assumed a passive stance which in a certain sense "forced" Martin to act, for instance by commenting upon the divisional managers´ contibutions in order to liven things up a bit. As a little thought experiment, let us try to imagine what would have happened if the person who asked a question and was promptly assured he need not worry, had replied that he was not worried at all and that a simple factual question did not imply anxiety. By thus questioning the legitimacy of imputing anxiety to him in this manner, he would have struck a note that was more in tune with the communicative ideal; it would have been an attempt to reduce the asymmetry of the social relations. Contributions like this might, at least marginally, have given the meeting a different character. Social situations are usually "open" to the extent that proceedings can change character, if something occurs to subvert previously dominant norms. Power is often more precarious than people believe. In modern companies there are some elements of cultural values and subjective orientations associated with late modern society in general, for instance, democracy, autonomy and freedom of speech – which are sometimes also locally espoused in the form of positive values associated with decentralization, initiative and the contribution of the individual – which provide some underpinning for communicative ideals. Even if free speech and open dialogue are far from being central principles in a corporation, and even if they contradict the dominating ideals, there is still often room for some heterogeneity and variation in terms of values and norms. (Contradiction and variation exist parallel with consistency and homogeneity in corporate as well as other cultural contexts. See Alvesson, 1993a; Martin, 1992.) Perhaps an opportunity for invoking these cultural resources for reducing the distance to the communicative ideals – and a better one than the case of the person who was attributed feelings of anxiety – could have been the question time at the end of the meeting. Here it would not have been impossible, nor would it have been considered inappropriate, to engage in some modest checking of validity claims. Any participant could say, "Given that this is an information meeting, could you tell us more about ..." or, "Please explain why you have decided to ..."

However, we cannot be sure that more activity on the part of the participants would have reduced the asymmetry of the power relations. More active participation by the subordinates could easily have reinforced the character of the situation as an expression of successful, but effectively concealed, strategic action. That the boss did encourage participation, i.e. that people should ask questions, could be seen not only as a way of livening things up but also as a means of eliciting a response to his message. Dominance requires endorsement in the shape of a visible response, for instance in subordination, albeit a subordination that is hidden (not too marked) and in which the subordinates exhibit willingness and enthusiasm. Pronounced passivity does not look as good as "subordinate independence" or "committed compliance". Depending on exactly what form it took and what ensued, more participation on the part of the underlings could have either improved or aggravated the situation as regards communicative action.

5.2.3   The situation in a wider communicative context

We can assume, however, that the company´s traditions and its "corporate culture" (communicative infrastructure) – of which the information meeting perhaps gives us some idea – have provoked the employees to adapt and subordinate themselves to (and thus to reproduce) the company´s hierarchical structures, as well as such social and corporate ideologies as underpin the ideals that imbued the meeting. The identities corresponding to this cultural convention are not instantly produced, but are marked by experiences and habits developed in other settings.[4] Without having studied the question in any detail, I feel strongly that the event described here is not untypical of conditions in this company (cf. Chapter 2). Life in a fairly large and long-established industrial corporation probably teaches its personnel, including middle and lower management, that initiative and important decisions are top management´s prerogative, with which lower ranks should not meddle. In a capitalist society – with the goal priorities and the institutionalization of social relations that it involves – the "objective" opportunities for participation are limited (if not as limited as the meeting would suggest). The fundamentally undemocratic character of companies as a whole – despite their political importance in a number of ways – is regarded as self-evident and unproblematic. It is taken for granted that management should make important decisions concerning people´s working lives, without consulting those who are affected.

---

[4]   An alternative interpretation could be linked to the participants' lack of familiarity with situations such as the information meeting. This kind of situation is relatively rare in the company, which means that people feel insecure and passive. We could then point out that social boundaries and the absence of social interaction across organizational levels or in public situations, for instance, rather than learned passivity engendered by repetitive acts of power might account for the behaviour observed at the meeting. The infrequent use of situations such as the information meeting would then be a powerful means of exercising control. This interpretation would be more in line with a cultural and Habermasian view than with a Foucault-inspired understanding of power. (Foucault does not take an interest in episodic, symbolically loaded examples of the exercise of power.) It is of course possible to combine the view that the behaviour of the (passive) participants during the meeting is a function of identities developed in some other settings (not necessarily similar to the present situation) with the (temporary) effect of the existential uncertainty produced by a situation with which they feel (relatively) unfamiliar. Given a certain level of uncertainty or anxiety, people easily fall back on rules which are familiar from other similar situations.

The most active role envisaged in any wider context for those present at the meeting in this study was that of questioners. In view of the dearth of questions actually asked, it seems that as a result of the prevailing relations of domination, even this role may be too active for lower-level managers at a (mass) "meeting" with top management.

An effect of the meeting was thus to constitute those attending it as listeners and recipients rather than participants in a qualified discussion about and preconditions for business activities and organizational design.[5] As such, the meeting is one of many, possibly quite diverse, micro-events which socialize people in this way. The exclusion of individuals, by definition, from such qualified discussion helps to normalize the basic views on major decisions and attitudes, such that it becomes "normal" for the individuals to accept these views. As I have pointed out before, corporations – as well as other social settings – are far from consistent in terms of the way speaker and listener positions are distributed. Everyone is both, but to a varying degree and in different sorts of situation. The initiative tends to be with the person who occupies the superior position. This can even be observed when the production and reproduction of shared beliefs and consent are less obviously marked by asymmetrical roles than they are at the information meeting. A good example is provided by the secretary quoted in Chapter 2, who said that her boss always had to go up to Martin´s office when the two were to meet, which meant that the top manager never met his subordinate in the latter´s own office. It then appears reasonable to assume that this staging of the event (their discussion) would foster certain asymmetries in terms of initiative and the framing of the conversation. (Here one could raise the warning flag for communicative distortion, although it should be remembered that this is not an automatic result of the staging of a situation, since the stage does not completely determine the action, at least not in detail.)

In much management literature, top management is regarded as entitled to – and often as actually having – an almost complete monopoly on establishing important values, norms and ideals, as well as determining what is true and correct. Modern literature in the field of management

---

5   An interesting but difficult research task would be to study people in a company in the role as "listeners", and as an "audience" – special characters attaching to them as the led (and to a lesser degree to the leaders).

zealously advocates that managers, by way of leadership, establish ideals and meaning for others (see e.g. Peters and Waterman, 1982; Pfeffer, 1981a). It is the establishment of such "expert cultures" in every possible social sphere that leads to a lack of independence and fragmented forms of consciousness (White, 1988).

In the case studied here the head of the business area exhibited such a monopoly during the information meeting, and by their passivity the staff endorsed it. The undemocratic spirit that pervades much of organizational life in the company is reinforced and reproduced in social situations such as this one. We may thus define the information meeting as anti-communicative action, in which hierarchical and ideological conditions were reinforced, and individuals disciplined in such a way as to obstruct the questioning of general conditions and social relations or specific statements, or the holding of free and rational discussions. Like many other institutions, companies are permeated by such anti-communicative actions. As one of these, the meeting reproduced, reinforced and normalized a low level of communicative rationality, as well as endorsing the view that the discussion of important issues, at least in the public sphere, is an exclusively top management prerogative. Structural communicative distortions are normalized.

This was nevertheless obscured to some extent by certain elements in the boss´s behaviour, primarily his question-and-answer technique, his references to "us" as the self-evident base of everything, and his jokes about his own role. The effect of all this was to de-dramatise the hierarchy. Hierarchy and one-way communication was thus complemented by an attempt to create involvement and belongingness ("us"). By way of this pseudo-participation the otherwise sharp line between speakers and audience that was manifest and reinforced by the meeting, became a little blurred. Yet this pseudo-participation cast people in the role at best – or perhaps at worst – of contented listeners, who felt involved, not of real participants, who were involved.

5.2.4   Final comments

The value of using a Habermasian framework is not only or even primarily a matter of contributing to the philosophy of organizing or calling for grand blueprints of organizational change with a view to realizing ideas about ideal speech or undistorted communications. Even if problematic communicative qualities in structures, events or actions are revealed, this does not automatically mean that these should all be altered or redesigned. Corporate life calls for space for instrumental or strategic goals and acts. During the normal work day they must be central.[6] Perhaps the communicative ideals can only very occasionally lead to a break in smooth interaction and the call for ambitious dialogue processes, in which validity claims are checked. This also means engaging in social interaction of the sort that aims to develop a more communicatively grounded set of shared beliefs, as well as consent, trust and common foci of attention. But the potential for such action – at structural, cultural and identity levels – and the rationalization of the corporation as a lifeworld should be encouraged and enriched, thus changing the quality of organizational life.

In this chapter I have not argued that the studied meeting should have been differently designed, although it is important to consider other structural arrangements apart from those currently dominant in corporate life. Instead I have had two other aims. First, I have indicated some openings for fruitful tension and conflict, and suggested that a Habermasian framework could alert corporate actors to the possibility of exploiting such openings to make their voices heard, if they feel it is motivated to do so. Secondly, I have thrown some light on the way the positions of speaker and listener are produced and reproduced. The point I want to make is not so much that the distribution of voice and silence in organizations is largely determined by asymmetries – indeed it is sometimes necessary that they should be. What concerns me more is that people´s ability to judge when and to what extent asymmetries are legitimated and when they are "surplus" is being undermined, and their capacity to take counteractive action inhibited.

The situation focused here may not be problematic in terms of the absence of voices against the top management rhetoric on the specific matters at hand and in the specific setting. The problem lies rather in its

---

6 According to Clegg (1994) dialogue "will not be ideal where it is organizational. Organization means more or less domination and distorted communication" (p. 169, see also Clegg and Higgins, 1987). For me, the emphasis should be on "more or less" with the hope of increasing the emphasis on "less", while Clegg concludes that organizations can never be ideal speech situations.

(re)production of structures, cultural beliefs and identities which form a communicative infrastructure characterized by a surplus of asymmetrical communicative relations. The legitimacy and hegemonic position of instrumental rationality and strategic action are central here. Habermas communicative theory offers a powerful counter idea, available for pragmatic use (Forester, 1989, 1993). It offers cultural values and a means for strengthening the socialization (through education) of identities which are less tolerant in face of structures and norms for silencing people in corporate settings.

6   Summary and comments

In this final chapter I shall first recapitulate and clarify some of the conclusions suggested by our three readings of the empirical material. I will then make a brief comparison of the three interpretations. In the following section I shall look a little more closely at the behaviour of subordinates in power relationships in terms of resistance – an aspect that has barely been touched upon in the earlier chapters. I will also say something about the advantage of the specific combination of approaches used in this study, while also briefly addressing some of the blind spots that can occur in critically oriented readings, even when these are conducted within a multiple perspective framework. Finally I will address some problems of methodology.

6.1   The three interpretations

According to the critical-cultural reading, which is the broadest and least specific, the information meeting is seen as a social drama aimed at creating and recreating the organization as a set of shared meanings and common understandings of social practices. There are two fundamental themes here: on the one hand, the creation of hierarchy, of a clear social stratification which is taken for granted and regarded as unproblematic; on the other, the building of a sense of community, a feeling of consensus and belonging, a shared social identity associated with senior corporate membership. These two themes are the cornerstones of social order (Duncan, 1968; Nilson, 1976). In social drama, where the good and the right are elucidated and the common value system endorsed, social order is recreated.

Growth, profit and financial control, "us", "the boss decides" – these were all important messages at the information meeting; they, more than anything else, set the tone. Those attending the meeting learned (all over again) that these conditions and values reigned supreme. They were presented as both natural and reasonable, the prime aims in the world depicted here. This hegemony presupposes that other good things or desirable ideals must either accord reasonably well with the dominant aims, or must be clearly subordinated to them. Such alternative ideals could include participation, self-determination, open discussion, job satisfaction and security. These are interwoven by various means with the main message, which thus becomes sufficiently ambiguous and blurred around the edges, so that people can read into it more or less what they like and can then accept the bundle of messages as a whole. The use of ambiguity in communication is recommended by many authors as an effective management technique for gaining acceptance, and avoiding doubt and debate (Pfeffer, 1981a; Pondy, 1983; Weick and Browning, 1986). This is the very antithesis of Habermas´s communicative rationality. "Good" communicative action thus appears in two totally different guises according to the ideals of the (conventional) management writers and those of Critical Theory (Alvesson, 1991).

The difference between a management-oriented and a critical-theoretical focus is that the first regards contradictions and opposition as potentially problematic, something that has to be dealt with (hidden, overcome) perhaps by symbolic means, while the second sees the same phenomena as a potential force for positive development: social reality is "opened up" and organization members are encouraged to a greater awareness, to reflection upon their situation, which in turn can lead to a questioning of the prevailing dominance relations. In our case, where it is lower and middle-level managers who are being persuaded, it is certainly not a question of countering rebellious tendencies or criticism of capitalist ventures; rather, it is a case of maximizing acceptance and commitment to the goals, values and objectives that top management has established as being fundamental to the company. Certain values and norms must be secured in the ranks of the subordinate managers: on the one hand, hierarchy, subordination, a willingness to change and to accept top-down communication, and on the other, a sense of community, managerial identity, involvement, influence, security and respect. The contradictions between these various themes and orientations, which management had to handle, contributed to the complexity of the overall cultural communication. Management´s concern was to counteract doubt and worry, which undermine legitimacy, faith, motivation and drive.

According to a Foucault-inspired thesis the information meeting can be said to represent a situation in which power techniques are activated. Information is seen here as the formation of the subjects present. The exercise of power is steered in part by management discourses, which define and circumscribe not only the subordinates but also the top manager himself. That these power techniques have economic and productive effects is obvious, although as we have seen above there are many other (possibly "better") ways of exerting effective influence. "Organization" presupposes discipline – implies it, indeed, almost by definition. Two aspects of this are particularly important: to establish that the total activities and achievements of the subordinates can be evaluated and controlled, and to define the combination of "decentralization" and control as being rational and in the interests of all. The individual as "independent", responsible and subordinate all at the same time, is a typical expression of contemporary management discourse with its frequent references to "decentralization". Subordination is ensured mainly by gearing the individual to the idea of striving for the "best" possible results. "Result-orientation" denotes normality, regulates the individual´s compliancy, and provides a means of motivation and control. Disciplinary power is exercised by defining the subject´s identity in relation to this orientation – a power which, in our case, worked in the sense of disciplining (and producing) everyone at the meeting (not least the highest-ranking managers).

The Habermasian interpretation is based on a fundamental attitude toward social interaction, namely that communication is dependent on the anticipation that statements can be subjected to questioning and critical testing in dialogue between equal partners. A Habermasian reading indicates two interesting aspects of the meeting and the organization. One of these concerns specific elements in the speech acts which occurred; it was quite clear that these could have been challenged as regards their claims to validity, and could therefore have led to the kind of dialogue that would have tested them (although not necessarily in the specific situation). A Habermasian reading, according to the present author, is productive in the sense that it indicates openings for the checking of problematic statements and offers a more rational idea of the shared production of beliefs, consent, trust and attention. The other more general aspect concerns the gap which existed between the ideal of high communicative rationality or undistorted discussion, and the social relations and identities that the information meeting actually suggested as it ran its course, i.e. the establishment of top managers as speakers and the rest of the staff as listeners (and consumers of decisions) with regard to "strategically significant" considerations and decisions. Patterns of belief and identities associated with surplus asymmetries – extensive unequal opportunities and/or actions regarding voice or silence beyond what is motivated by the division of labour – were indicated as a systematic distortion in communications.

6.2   Comparison of approaches

Since the main objective of this study is to provide distinct interpretations based on the different angles of approach, there is no reason to try to integrate the approaches or to present any synthesis of "research results". However, a few comments on the relation between the three perspectives seems necessary, and some clarification of the elements of cross-fertilization and confrontation that exist between them, and which I touched upon at the beginning of this book.

The cultural reading of the empirical material provides a broad basis for other interpretations. It can offer a means of determining the meaning of several elements of the information meeting. The other two readings are based on more specific theories and focus on certain aspects, i.e. particular conceptions of power and communicative action. Up to a point they also build on a cultural understanding focusing on shared ideas and meanings. The Foucault reading, for instance, only touches briefly upon the role of the body (control of physical presence during the meeting), which is Foucault´s favourite subject. In our present case the techniques of power are of course directed primarily towards the conceptual world, towards the exercise of discipline by establishing subordination and determining identity and normality. My interpretation is thus at variance with Foucault´s genealogical stance, which focuses on power and "knowledge" in relation to the historical view of the body, whereas I adopt a more cultural approach directed at ideas about social and economic matters. The interpretation of the cultural communication and of the exercise of power in terms of controlling meanings and world views, can help us to understand the communicative distortions revealed by the spotlight of Habermas´s theory.

We can thus see certain "carry-over effects" from the cultural interpretation to the other readings, which is in part the result of the amplitude of the cultural approach and its general nature. However, it is also important to note that this reading was the first to be performed and the first to be presented in this book. In reality, related theories – even if they possess distinct characteristics – always up to a point attend to (almost) the same phenomena or details, and do so in a similar way, especially if they are used by one and the same author. The ideal approaches of many theoretical studies do not altogether stand up in their pure form when confronted by empirical "reality". Empirical observation and interpretation are never independent of the theory and language of the researcher, but nor are simple projections of the theoretical framework. The researcher´s vocabulary must be adapted to the particular empirical phenomenon at hand: something out there has an input on the construction of the phenomenon in the research process. The phenomenon under study tends to "peel off" certain theoretical dissimilarities in the empirical analysis. This means that there are some overlapping points of contact between those aspects and interpretations that the different approaches are able to attend to. (For this reason, if a phenomenon had already been interpreted in terms of one theory above, I did not repeat it in subsequent interpretations, even if the theory concerned could have made much the same point.) However, the overlapping areas where identical interpretations could have been made from all three perspectives, were in fact limited. The different vocabularies lead to at least some variation, even when similar dimensions are being focused on from the different theoretical angles. Issues are framed at least a little differently. As well as stealing the odd point from the other theories, the cultural interpretation does also provide some openings that both facilitate and fertilize the other two. At the same time the Foucault and Habermas readings add a certain depth and support to the cultural interpretation of the meeting. There is thus some cross-fertilization between the various perspectives.

The fact that the three interpretations in some ways express similar views on the general nature of power, at least in relation to hard-core functionalist and "positivist" analyses of power, and can all encourage the questioning of perceptions and reactions to everyday experiences such as the one described here, may also be seen as a sort of co-ordinating link between them. All three readings concur with Latour (1986: 273) when he proposes that power be treated "not as a cause of people´s behaviour, but as a consequence of an instance activity of enrolling, convincing and enlisting". The information meeting seems to me to be a typical instance of such an activity. The impact made by the boss – in so far as he makes any – is not therefore an automatic consequence of his formal position, but must rather be understood on a basis of his concrete actions and their effect in terms of responsiveness on the part of other actors and on the development of social relations. The different theoretical approaches also help to undermine trained incapacities, common sense, standard social recipes, and the natural self-evidence of everyday experience, which all conspire to preclude examination, and seek instead to trigger "the plurivocality of human exerience" (Deetz, 1992a: 65). Thus a critical interest in the details of the operations of power – which is intent on moulding the subjectivity of individuals – can serve to increase just this plurality of human experience. As regards the possible effects of such plurality, the various approaches diverge, depending on their differing conceptions of the individual.

Alongside these somewhat general similarities, there are also fundamental differences between the theories and the related readings of the case. The cultural perspective, for instance, differs from the other two on several important counts. In Foucault´s version there is relatively little room for those significations and meanings that the subjects may impute to phenomena. This approach, unlike the cultural perspective, has somewhat less time for the subject as one who actively interprets and endows things with meaning. The subject appears not so much as an interpreter, as an effect, of power.[1] The interest concerns the processes that form and

---

[1] In the present case my empirical material regarding the subjects' own ideas and meanings was limited. As mentioned in Chapter 2, my interpretations are based upon some general knowledge of cultural relations in Western and particularly Swedish society and organizations, and on insights from an ethnographic study of parts of the corporation. I have assumed that those attending the meeting attached particular meanings to the symbolism of expressions such as "we" or of the degree of visibility at the meeting and so on, and that these meanings then affected their view of the social reality. This perspective presupposes the notion of the subjects as interpretation-making beings who, in relation to their own social

prestructure the ways in which meanings are developed rather than the active development of meanings. Whereas the cultural interpretation concentrates on the collective ideational world, including ideologies and conceptions of the world, the Foucault-inspired reading concentrates on the constituting of the individual´s subjectivity and identity. Foucault´s strong emphasis on practices leads to a more immediately "material" analysis. There is certainly some overlapping, and it is not out of the question that the different approaches may lead to the conclusion that individuals are influenced in a similar way, in terms of the subjectivity that is developed. Yet, whereas the conceptual world is a collective phenomenon or a common symbolic environment in which the separate individuals are not very important (meaning is social and public, as Geertz says), discipline is a question of disciplining individual subjects (bodies). Thus the readings emphasize different ways of ensuring control and slightly different targets for it.

By combining these perspectives we may be able to clarify certain insights. In Chapter 3 I stressed the paradoxical nature of communication in this organization. Double binds, i.e. double messages that block the individual, do seem to occur fairly regularly in organizational life (cf. Hennestad, 1989). The members of the audience at the meeting were addressed as managers, but treated as subordinates. The importance of the individual having options for influence was emphasized, yet the meeting suggested nothing approaching co-determination. It seems that the more explicit attention-grabbing communication (well elucidated by the cultural interpretation), represents the more "positive" side of things, while the more subtle expressions of power secure the other less "positive" aspect. While the first touches upon the shared perception of reality, the second works on an individualized level. In the "good" ideas about managerial identity, self-determination etc., all are united; when it comes to securing subordination, people are addressed as separate and socially isolated individuals. This time there is no similar evocation of a shared and easily articulated area of experience.

---

world, are both subordinated and active. Dominance is maintained by representing the world in a particular way, sometimes to the detriment of the subjects themselves.

Another important difference between the cultural theory and Foucault's approach concerns attitudes to ideology. Foucault is not interested in it, as, in his view, it is generally used pejoratively, referring to false or restrictive conceptual systems which are explicitly or implicitly compared with "true" or correct views. (There are nevertheless several instances in the literature of more sophisticated views of ideology, avoiding such crude confrontations; see, for example, Alvesson, 1991; Czarniawska-Joerges, 1988; Mumby, 1988; Therborn, 1980). In the critical-cultural perspective there is at least the implicit notion that dominant views can be replaced, if not by "true" ideas and conceptions then at least by such as are less constricting and more liberating.

The Habermas interpretation, compared with the cultural variant, is particularly notable for assumptions regarding the explorable and testable nature of social reality. The cultural interpretation, on the other hand, emphasizes the ambiguous and symbolical nature of this reality. According to cultural theory possible meanings can be indicated, but their often uncertain and multiple character makes them difficult to pin down with the help of critical reason. Whereas Habermas emphasizes the individual's intellectual and linguistic capacity and potential for open discussion, cultural theory (at least our variant) advances a more holistic and "foggier" notion of the individual, in which imagination and emotional attitudes are regarded as important. The capacity or potential for rational argument is not seen as the most outstanding human characteristic by the cultural theorists. A further difference between the Habermasian view and the cultural perspective is the more patently normative quality of the former.

In terms of normativity Habermas pursues clear ideals, Foucault is sceptical of every effort to be normative, while culture theory in the (critical) version used in this book avoids adopting a clear stance, apart from questioning and counteracting attempts to hold a certain set of meanings and values as self-evidently privileged over others.

Although Habermas has a different idea about the possibility of reaching any form of "truth" (a conception qualitatively superior to any other), he does in fact resemble Foucault in his disinclination to focus on ideology, albeit for other reasons; in this, of course, he differs somewhat from the cultural theorists. The critique of ideology advanced by traditional Critical Theory is replaced by a critique of cultural impoverishment and the

fragmentation of everyday consciousness, which undermines communicative action (White, 1988).

The dissimilarities between the cultural-theoretical reading and the other
two interpretations are nevertheless much less marked than the differences
between the Foucault-inspired and the Habermasian readings. The former
tends to emphasize the "negative" element – albeit seeing it as associated
with productive functions – in that it leaves little room for the possibility of
a more "positive" and power-free form of collaboration or dialogue;
Habermas's concept of communicative rationality, on the other hand,
signals the possibility of variation in this respect. We could say that while
Foucault sees the two qualities of enabling and constraining as inseparable,
Habermas hopes that a mix of the two can be modified to the advantage of
the former, that is to say he believes in non-constrained social forms of
enablement. As we have seen, Habermas emphasizes that social institutions
and organizational forms can be "better" or "worse" in a communicative
sense. Conversely, it is assumed that power can be more, or less,
conspicuous. The critique that arises from such a reading may throw light
on certain weaknesses in contemporary practices, thus – unlike a Foucault
interpretation – inspiring a call for more democratic forms of organization.
Admittedly it would hardly be feasible to try to maximize communicative
action in a company (especially not of the type discussed here and in a
similar social setting), but some sources of distorted communication can
perhaps be counteracted. A Habermas-inspired reading directs our attention
towards such a possibility. The processes in which shared beliefs and
consent are constructed may offer variously effective opportunities for
checking, and the (temporary) outcomes of these processes may bear
variously strong imprints of such checking. The Utopian element here –
which is not of the "all-or-nothing" sort, but which merely indicates the
possibility of reducing distortion and improving communicative rationality
– can thus serve to generate action in a way that the Foucault reading does
not.

Foucault insists that the forms and practices of power are not a simple
consequence of will and decision. On the contrary, they have considerable
anonymity and independence. They seem to have a dynamic of their own,
consisting of the recoils and transformations that are created by the relation

to adjacent practices as well as to historical chance (Beronius, 1991: 79). Thus, according to this view, attempts at changing social situations, such as the information meeting, would not necessarily turn out well, in the sense that the good intentions could lead to undesirable effects. Other practices similar to or different from those observed at the meeting, which would bind the subjects just as strongly to prescribed forms of subjectivities, could be accentuated. Foucault-inspired interpretations of power can encourage defensive reactions – attempts at evasive action and temporary measures of protection – but resistance does not indicate any route towards real improvement, in the sense of a possible ideal situation for which to strive or even a less problematic route to embark upon. Rather, it is claimed that such ideal situations – emancipation instead of dominance – come to imply a new form of power. It is not the good intentions that are doubted – these are uninteresting, according to Foucault – but their consequences. We soon discover, if we scrutinize history with Foucault's eyes, that attempts to turn good ideals into practice do not lead to the results intended (insofar as it makes sense to talk about intentions). In this perspective, it is not clear why people should resist at all. In Foucault's view, the notion of the rational subject who is guided by reason and does not allow him- or herself to be controlled by extraneous forces, is a fiction; it may also be instrumental in farreaching social control, whereby the subject is characterized by self-supervision and self-discipline and where the sources of this seemingly autonomous control are not recognized. Perhaps, under Foucault's interpretation, it could even be claimed that an event such as the one studied here – which in many ways demonstrates a fairly obvious example of power behaviour and asymmetric power relations – is a less insidious and thus less dangerous way of wielding power and disciplining people than attempts at realizing a more "humanistic" and progressive ideal would be, for instance, ideals associated with workplace democracy or maybe even the Habermasian ideal itself.

There are two elements in phenomena that warrant suspicion and may motivate the researcher to write in such a way that reflection (culture theory, Habermas), resistance (Foucault) or, in a practical context, communicative action (Habermas) are encouraged and facilitated: judgements about (a) the potential harm involved and (b) the subtleties in the power effects. It could be argued, perhaps not so much against Foucault but in a way quite different from his (non-judgemental) style, that political totalitarianism is more dangerous than psychotherapy, or that death from AIDS is more troublesome than the efforts to produce bodies incorporating the kind of self-survellience leading to "safe sex". At the same time, the subtle mechanisms involved in the network of the micro-physics of power are crucial to an understanding of contemporary forms of power, and the added knowledge value may sometimes be greater than addressing comparatively visible and well understood social problems and forms of power (or violence). When evaluating phenomena and proposals, both these elements should, in my view, be borne in mind. Habermas tends to be most worried about the bigger threats to democracy and human wellbeing, and possibly neglects or downplays some of the potential dangers of establishing a bastion against these threats. Foucault focuses on the subtleties of power and may therefore lose sight of the larger, perhaps centralized, sources of threat to human wellbeing and political rights and possibilities ("progress"), including centralized economic power, ecological catastrophe, religious fundamentalism, the technocratization of politics, the mass-media creation of hyperrealities, etc.

The event focused on in this book may represent a balance between these two criteria, at least in the context of modern management practice. The information meeting is significant and visible in terms of creating strongly asymmetrical social relations, at the same time that it includes a number of rather subtle means for doing this. In my opinion it thus provides a good case for the critical analyst: it is important and problematic enough to motivate the effort, subtle enough to allow nuanced critical-interpretive insights. When considering, for example, participative or progressive efforts and practices in working life, it is important to consider the amount of harm (constraints) involved, before letting a powerful apparatus of micro-physics of power-interpretations loose on these practices. Even though these could be described as, among other things, power games, it does not follow that resistance is to be encouraged. The clinical judgement of the researcher is, of course, vital here.

In view of Foucault´s profound scepticism and his interest in the subtleties of power, and Habermas´s preference for finding rational solutions beyond power in the sense of force or (avoidable) constraint, it might be thought that the two approaches are mutually exclusive, and that criticism and disassociation must be typical of the relation between the two. But even if the strongest and most conspicuous statements emanating from different approaches may seem to point in opposite directions, there are often a number of implicit assumptions and attitudes that do not indicate discord quite so blatantly. Expressed criticism and disagreement often spring from a basis of shared or at least not altogether incompatible premises, which are not emphasized because they are not central to the current debate (Bernstein, 1983). Both Foucault and Habermas – albeit in the case of the latter in slightly more mixed terms – have made more or less direct positive noises about the other's work.[2] Foucault's critique of the humanistic idea of the potentially autonomous, integrated and responsible individual, for example, can be seen as a call to reconsider the idea, rather than to abandon any notion of emancipation at all.[3] Foucault's works can also be seen as attempts to come to terms with naive, dominating forms of human self-understanding, in a way that allows, at least to some extent, space for thinking and acting independently of present and past power relations.

> Foucault paints the picture of a totally normalized society, not because he believes our present society is one, but because he hopes we will find the picture threatening. He could hope for this effect on us only if we have not been completely normalized. (Hoy, 1986: 14)

It can also be claimed that emancipatory ambitions are not necessarily best realized by focusing too hard on emancipation. The important point is not the potential optimism this implies, but the degree of emancipatory relevance in the project. Foucault's works may be said to have such

---

2 See e.g. Foucault (1983), Habermas (1986). Foucault's kinship with the Frankfurt school is clarified by the following quotation from an interview:

   Now, obviously, if I had been familar with the Frankfurt School, if I had been aware of it at the time, I would not have said a number of stupid things that I did say and I would have avoided many of the detours which I made while trying to pursue my own humble path - when, meanwhile, avenues had been opened up by the Frankfurt School. (Foucault, 1983: 200)

3 Fay (1987), for example, agrees in part with Foucault's critique of the emancipatory concept of Critical Theory, which he regards as too intellectual. In his view, the impact of dominance relations on the body means that the emancipatory project cannot be limited to the social and psychological levels; it must also encompass biology, for instance with the help of body therapy.

relevance, without urging optimism as regards the final goal.[4] To paraphrase Foucault himself, a "nihilistic intention" need not entail effects in line with itself.

There is another idea which can help to pave the way for agreement between the Habermasian and Foucauldian approaches (and the interpretations made in this book), namely that emancipation should not be seen as a clearcut project, in which liberation from dominance relations progresses in a straight line from the "bad" to the "good". Emancipation can be envisaged instead as a continuous struggle without any clear goal in the shape of an eternal, unproblematic state, as a permanent attempt to resist and ward off power and normalization and, possibly, to enhance the autonomy and capacity of individuals to critical thinking without claiming the possibility of full autonomy, reflectivity and rationality (cf. Alvesson and Willmott, 1996, Ch. 7; Castoriadis, 1992; Deetz, 1992a, b). Foucault was not to pursue this line of argument to its conclusion (particularly the issue of autonomy), and Habermas might see it as a failure to appreciate the full potential of the project of communicative action and rationality. However, this gives us some idea of how the rivalry and tension between the two approaches can be handled as part of a study based on multiple interpretations.

The tension between these three approaches, and particularly between Foucault and Habermas, is in my view just as interesting as any common base might be, and it is not the similarities that I want to emphasize here. In the present book I have tried to show that tension can be very fruitful, and that even – perhaps particularly – Foucault and Habermas can complement one another very nicely in a study devoted to exploring multiple interpretations. Interpretations based on these approaches function well

---

4 It is also debatable whether Foucault's idea about the impossibility of the subject's emancipation (or at least his consistent warnings about optimistic attempts in this direction), does actually prevent anyone from trying to use these ideas for emancipatory purposes. A slightly selective but pro-emancipation reading of his work is certainly possible. It is possible to accept his empirical work on the exercise of power without necessarily taking on board his more philosophical ideas about the inevitable nature of power, e.g. as something that is present in the development and use of knowledge. The emancipatory potential of Foucault's revealing studies may in fact score better than many of the more abstract and philosophical writings of critical theorists such as Habermas.

together, in my opinion, like voices in an ongoing conversation sharpening our awareness of different ways of understanding organizational life. There is wide support for the idea that a paradigmatic shift is needed in social science. I touched upon this myself in Chapters 1 and 2, in line with a massive amount of post-empiricist literature:

> the assumption of an already stable, well-formed, systematic reality "behind appearances", full of "things" identifiable independently of language, awaiting discovery by the appropriate methods, must be replaced by another reality of a more social and more historical kind: that of vague, still developing, still only partially specified, unstable, contestable reality, "furnished" and "furnishing" a two-sided fore-structure of understanding, open to further specification as a result of human, communicative activity. (Shotter and Gergen, 1994: 14-15).

The conversational approach to inquiry suggested by Shotter and Gergen, Morgan (1983) and others may be specified through a multiple interpretation method. Here the element of communication is salient within a specific study, thus facilitating interaction between standpoints and ways of understanding. One important criterion for assessing a study of this nature, in addition to the common post empiricist ideals such as novelty, conceptual appeal, empirical support for interpretations (plausibility rather than verification/falsification of hypotheses) and elegance (aesthetics), would then consist of how the different perspectives adopted function together in an intra-textual conversation. The criteria discussed earlier for the choice of the combination of the theories used in a multiple perspective approach are relevant here. A good conversation involves a combination of consensus, variation in views and dissensus. Too much of any of these elements means that the conversation becomes uninteresting; it becomes repetitive, it comes to consist of monologues or turns into a quarrel. The voices involved should thus address similar problems and should to a certain degree have a shared vocabulary. They should indicate new (different) understandings in relation to interpretations made from the other perspectives involved, thus adding something to them. They should also be critical, challenging the assumptions and arguments of the other perspectives. This also means that the mix of interpretations should facilitate reflection about the strengths and limitations of the perspectives and interpretations concerned. Not only should the conversation produced in a specific case be critically considered, but also the voices that are absent from it – bearing in mind that the presence of too many or too diverse voices obstructs a good conversation, which may degenerate into mere babble. Later in this chapter I will briefly comment upon one missing perspective: the managerial.

6.3   Commentary on countervailing power

Obviously the choice of a particular focus means leaving out other important angles. In the present study I have not followed up the exercise of power beyond the limits of the information meeting, which obviously means that several interesting aspects associated with the power process lie outside the scope of the book. In this final chapter, however, I would like to touch upon one crucial dimension which the studied event was unable to capture, namely the way in which the subordinates relate to the exercise of power.

During the information meeting it was top management (represented by Martin) who controlled the course of events. (Such a description is hardly acceptable in a Foucauldian perspective, in which a human agent is not the locus of control, but I am content here with a more commonsensical description.) Activity and initiative are unequivocally on the side of the top manager. There seem to have been few of the prerequisites of counter-vailing power – which can express itself in questioning, launching symbols to undermine management´s influence, for example by making humorous comments, mild sabotage (explicit lack of interest, ritualistic behaviour or negative remarks) and so on – although these were probably not as non-existent in other contexts as the actions of those present might suggest. The situation gives us a picture of top management, in which the boss appears as subject, and the subordinates more or less as objects. Both the situation and the resulting portrayal of the corporation and its management are of course limited and not necessarily representative, but both are nevertheless significant. Although this particular situation can tell us a good deal about top management and expressions of dominance in organizations, it says less about the actions-in-terms-of-power of the subordinates attending the meeting (i.e. the managers below the top level). Our material indicates a certain passivity and general submissiveness, but it does not clarify the nature of the orientations and actions which would be interesting to examine – and which must have occurred at least to a limited extent – in the perspective of countervailing power. There is increasing recognition that even asymmetrical relations of power (almost) never mean that the weaker actor is totally devoid of some resources or scope for action or resistance. As Crozier and Friedberg (1980: 32) put it, power "lies at the margin of liberty available to each partner in a relation of power".

Top management is obviously not omnipotent, either in terms of an actor who represents the centre of power in action, or as an envelope term for all the techniques and functions of power in use in the organization. Latour (1986) compares a "transmission" model of power on the one hand, whereby various links in the chain of power can transmit or resist a force exercised upon them, with a model of power as "translation" on the other:

> in the translation approach the initial force does not count for more than any other; force is never transmitted in its entirety and no matter what happened earlier, it can stop at any time depending on the action of the person next along the chain; again, instead of a passive medium through which the force is exerted, there are active members shaping and changing the token as it is moved. (p. 268)

It is not thus a matter of social mechanics; it is an open question how far and in what way power will make an impact. Up to a point this even applies in a Foucauldian perspective. Although the subject may be moulded by the disciplinary techniques of power, resistance will not be lacking. But my interest has been to interpret a situation from different angles, not to try to measure effects or to follow the thinking or acting of actors and to discover the transmissions or translations that occur as a result of the situation concerned. Empirically speaking, this would anyway be very difficult to do, especially if one adheres to the ideals of close readings and good access to core empirical phenomena (which at least to some extent can be directly observed in a natural context). Latour seems to exaggerate the voluntary and precarious elements in the exercise of power. The comparative success that marks modern Western (and Japanese) companies in terms of productivity suggests that the process of translation does not usually diverge unduly from the forces that originally initiated it. At least this appears to be the case in tightly connected and controlled companies such as McDonalds and other machine bureaucracies. In some other corporate contexts, the level of ambiguity is higher, and we then have more space for quite different types of interpretations and translations which radically transform the meaning and effect of the initial force. This is contingent upon the complexity of the situations and the level of antagonism in the social relations. We must take into account that, in a power perspective, the sum total of actions in a company is multifaceted and that translations of initial forces may lead to quite varied outcomes. Clegg (1989b: 105) puts it as follows:

> Organizational action is an indeterminate outcome of substantial struggles between different agencies; between people who deploy different resources; people whose organizational identities will be shaped by the way in which disciplinary practices work through and on them.

Power relations include a variety of groups and constellations; moreover, these are expressed in a number of different contexts and situations. Clegg talks about nodal points where the interests of various actors come together and battles are fought out, whereby social relations are reproduced or transmitted. Organizations consist of innumerable nodes of this kind, ranging from employment contracts to the allocation of office space, as well as open struggles or tacit negotiations about the use of words (control of meaning) and modes of working. Social relations are important in this context, although material arrangements, perhaps partly the sediments of history, exercise power – constrain behaviour and affect ideas and understandings (Østerberg, 1971). Different nodes can favour or disfavour different actors to a greater or lesser extent. Our information meeting provides an example, in which management (Martin) is clearly in control, thus giving us one picture of the expression of power and of certain social relations in the company. At other nodes the (a)symmetry of power in social relations may be quite different. This has to be borne in mind in any attempt to evaluate the event concerned. The extent to which other meetings between higher and lower-level managers either confirm or negate the implications of the information meeting, remains an open question.

If I limit myself to the relation between top management and those at lower levels – while recognizing that this constitutes one part only of the important power relations to be found in organizations – then the reactions of the lower levels to the measures imposed by top management do appear to play a significant part in the shaping of broader (not necessarily coherent) patterns of power in organizations. If we further limit ourselves to attitudes and reactions to managerial initiatives – which seems a reasonable thing to do, given the empirical focus of this study – we can see that countervailing reactions take on a different hue according to which of our theoretical approaches we adopt. In cultural-theoretical terms it is a question of the redefinition from below of meanings that management tries to impose, and the creation of alternative meanings; in Foucault´s terms we are talking of resistance to power, and in a Habermasian perspective of the critical checking of claims to validity in dialogue form.

The information meeting offers us little empirical material for use in discussing these aspects, but another example from the same organization can serve to illustrate subordinate reactions and the possibilities of countervailing power. The reader may recall that Martin was said by one interviewee to lack sufficient knowledge of the company´s operation. "He´s spent most of his life selling socks and underwear." We cannot tell how many people held this view, nor judge its relative importance in overall attitudes to this manager, but it does probably represent some sort of popular conviction. People did obviously discuss Martin quite often, and this comment is likely to be based on opinions that were being generally bandied about. In a company in which most people had worked for a long time and internal promotion was common, a certain proneness to question the ideas and style of an outsider may not simply be an expression of inertia and conservatism; it could also represent an input into critical thinking in the evaluation of authority.

More generally, employees always have access to forms of knowledge that are an important resource in conflicts and the regulation of social relations (Collinson, 1994). In Taylorized labour processes this resource may sometimes be weak, but in other settings it may be more significant. Knowledge and knowledge distribution are not simple or static; they are multiple, contested and shifting. Different actors and groups may be more or less successful in their claims for the importance of their own particular knowledge, and their success differs depending on the specific context. In the case of Multi, the top manager Martin appears to be successful in his claims to represent knowledge totally superior to that of his audience in the context of the reorganization. But as the remarks cited above about his lack of knowledge of the business indicate, there are other contexts in which the asymmetry between the top manager and his subordinates may shift.

In a cultural-theoretical perspective the view that the manager was regarded at least occasionally as having rather meagre knowledge of the particular field of business, may endow the meaning ascribed to his actions and statements with a slightly different flavour than if he were believed to be knowledgeable about the industry. Or at any rate one may presume that this is the case if and when slightly sceptical ideas about his background and knowledge are introduced into the interpretive context in specific areas. Authority thus runs the risk of being undermined; he would also be seen as a person who had to depend on others in the company to a higher degree than many other managing directors with longer experience in the industry.[5] All this is connected with ideas and claims about the crucial importance and value of specialized knowledge and the distinctive nature of the business, as well as a certain downplaying of the value of marketing and sales experience, and of general management capacity. In the specific context of the information meeting, such views could be used to reduce the effects of the top manager´s charisma (his persuasive style). By defining him as a performer or artist, the rhetorical power of his accounts would come over as a good talk, rather loosely coupled to (more substantive parts of) corporate reality. People in general realize the difference, but the looseness of the coupling – and thus a certain weakening of the persuasive effects – may be greater if the top manager is regarded partly as an outsider. The perception of the manager as an actor, expressed by an interviewee quoted in Chapter 2, suggests there is some relevance in this comment. Even though the person quoted seemed to be more impressed by the top manager, than sceptical about him, some distancing from the content of the messages delivered may be involved here.

---

[5] The idea of resource-dependence as the basis of power is very widespread in organization theory. It is held that access to scarce resources or to resources that are hard to replace, such as information or professional competence, is a source of power. This functionalist notion of power is a long way from the view put forward in the present study, and I will not therefore elaborate upon it here.

Similar indications of dependence relations and of the relative value of different activities and competences, can also affect the boss´s attempts at creating the right forms of subjectivity, among other things by a process of normalization. Superficially Martin is the very linchpin of these forms, but at a slightly deeper level he merely acts as a channel for them. Questioning his authority might have the effect of undermining the control techniques adopted in the meeting, which are to some extent associated with the person of the boss. The games of truth that are presented through the intermediation of Martin lose some of their efficiency in "producing" specific forms of subjectivities, if the medium himself is regarded with some scepticism. We should not make too much of this point, as the effect of a particular person is anyway fairly marginal, at least in a Foucauldian perspective. Stretching the inspiration of Foucault a bit, some sort of platform can nevertheless be identified here, from which resistance could be launched against some of the weapons of power that top management commands, i.e. discourses mediated by management. In concrete terms, the idea that the boss is a bit short on knowledge about the business might inspire some of his centrally located subordinates to employ various power strategies of their own against him. But about this we can of course only guess as the available empirical material does not cover these aspects.

We can express this kind of power relationship in terms of the two management discourses on strategic management and core competence. As against a strategy discourse emphasizing analytical skills and general management knowledge, a discourse has been developed which focuses on management as a core competence, in which a profound knowledge of the particular business is crucial (Mintzberg, 1990). Any form of knowledge includes power effects, not only for the (managers) who are "called upon" or constituted through the discursive and material practices associated with this knowledge, but also for others whose identities, status and resource base are affected by it. In the competition between the different discourses on strategy and management, the positions of various groups and actors in management are strengthened or weakened, depending on the relationship between the discourses in society in general at the particular time, on the specific business situation of a particular company and the way this is defined in terms of the discourses. In the present context, Martin relies on the discourse on strategic management, while many of the lower managers were able to exploit the core competence discourse as a resource for their resistance, or even to help them to engage in more active and "offensive" types of behaviour going beyond resistance.[6] It could be added here that the present time appears to be characterized by a diversity of discourses in many areas. This is particularly clear in organization studies (e.g. Morgan, 1986) and also in management and strategy areas in general. As a result of higher education the diverse forms of knowledge and discourse are also available to practitioners. This means that corporate life may become pluralized in a way that weakens the grip of discursively mediated power. Disciplinary power becomes more precarious and contested than it is in institutionalized settings, where the shifts and diversity of knowledge are less pronounced.

In a communicative action framework the assertion regarding the boss´s limited knowledge of the business, provides a basis for questioning the validity of his statements. The correctness (or "truth") of statements about matters of fact, and the legitimacy of pronouncements intended to represent the members of the organization (who do "know" the business), may be regarded with a certain scepticism. The belief in the boss´s limited knowledge in certain respects can therefore sharpen the audience´s sensitivity to such statements as are not self-evidently legitimate or correct. Moreover, observations and opinions like this can help to modify the asymmetry that otherwise dictates the conditions for saying what is "true" and "good" about the business. There may be a stronger inclination to say (or think) "No, I dispute that", as regards claims to validity. Nevertheless, this does not tell us anything about the "external" prerequisites for achieving symmetric communication, the perceived possibility for subordinates to test in discussions the validity and legitimacy of the various statements emanating from above, and to establish themselves not merely as listeners but also as speakers in important contexts. (The impression is that the people at DMT are not very inclined to act in accordance with Habermasian ideals, in relation to top management.)

---

6 In the literature on power and resistance the second term is normally used to refer to the actions of subordinates, which are often seen as reactive. It makes sense to be open to the idea that even actors not in high positions when it comes to taking the initiative, can still use discursive resources for their own advantage. Subordinate positions do not have to be regarded as automatically and exclusively leading to passivity or defensive reactions.

Another interesting topic connected with counterpower or resistance concerns hierarchical distance. This element is prominent at the meeting and only superficially counteracted by references to "decentralization", "we" and the shared managerial identity of those present. As we saw in Chapter 2, the example of the person not wearing a tie shows clearly that many low- and middle-level managers see the company as relatively hierarchical and experience considerable social distance between themselves and top management. What implications could such a perception of distance have as regards countervailing power and resistance? They may of course be very different for different people in different contexts, but in principle the stressing of social distance is more likely to function as an element in passive resistance than as a countervailing power. (The two concepts overlap, but while resistance works reactively against a dominant part in a relationship of power, or against a specific technology of power, countervailing power may also involve more activity and the possibility of abolishing asymmetrical relations.) Collinson (1994) uses the term "resistance through distance" and refers to efforts to minimize the social distance and the "otherness of" top management. This involves a denial or reduction of involvement and interest in key organizational issues outside one's own job sphere. For low- and middle-level managers, such distance is normally less pronounced than it may be in the case of blue-collar workers, but it would be a mistake not to recognize that the social gap between top and low-level managers may be significant. Due to the importance of this last group, even a moderate expression of distance may undermine top management's position or trigger changes. In many companies which rely heavily on normative control, i.e. through the use of corporate culture, the creation of a corporate "we" and the reduction of perceived distance and pronounced social differences is an integral part of this control, and one which is of vital importance in facilitating the identification with core values and ideas (Alvesson, 1993b, 1995a; Kunda, 1992).

In cultural terms the perception of social distance within the company, and ways of talking that indicate such a distance, may weaken the efficiency of communication from top management down. Meanings communicated by a person perceived as belonging to an out-group ("them") are taken less seriously than those expressed by a member of an in-group ("us"). But this effect is not mechanical. Social distance may not be perceived negatively (or referred to in this way). A legitimate authority occupying a high status position may be seen as far "above" its followers and precisely because of this may be able to express something in a powerful way. Its actions and words may be ascribed a certain aura. The concept of charisma is relevant here. Charisma is often confused with a set of personal traits, but should be seen rather as a quality in a relationship and as something attributed by followers to a leader (Alvesson, 1995a; Bryman, 1993). The leader in this case may not be seen as an outsider – one of "them" – even if he or she is perceived as being above "us". Martin seems to be regarded as "rather charismatic" by at least some of his subordinates in situations such as the one described here. Such an impression may well be underpinned by the scarcity of areas of contact between him and the lower-level managers – making the latter more inclined to respond to images produced in orchestrated performances such as the information meeting than to a variety of everyday situations. A person skilled in public presentations typically scores much better in public settings, than in the less controlled, less prestructured and more varied situations of everyday life.

We thus have mixed effects as regards Martin´s impact in terms of social distance. Emphasis on distance in many situations, such as in the tie episode or the reference to golf playing referred to in Chapter 2, weakens the effect of the messages communicated. Through such talk and thinking the employees stress their relative independence of the slightly alien world of top management – the world of ties and golf. But in contexts where this world – or a person representing it – becomes perceived as less remote, as when the top manager talks directly to his subordinates, "the bureaucratic charisma" attributed to a top management position in combination with persuasive skills (and the utilization of a set of symbolic and discursive resources) draws upon this distance and may weaken resistance, at least temporarily.[7] Rather than emphasizing a uniform pattern in the meaning of

---

[7] The shopfloor workers engaged in resistance through distance, who were studied by Collinson (1994), tried to minimize interpersonal interaction with management. Such interaction was perceived by the researcher as leading to greater management control and ultimately to a weakening of the workers´ position.

Another case illustrates the combined effect of the aura associated with a higher position and social interaction. When a high-status person, perceived as totally different from "normal"

hierarchical distance and in responses to such distance, it is necessary to pay attention to variety. Hierarchy and distance are not static, but must be considered in relation to the particular local context.

The emphasis on social distance may thus encourage, or become part of, the resistance to management control, but it may also reinforce "the bureaucratic charisma" that arouses a strong response and provokes subordinateship, especially perhaps when the distance is temporarily bridged (with more or less transitory effect) and top management becomes visible.

In terms of communicative action, distance – as something constructed in interpretation and talk – has mainly a negative impact. The element of scepticism involved may open the way for an inclination to raise doubts about validity claims, but actual consensus-seeking discussions are unlikely to take place. Resistance through distance is basically passive, and it may lock people into rigid superior-subordinate relationships and discourage subordinates from active participation. As Collinson (1994: 57) says, "oppositional strategies that seek to increase employee involvement in organizational processes and to render managerial practices visible and accountable have greater effectiveness than those primarily concerned with distancing". Of course, obstacles to the realization of this ideal may be strong. There is always a chance that the processes end in the accomplishment of highly effective management control, including the passivization of opposition. Involvement presupposes that there is a minimum level of shared experiences, interests and orientations. How far it makes sense to talk about such common frameworks will always differ. Various individuals or groups possess (or perceive) similarities as well as differences. The ratio is not static, but depends partly upon whether cross-group social interaction takes place and participative processes emerge. (As a result of such interactions and processes, group boundaries change.) Defining top management as alien may reduce the scope for communicative action and participation in which top management´s prerogative is

---

people, behaves in a normal way – for example Thomas Watson of IBM obeying a request to follow the safety rules by a (nervous) junior employee during a visit to a factory – it is perceived as extraordinary and may lead to story-telling in the organization (Martin et al., 1983; Mumby, 1988).

challenged. It may reinforce resistance, but it may also lead people to abstain from engaging in communicative action in which distance as well as asymmetries in power may be weakened.

6.4   Some less critical views on the information meeting

As I approach the end of this text I would like to reflect further upon my own position, and to consider for a moment what tends to be neglected by the specific multiple-perspective combination used here and to see what connections there may be with the concerns and agendas of more "conventional" management and organization studies.

Critical-emancipatory studies can all too easily be read as implying that things could and should be done in way that radically differs from the way they are done at present. Such readings are not wrong, but it is often wise to be cautious about possible normative implications. The present text has not been intended as an exercise in fault finding. Showing how power works in management as a practical accomplishment may alert the readers – be they students or practitioners in the field – to the way in which social reality, identities and standards for social interaction can become fixed in organizational life. Such sensitizing interpretations may have a general intellectual as well as a more practically oriented relevance, thus encouraging the development and consideration of a more varied set of meanings and understandings, acts of resistance and/or a potential for involvement in validity-questioning critical dialogues in corporate settings. This is not the same thing as suggesting that the top manager in a case necessarily acts wrongly or should behave according to another set of values or another leadership formula.

The top manager in this case may in fact be seen as an example of efficient leadership. Given his goals – to overcome resistance to a reorganization and to create acceptance for new organizational arrangements – he probably performed well. In this sense, our case could be taken as an example of leadership behaviour from which various kinds of pro-managerial lessons can be learnt, e.g. how to present a particular issue in a larger frame, which makes it appear logical in terms of history, zeit-geist, certain aspects of the business context or visions about the future, how to alternate between different tones of voice in order to dramatize the story, to refer to a broad spectrum of concerns so that nobody feels their own core issue has been neglected, to refer to the staff´s opinions and feedback so that they feel involved and respected and that they are sharing some of the responsibility for the new arrangements, etc.

In evaluating the efficiency of leadership or other forms of normative control, it is important to recognize that few if any outcomes can be evaluated simply in terms of good or bad. Outcomes are often ambiguous, dynamic, local and very difficult to measure or to describe in qualitative terms (see the discussion on method in Chapter 2). In addition, almost everything that can be described as "positive" can also be described in less favourable terms: "strong" leadership may imply a high degree of subordination by others (at least in certain core respects) to the ideas and wishes of the leader; broad acceptance and consensus on a particular line of development may mean a freezing of meaning, "group-think" and intolerance to oppositional or critical thinking; a powerful vision is likely to provoke contradictions between ideals and (perceived) reality, and so on. The exercise of disciplinary power and the blocking of communicative action may reduce criticism and reflective capacity, while at the same time producing a less negative workplace climate and more secure self-identities.

The "interests" of the employees – and it should be borne in mind that employees are not the only legitimate shareholders in corporations – can hardly be defined by a researcher. However, a certain degree of autonomy (the possibility of questioning) in the creation of meaning, resistance to the machinery of disciplinary power and some chance of raising one´s voice and being listened to, do seem to represent one set of valid concerns. Another could comprise the capable management and coordination of organizational activities to increase deliveries to consumers, and to improve the chances of corporate survival and continued employment. These two sets of "interests" to some extent co-exist and may occasionally support each other, but they may also conflict. Effective production on a capitalist market implies restrictions in terms of autonomy, free dialogue, critical reflection and persistent resistance. One may well question the domination of the money medium in the capitalist market economy and its distorting effects on the relationship between material well-being and other ways of achieving satisfaction in and outside working life, but in a short- and middle-term corporate context such considerations appear to be of limited relevance. Thus the concerns of critical-emancipatory research in management and organization studies may not be to try to establish an alternative to mainstream management thinking and concerns, but to encourage a critical appreciation of management practices. To some extent such an appreciation may lead to new organizational forms and practices, but more often the probable – and perhaps sufficiently positive – effect will be on an intellectual level. The power effects of the meeting focused on in this book – like most examples of power in modern institutions – work at the level of ideas (meanings, subjectivities, communicative distortions) and by supporting "anti-power readings" and mobilizating alternative meanings, a resistent form of subjectivity and the recognition of distortive elements can be encouraged. This may well be an effective way of achieving a balance between the principle (and constraint) that organizations exist for the production of material goods and services on the one hand, and on the other the idea that autonomy, reflection and kicking against power are values worth pursuing.

One element in this balance is that critical studies refrain from expressing an exclusively or mainly pejorative view of conventional leadership and management research, thus closing doors on intellectual commitments other than those broadly represented by Habermas, Foucault and like-minded scholars. In the present book I am not primarily interested in making a contribution to conventional research, nor to the improvement of managerial practice. Not because I reject such work – although I often have mixed feelings about it – but because many people are already engaged in it, and I feel that there is a shortage of studies which seek to develop a more critical understanding of corporate life and to support people in their autonomy projects. (For overviews of these, see Alvesson and Willmott, 1996)

These projects are important and deserve much more support than is currently offered by management and organization research and education or by various practitioner-oriented texts. In order to be relevant in the latter context as well as avoiding the holier-than-thou attitude that is often so prominent in critical work, and to be more relevant to (and less outflanked by) mainstream management, some room should also be given, even in critical texts, to the consideration of virtues and constraints other than the maximization of critical insights in the cause of autonomy (Alvesson and Willmott, 1996, Chapter 7). One modest way of accomplishing this – and all in accordance with the ideal of offering multiple perspectives and opening up texts – is to remind the reader and oneself of legitimate cognitive interests and lines of interpretation other than those represented in the set of perspectives chosen.

6.5   On the methodology of multiple interpretations of situations

One of the aims of this book has been to contribute to the development of a methodology for multiple interpretations of situations. The two central elements in this – multiple interpretations and a focus on a single core situation limited in time and space – can be treated as separate choices. It is of course possible to carry out multiple interpretations on broader and, often more superficially described empirical material, and it is also perfectly possible to use a single theoretical framework in an in-depth study of a particular event. Both these alternatives have in fact sometimes been used, while I am not familiar with any examples of the method (or combination of methodological principles) suggested here. The great majority of qualitative organizational research draws upon one integrated theoretical framework for the study of a broader extract of organizations, generally elucidated in a series of interviews and, less commonly, in a period of observation of natural settings (sometimes supplemented by other less significant methods, such as the study of documents).

I will not repeat here the points made in Chapter 2 about the advantages and problems of the multiple-situational methodology, but will simply describe a few working principles for this kind of research. I will start with the empirical aspect (the situational focus) and proceed to the theoretical (a framework of multiple perspectives). I should perhaps emphasize that what follows below is of general relevance, irrespective of the choice between critical or more conventional research.

6.5.1   Empirical work – on finding, choosing and documenting the focused situation

Contrary to what one might believe, the principal advantage of focusing on a particular situation is not that it saves the researcher a lot of time and work. It may well be economical in this sense, but the benefit is rather doubtful. A certain amount of ethnographic work is needed in order to become familiar with the local setting and to acquire enough background knowledge to appreciate what is taking place in the situation concerned. Such work – which includes talking to people – reduces both the distance between the researcher´s and the organization members´ horizons, and the risk of error in interpreting the case. Being around for a time is also necessary in order to find a situation suitable for detailed investigation, and to learn to appreciate the focused on situation in relation to other situations in the organization. But a study that involves in-depth interpretations of a situation differs from an ethnography, since much less work is used in documenting and analysing larger excerpts of the setting. Instead, the level of ambition in a multiple-situational study is higher with regard to theoretical work and the intensive interpretation of the focused situation. In other words, less time and effort are spent on the mechanics of data collection and categorization, and more on a deep exploration of the meaning of the empirical material. The approach is grounded in the assumption that the interpretive acts whereby the meaning of empirical material is created are never clear or simple, and that a concentrated empirical material may allow a rich body of insights.

Naturally, not all situations correspond to these assumptions or qualify for this kind of study. I shall develop some general ideas (already touched upon in Chapter 2) about what attributes a good situation requires to be the focus of an organization study, and how the researcher should relate to it.

The focal situation should reflect significant elements of organizational life. This does not mean that it must be an average situation – I wonder if there are any such and suspect that if there are, they are probably rather dull and not very illuminating – but it should function as a suitable entry point for an understanding of wider sections of organizations. This does not mean of course that no other interestingly "different" situations are present. In organizational settings there is usually a rich variety of situations and interactions, which, to varying degrees, are valuable as an expression of broader aspects of organizational life. Some may be extreme, others less untypical. One could perhaps say that the focused situation should not be atypical. Actions, designs, statements, agendas, etc that are exhibited in a focal situation should ideally have been perceived (interpreted) and documented by the researcher in one or more other situations as well, and/or described in interview statements. Brief illustrations indicating that what has been observed in the core situation has also been noted in other situations may then be included in the research text. To a limited extent this has been done in the present book. Alternatively, the researcher could treat the situation as unique but interesting, which means that it can indicate quite little about the specific corporate context (or organizations in general), but may offer other kinds of insight. Atypical situations may be harder to make sense of – the prestructured understanding associated with the local knowledge acquired may not be altogether relevant. Descriptions of such situations may also mislead the reader. Even if the researcher is well aware of the relative autonomy of a specific situation, in particular an atypical one, the reader may all too readily construct a broader and more general picture based on the description available. The general or broader relevance of an atypical situation may thus be rather unclear.

A core assumption behind the idea of focusing on situations is that organizations are not (normally) tightly structured systems, in which every part stands in a one-to-one relationship with the organizational whole. This is partly an effect of the functional demands imposed by the variety of tasks and competencies in complex organizations which call for diversity and loose coupling, and partly of the variety of people and groups who diverge in their actions and interactions depending on their occupational background, gender, age, life trajectory and the way their work tasks talk to them. Organizational life is characterized by various context-dependent social orders and dominant modes of ordering (Law, 1994), rather than by a single order which puts its imprint on all or even most situations. One approach could be to try to illuminate part of that variety by focusing on a suitable situation. This means that the researcher should avoid – or at least be very careful about – generalizing about the organization as a whole, while nonetheless striving to reach beyond the focused situation.[8] For example, the present case may be illuminating when it comes to understanding that part of organizational life which concerns interaction between top and middle management, or, more specifically, the top-down communication between the two. There is a delicate balance here between saying too much and too little, between concentrating on the focused situation as a means for understanding broader segments of organizational life and making claims about this, or treating the focused situation as a closed, self-contained event, which cannot be related to the organizational context (or to any other situations in other organizational settings) in a clear straightforward way.

Another important point is that it should be possible to describe the focal situation concisely, i.e. without the researcher being forced to explain at length what is taking place. This means that the situation can also be interpreted by readers without any pre-structured knowledge of the local setting (even though such knowledge always facilitates interpretation). Thus relatively well-structured situations may be more suitable than certain other events which might appear messy and incomprehensible to the outsider. Such situations call for a lot of authorial editing, interpretation and explanation, making the readers highly dependent on the author and often reducing their chances of making their own independent inter-pretations. Even if the readers are given sufficient background information by a helpful author, their dependence on this information can give rise to feelings of inferiority and may discourage active reading.

The need to seek the views and meanings of the participants in a studied situation can vary from case to case. The researcher may feel that it is vital to talk to people in order to grasp what has happened and/or to get their views on certain things. If this is the case, it is important to recognize the difference between the meanings spontaneously ascribed to elements in the focal situation and the meanings that are developed and reported about these in the interview context, and to avoid seeing the latter as a simple

---

8   In the present case I have invoked some other empirical elements beside the focal situation in order to show that this is not atypical for the organization. That hierarchical relations and top-down communication are at least sometimes part of organizational reality also outside the events focused on, has been briefly illustrated.

reflection of the former (Potter and Wetherell, 1987; Silverman, 1985). Interviews create their own social dynamics. Analytical work is needed here to produce good guesses of the way interview statements may throw light on sense-making processes and meanings, feelings and ideas developed in and about the situations in question. Simple empiricism – believing that the "truth" comes through unvarnished in the interview transcripts – will not do.

6.5.2   Theoretical work – coping with multiple interpretations

The multiple-situational methodology places a heavy burden on the theories used. The basic idea is that the (self-)critical and reflective application of powerful theories should compensate for the absence of a large number of descriptions based on broad, rich and varied empirical material. A powerful theory has a strong interpretive capacity, i.e. it can indicate aspects and dimensions of the phenomenon studied which go well beyond common sense. It can generate a new way of seeing the phenomenon. This means that a powerful theory can never stand in a simple relation to empirical data.[9] It escapes the strict positivist criteria for verification/falsification, while its analytical structure is not close to that of data. Its value is related more to imagination and creativity than to those virtues beloved of traditional positivist and neo-positivist epistemology, e.g. caution, reliability and replicability, guaranteed by a strong adherence to techniques and protocol.

There must be an interplay between observations of situations and theory in the sense that the evaluation as to which situations are interesting is affected by the theories favoured by the researcher. (In addition, theories affect the way situations are perceived and described – although descriptions may be more or less open in relation to various theories,

---

[9] As noted before, theory never stands in a simple relationship to data, partly because theory (in a broad sense of the word) is needed in order to construct "data". However, we may differentiate between "low-brow" theories whose principal advantage is that they facilitate the sorting of empirical observations and offer hypotheses, and "high-brow" theories which stimulate abstract thinking about how to understand complexities beyond the directly observable.

making different interpretations possible.) It is important that the situation functions in relation to the researcher´s interpretive repertoire, i.e. the range of aspects that the researcher is capable of observing and making sense of (Alvesson and Sköldberg, 1996). The repertoire depends, amongst other things, on the theories which the researcher commands as well as on other cultural frameworks adopted by groups of which the researcher is a member. What falls outside the interpretive repertoire is not perceived, or is perceived as without meaning (in the scientific context). The focal situation must thus not only say something about broader organizational patterns, but it must also allow the theories used to function well in relation to the situation. This is not necessarily so very tricky, since powerful theories can say something about most situations (which in turn is not unproblematic, as noted in the critique of Foucault above). Nevertheless the theories which the researcher wants or is able to utilize may function better or worse in relation to different kinds of empirical material, and must therefore affect the particular situation in focus. In practice this means that the choice of situation for the in-depth study will be based in part on theoretical criteria. (In a sense this is always the case, as the researcher´s theoretical background affects what he or she considers to be interesting, but these criteria may be even more significant here than in "normal" research with a more definite empirical orientation, where "high-brow" theories may matter less than common sense.)

The use of powerful theories is not without risk – perhaps more so than theories in general – in that they have "command" over the empirical material. The interpretive tendency may be so strong that it sweeps the empirical material along with it. Disciplinary power and communicative distortions, for example may be observed anywhere. The theories influence what is perceived, what will be emphasized as the focal situation, and how it will be interpreted. As we have noted before, it is a general tenet of the philosophy of science that empirical data never emerge in pure form, free of interpretation. Formal theory and other interpretive devices (language, culturally taken-for-granted ideas) are always crucial in the construction of data (Alvesson and Sköldberg, 1996). Powerful theories are thus not necessarily more risky than cultural conventions when it comes to mis- or overinterpretations of "reality". Nevertheless, in the interpretive act, a good fusion between theory or framework and empirical material will not be achieved if the researcher is overpowered by, or is uncritical of, a "strong" theory. What is crucial here is the researcher´s way of relating to the theoretical source of inspiration – to be aware of the critique and of other theories, and to be genuinely interested in empirical phenomena and the possibility that these may be interpreted in a way that kicks back against one´s theoretical preferences, or that can at least be interpreted by using an alternative vocabulary.

The significant advantage of multiple interpretations is that they offer a way of handling this problem (if that is the right word). The use of different theories means that the selective focusing and blind spots of each are indirectly highlighted. The multiple perspectives approach facilitates a high degree of reflexivity in research (Alvesson and Sköldberg, 1996). The situational focus is also beneficial as a way of constraining and counteracting the potentially totalizing influence of theories, through the possibility it allows the reader of acquiring a good view of the core situation and through the care that is taken to avoid overgeneralization from the situation (see also the section on empirical work above).

Several possible paths are available for choosing which theories to use. Just as theoretical preferences and knowledge may influence what event is targeted, the event itself can also influence the choice of theories to be used. If the researcher has a broad interpretive repertoire – is well-read and is positively disposed several perspectives and alternative vocabularies – then a great many situations can be opened up for in-depth studies. The researcher can grasp a rich variety of dimensions and aspects and is capable of the in-depth analysis of a wide range of phenomena or situations. It becomes easier to find a good situation. If, in contrast, the researcher is thoroughly familiar with two or three theoretical perspectives only, then a situation has to be found which functions in relation to just these perspectives.

It is important, as I indicated in Chapter 1, that researchers primarily use theories with which they are intellectually familiar and for which they feel an emotional preference. Very few researchers can successfully hop between theories with different paradigmatic roots. It is possible to operate within a particular intellectual horizon, which may incorporate some related intellectual traditions. If we broaden our horizon in one direction, it is not unlikely that we narrow it in another. However, researchers may also conduct secondary or complementary interpretations taken from frameworks or positions from the set of theories to which thery are mainly committed. One or two creative interpretations may also be made from frameworks of which they have little expert knowledge. By making comments from alternative positions it becomes possible to throw critical light on the set of perspectives favoured, and to encourage the reader to consider yet other alternative interpretations, thus further counteracting the totalizing element that is more or less pronounced in all research, and about which postmodernists are with some justification so worried.

It is my experience that it is necessary to concentrate the work with a particular theory, in order to be able to exploit its interpretive powers. I think it is difficult to move freely and immediately between different positions in multiple interpretive work. "Intellectual jumping" is a difficult sport. Moving to a new position calls for "unfreezing" and desocialization from the previous position. It is necessary to distance yourself temporarily from the theory in which you were previously engaged. Perhaps the research process should be divided into distinct phases. Paradigmatically related theories make changes possible, but may also make it difficult to exploit the differences to the full. (It is like talking two similar languages. The similarities make it easier to get a fairly good understanding of both of them, but they also often make it more difficult to master either altogether, as it is so easy to mix and confuse the two.) Even if you are well read in the particular theoretical positions used in a multiple interpretation framework, it still takes a lot of re-reading to change from working with one theory to another. Never underestimate the hard work involved in using several theories!

6.6   Conclusion

Underlying this study were three purposes, all of them theoretical but each separately including some other element: the empirical element of exploring power in an organizational context, the pedagogical one of illustrating the relevance and usefulness of Foucault and Habermas in empirical management and organization studies and the methodological one of developing ideas for a multiperspective situational approach and providing relevant illustrations of this.

With my attempts at dense, close-up readings and interpretations of a typical (?) company situation, I have tried to contribute something to an organization theory and a way of thinking that allows for a sensitive response to the more subtle aspects of communicative actions, in particular the way in which such actions can permit the insidious exercise of power and the regulation of people´s ideas values, and subjectivities. To put it another way, I have tried to encourage reflection upon the question of legitimacy or illegitimacy in management and corporate contexts. Perhaps, as a result of the development and diffusion of knowledge guided by this ambition, the political formation of everyday experience – "power and politics as a matter not only of competing experiences, but as the production of the experiences at hand" (Deetz, 1992a: 128) – might be brought to run a little less smoothly.

An important overall ambition has also been to remind the reader, in one and the same text, of two things: that the level of communicative rationality is not a constant, and that the forms of power can assume many different, impenetrable and even productive guises. I have sought to encourage a type of thinking that admits the possibility of better, non-repressive and non-elitist social forms, but that is also suspicious of the idea that power can simply be swept away. In the main the study sticks to the critical tradition, pointing out possible expressions of repression and dominance, in the hope of stimulating the development of knowledge in an emancipatory spirit. Foucault serves to remind us of the difficulties this involves, and to arouse wholesome doubts in our minds regarding the unequivocal nature of either the emancipatory or the repressive categories. The idea of power as a pervasive and central element in all social interaction – and as a permanent source of suspicion and doubt – is thus juxtaposed with a social critique which points towards social forms that are in a broad sense more rational than those which can be seen in the current world.

References

Aktouf, O. 1992. "Management and theories of organizations in the 1990s: toward a critical radical humanism?" *Academy of Management Review.* 17, 407-431.

Allen, M. W., J. Gotcher and J. H. Seibert. 1993. "A decade of organizational communication research: journal articles 1980–1991". In S. Deetz (ed.). *Communication Yearbook, Vol. 16.* Newbury Park, Ca: Sage.

Alvesson, M. 1987. *Organization Theory and Technocratic Consciousness. Rationality, Ideology and Quality of Work.* Berlin/New York: de Gruyter.

Alvesson, M. 1990. "Organization: from substance to image?" *Organization Studies.* 11, 3, 373–394.

Alvesson, M. 1991. "Organizational symbolism and ideology". *Journal of Management Studies.* 28, 3, 207–225.

Alvesson, M. 1993a. *Cultural Perspectives on Organizations.* Cambridge: Cambridge University Press.

Alvesson, M. 1993b. "Cultural-ideological modes of management control". In S. Deetz (ed.). *Communication Yearbook, Vol. 16.* Newbury Park, Ca: Sage.

Alvesson, M. 1995a. *Management of Knowledge-Intensive Companies.* Berlin/New York: de Gruyter.

Alvesson, M. 1995b. "The meaning and meaninglessness of post-modernism". *Organization Studies.* 16, 6, 1049–1077.

Alvesson, M. and P. O. Berg. 1992. *Corporate Culture and Organizational Symbolism.* Berlin/New York: de Gruyter.

Alvesson, M. and I. Björkman. 1992. *Organisationsidentitet och organisationsbyggande. En studie av ett industriföretag.* Lund: Studentlitteratur.

Alvesson, M. and S. Deetz. 1996. "Critical theory and postmodern approaches in organization studies". In S. Clegg, C. Hardy and W. Nord (eds.). *Handbook of Organization Studies.* London: Sage.

Alvessson, M and K. Sköldberg. 1996. *Towards a Reflexive Methodology.* London: Sage. (In press).

Alvesson, M. and H. Willmott (eds.). 1992. *Critical Management Studies.* London: Sage.

Alvesson, M. and H. Willmott. 1995. "Strategic management as domination and emancipation: from planning and process to communication and praxis". In P. Shrivastava and C. Stubbart (eds.). *Advances in Strategic Management, Vol. 11.* Greenwich: JAI Press.

Alvesson, M. and H. Willmott. 1996. *Making Sense of Management. A Critical Analysis.* London: Sage.

Arbnor, I. and B. Bjerke. 1977. *Företagsekonomisk Metodlära.* Lund: Studentlitteratur.

Argyris, C. 1982. "How learning and reasoning processes affect organizational change". In P. Goodman (ed.). *Change in Organizations.* San Francisco: Jossey-Bass.

Armstrong, P. 1994. "The influence of Michel Foucault on accounting research". *Critical Perspectives on Accounting.* 5, 25–55.

Arnason, J. 1992. "World interpretation and mutual understanding". In A. Honneth et al. (eds.). *Cultural-Political Interventions in the Unfinished Project of Enlightenment.* Cambridge, Ma: MIT Press.

Aronowitz, S. 1992. "The tensions of critical theory: is negative dialectics all there is?". In S. Seidman and D. Wagner (eds.). *Postmodernism & Social Theory.* Cambridge, Ma/Oxford: Blackwell.

Ashforth, B. and F. Mael. 1989. "Social identity theory and the organization". *Academy of Management Review.* 14, 20–39.

Asplund, J. 1970. *Om undran inför samhället.* Lund: Argos.

Astley, G. 1985. "Administrative science as socially constructed truth". *Administrative Science Quarterly.* 30, 497–513.

Baker, S. 1990. "Reflection, doubt, and the place of rhetoric in postmodern social theory". *Sociological Theory.* 8, 232–245.

Barley, S. and G. Kunda. 1992. "Design and devotion: surges of rational and normative ideologies of control in managerial discourse". *Administrative Science Quarterly.* 37, 363–399.

Barley, S., G. W. Meyer and D. C. Gash. 1988. "Cultures of culture: academics, practitioners and the pragmatics of normative control". *Administrative Science Quarterly.* 22, 1, 24–60.

Beckérus, Å. and A. Edström (ed). 1988. *Doktrinskiftet. Nya ideal i svenskt ledarskap.* Stockholm: Svenska Dagbladets Förlags AB.

Benson, J. K. 1977. "Organizations: a dialectical view. *Administrative Science Quarterly.* 22, 1–21.

Benson, J. K. 1983. "A dialectical method for the study of organizations". In G. Morgan (ed.). *Beyond Method.* Beverly Hills: Sage.

Benton, T. 1981. "'Objective interests' and the sociology of power". *Sociology.* 15, 161–184.

Bernstein, R. J. 1983. *Beyond Objectivism and Relativism.* Oxford: Basil Blackwell.

Bernstein, R. J. 1985. "Introduction". In R. J. Bernstein (ed.). *Habermas and Modernity.* Masschusetts: MIT Press.

Beronius, M. 1986. *Den disciplinära maktens organisering.* Lund: Arkiv.

Beronius, M. 1991. *Genealogi och sociologi.* Stehag: Symposion.

Borgert, L. 1994. "Contrasting images. An essay on the search for reflexivity in organizing and organization studies". Unpublished paper. University College of Falun/Borlänge, Sweden.

Brown, R. H. 1990. "Rhetoric, textuality, and the postmodern turn in sociological theory". *Sociological Theory*. 8, 188–197.

Brown, R. H. 1994. "Reconstructing social theory after the postmodern critique". In H. Simons and M. Billig (eds.). *After Postmodernism. Reconstructing Ideology Critique*. London: Sage.

Bryman, A. 1993. "Charismatic leadership in business organizations: some neglected issues". *Leadership Quarterly*. 4, 3/4, 289–304.

Bryman, A. 1996. "Leadership in organizations". In S. Clegg, C. Hardy and W. Nord (eds.). *Handbook of Organization Studies*. London: Sage.

Bubner, R. 1982. "Habermas's concept of Critical Theory". In J. B. Thompson and D. Held (eds.). *Habermas. Critical Debates*. London: Macmillan.

Burke, K. 1989. *On Symbols and Society*. Chicago: University of Chicago Press.

Burrell, G. 1988. "Modernism, postmodernism and organizational analysis 2: the contribution of Michel Foucault". *Organization Studies*. 9, 2, 221–235.

Burrell, G. and G. Morgan. 1979. *Sociological Paradigms and Organizational Analysis*. Aldershot: Gower.

Calás, M. and L. Smircich. 1987. "Post-culture: is the organizational culture literature dominant but dead?" Paper presented at the 3rd International Conference on Organizational Symbolism and Corporate Culture, Milan, June 1987.

Calhoun, C. 1992. "Culture, history, and the problem of specificity in social theory". In S. Seidman and D. Wagner (eds.). *Postmodernism & Social Theory*. Cambridge, Ma/Oxford: Blackwell.

Castoriadis, C. 1992. "Power, politics, autonomy". In A. Honneth et al. (eds.). *Cultural–Political Interventions in the Unfinished Project of Enlightenment*. Cambridge, Ma: MIT Press.

Clegg, S. 1987. "The power of language, the language of power". *Organization Studies*. 8, 1, 60–70.

Clegg, S. 1989a. *Frameworks of Power*. London: Sage.

Clegg, S. 1989b. "Radical revisions: power, discipline and organizations". *Organization Studies*. 10, 97–115.

Clegg, S. 1994. "Social theory for the study of organization: Weber and Foucault". *Organization*. 1, 1, 149–178.

Clegg, S., C. Hardy and W. Nord. 1996. "Some dare call it power". In S. Clegg, C. Hardy and W. Nord (eds.). *Handbook of Organization Studies*. London: Sage.

Clegg, S. and W. Higgins. 1987. "Against the current: organizational sociology and socialism". *Organization Studies.* 8, 201–221.

Clifford, J. 1986. "Introduction: partial truths". In J. Clifford and G. Marcus (eds.). *Writing Culture. The Poetics and Politics of Ethnography.* Los Angeles: University of California Press.

Coles, R. 1991. "Foucault´s dialogical artistic ethos". *Theory, Culture & Society.* 8, 99–120.

Collins, R. 1981. "Micro-translation as a theory-building strategy". In K. Knorr-Cetina and A. Cicourel (eds.). *Advances in Social Theory and Methodology.* Boston: Routledge and Kegan Paul.

Collins, R. 1988. "The micro contribution to macro sociology". *Sociological Theory.* 6, 242–253.

Collinson, D. 1994. "Strategies of resistance: power, knowledge and subjectivity in the workplace". In J. Jermier, D. Knights and W. Nord (eds.). *Resistance and Power in Organizations.* London: Routledge.

Cooper, R. and G. Burrell. 1988. "Modernism, postmodernism and organizational analysis: an introduction". *Organization Studies.* 9, 91–112.

Crozier, M. and E. Friedberg. 1980. *Actors & Systems.* Chicago: University of Chicago Press.

Czarniawska-Joerges, B. 1988. *Ideological Control in Nonideological Organizations.* New York: Praeger.

Czarniawska-Joerges, B. 1993. *The Three-Dimensional Organization.* Lund: Studentlitteratur.

Czarniawska-Joerges, B. 1994. "Narratives of individual and organizational identities". In S. Deetz (ed.). *Communication Yearbook, Vol. 17.* Newbury Park: Sage.

Dandridge, T. 1986. "Ceremony as an integration of work and play". *Organization Studies.* 7, 159–170.

Dandridge, T., I. Mitroff and W. Joyce. 1980. "Organizational symbolism: a topic to expand organizational analysis". *Academy of Management Review,* 5, 77–82.

Daudi, P. 1986. *Power in the Organization:.* Oxford: Basil Blackwell.

Deal, T. and A. Kennedy. 1982. *Corporate Cultures. The Rites and Rituals of Corporate Life.* Reading, Mass: Addison-Wesley.

Deetz, S. 1986. "Metaphors and the discursive production and reproduction of organization". In L. Thayer (ed.). *Communication – Organization.* Norwood, NJ: Ablex.

Deetz, S. 1992a. *Democracy in an Age of Corporate Colonization: Developments in Communication and the Politics of Everyday Life.* Albany: State University of New York Press.

Deetz, S. 1992b. "Disciplinary power in the modern corporation". In M. Alvesson and H. Willmott (eds.). *Critical Management Studies*. London: Sage.

Deetz, S. 1995. *Transforming Communication, Transforming Business: Building Responsive and Responsible Workplaces*. Cresskill, NJ: Hampton Press.

Deetz, S. 1996. Describing differences in approaches to organization science: rethinking Burrell and Morgan and their legacy". *Organization Science*. (in press)

Deetz, S. and A. Kersten. 1983. "Critical models of interpretive research". In L. Putnam and M. Pacanowsky (eds.). *Communication and Organizations*. Beverly Hills: Sage.

Deetz, S. and D. Mumby. 1986. "Metaphors, information, and power". In B. Reuben (ed.). *Information and Behavior*. New Brunswick, NJ: Transaction Books.

Dews, P. 1987. *Logics of Disintegration*. London: Verso.

Donaldson, L. 1985. *In Defence of Organization Theory*. Cambridge: Cambridge University Press.

Dreyfus, H. and P. Rabinow. 1986. "What is maturity? Habermas and Foucault on 'What is Enlightenment?'" In D. Hoy (ed.). *Foucault. A Critical Reader*. Oxford: Basil Blackwell.

Duncan, H. D. 1968. *Symbol and Society*. Oxford: Oxford University Press.

Eckberg, D. and R. Hill. 1980. "The paradigm concept and sociology: a critical review". In G. Gutting (ed.) *Paradigms and Revolutions*. Notre Dame, Ind.: University of Notre Dame Press.

Fay, B. 1987. *Critical Social Science*. Cambridge: Polity Press.

Featherstone, M. 1988. "In pursuit of the postmodern: an introduction". *Theory, Culture & Society*. 5, 195–215.

Fombrun, C. 1986. "Structural dynamics within and between organizations". *Administrative Science Quarterly*. 31, 403–421.

Forester, J. 1983. "Critical Theory and organizational analysis". In G. Morgan (ed.). *Beyond Method*. Beverly Hills: Sage.

Forester, J. 1988. "The contemporary relevance of Critical Theory to public administration: promises and problems". Paper. Dept of City and Regional Planning, Cornell University.

Forester, J. 1989. *Planning in the Face of Power*. Berkeley, CA: University of California Press.

Forester, J. 1992. "Critical ethnography: on fieldwork in a Habermasian way". In M. Alvesson and H. Willmott (eds.). *Critical Management Studies*. London: Sage.

Forester, J. 1993. *Critical Theory, Public Policy, and Planning Practice*. Albany: State University of New York Press.

Foster, H. (ed). 1984. *Postmodern Culture*. London: Pluto Press.

Foucault, M. 1974. *Discipline and Punish*. Harmondsworth: Penguin.

Foucault, M. 1976. *The History of Sexuality. Vol. 1*. New York: Pantheon.

Foucault, M. 1980. *Power/Knowledge*. New York: Pantheon.

Foucault, M. 1982. "The subject and power". *Critical Inquiry*. 8, 777–795.

Foucault, M. 1983. "Structuralism and post-structuralism: an interview with Michel Foucault, by G Raulet". *Telos*. 55, 195–211.

Foucault, M. 1984. "The ethic of care for the self as a practice of freedom: an interview with Michel Foucault". In J. Bernauer and D. Rasmussen (eds.). *The Final Foucault*. Cambridge, Ma: MIT Press.

Fromm, E. 1976. *To Have or to Be?* New York: Harper and Brothers.

Frost, P. J. 1987. "Power, politics, and influence". In F. Jablin et al. (eds.). *Handbook of Organizational Communication*. Newbury Park: Sage.

Frost, P. L. Moore, M. Louis, C. Lundberg and J. Martin (eds.) 1985. *Organizational Culture*. Beverly Hills: Sage.

Frost, P. L. Moore, M. Louis, C. Lundberg and J. Martin (eds.) 1991. *Reframing Organizational Culture*. Newbury Park: Sage.

Galbraith, J. K. 1983. *The Anatomy of Power*. New York: Simon and Schuster.

Geertz, C. 1973. *The Interpretation of Cultures*. New York: Basic Books.

Geertz, C. 1983. *Local Knowledge*. New York: Basic Books.

Giddens, A. 1979. *Central Problems in Social Theory*. London: Macmillan.

Giddens, A. 1982. "Labour and interaction". In J. B. Thompson and D. Held (eds.). *Habermas. Critical Debates*. London: Macmillan.

Gioia, D. and E. Pitre. 1990. "Multiparadigm perspectives on theory building". *Academy of Management Review*. 15, 584–602.

Gray, B., M. Bougon and A Donnellon. 1985. "Organizations as constructions and destructions of meaning". *Journal of Management*. 11, 2, 83–98.

Guba, E. and Y. Lincoln. 1994. "Competing paradigms in qualitative research". In N. Denzin and Y. Lincoln (eds.). *Handbook of Qualitative Research*. Thousand Oaks: Sage.

Gustavsen, B. 1985. "Workplace reform and democratic dialogue". *Economic and Industrial Democracy*. 6, 4, 461–479.

Habermas, J. 1971. *Toward a Rational Society*. London: Heinemann.

Habermas, J. 1972. *Knowledge and Human Interests*. London: Heinemann.

Habermas, J. 1977. "Hannah Arendt´s communications concept of power". *Social Research*. 44, 3–24.

Habermas, J. 1984. *The Theory of Communicative Action. Vol. 1*. Boston: Beacon Press.

Habermas, J. 1986. "Taking aim at the heart of the present". In D. C. Hoy (ed.) *Foucault. A Critical Reader.* Oxford: Basil Blackwell.

Hacking, I. 1982. "Language, truth and reason". In M. Hollis and S. Lukes (eds.) *Rationality and Relativism.* Oxford: Basil Blackwell.

Hackman, J. R., et al. 1975. "A new strategy for job enrichment". In B. Staw (ed.). *Psychological Foundations of Organizational Behaviour.* Santa Monica, CA: Goodyear.

Hammarsley, M. 1990. "What is wrong with ethnography? The myth of theoretical description". *Sociology.* 24, 597–615.

Hardy, C. 1994. "Power and politics in organizations". In *Managing Strategic Action.* London: Sage.

Hassard, J. 1991. "Multiple paradigms and organizational analysis: a case study". *Organization Studies.* 12, 275–299.

Hassard, J. and M. Parker (eds.). 1993. *Postmodernism and Organizations.* London: Sage.

Hatch, M. J. 1993. "The dynamics of organizational culture". *Academy of Management Review.* 18, 4, 657–693.

Hennestad, B. 1989. "The symbolic impact of double-bind leadership". Paper presented at the The Fourth International Conference on Organizational Symbolism and Corporate Culture, INSEAD, June 28–30, 1989.

Horkheimer, M. 1937. "Traditional and Critical Theory". In P. Connerton (ed.). *Critical Sociology.* Harmondsworth: Penguin 1976.

Horkheimer, M. and T. Adorno. 1947. *The Dialectics of Enlightenment.* London: Verso 1979.

Hosking, D. M. 1988. "Organizing, leadership and skilful process". *Journal of Management Studies.* 25, 2, 147–166.

Hoy, D. (ed.). 1986. *Foucault. A Critical Reader.* Oxford: Basil Blackwell.

Jablin, F. et al. (eds.). *Handbook of Organizational Communication.* Newbury Park: Sage.

Jackall, R. 1988. *Moral Mazes. The World of Corporate Managers.* Oxford: Oxford University Press.

Jackson, N. and P. Carter. 1991. "In defence of paradigm incommensurability". *Organization Studies,* 12, 109–127.

Jeffcutt, P. 1993. "From interpretation to representation". In J. Hassard and M. Parker (eds.). *Postmodernism and Organizations.* London: Sage.

Johansson, O. L. 1990. *Organisationsbegrepp och begreppsmedvetenhet.* Göteborg: BAS.

Kellner, D. 1988. "Postmodernism as social theory: some challenges and problems". *Theory, Culture & Society.* 5, 2–3, 239–269.

Kilmann, R., et al. (1985). *Gaining Control of the Corporate Culture.* San Francisco: Jossey-Bass.

Knights, D. 1992. "Changing spaces: the disruptive impact of a new epistemological location for the study of management". *Academy of Management Review.* 17, 514–536.

Knights, D. and G. Morgan. 1991. "Corporate strategy, organizations, and subjectivity: a critique". *Organization Studies.* 12, 251–273.

Knights, D. and T. Vurdubakis. 1994. "Foucault, power, resistance and all that". In J. Jermier, D. Knights and W. Nord (eds.). *Resistance and Power in Organizations.* London: Routledge.

Knights, D. and H. Willmott. 1985. "Power and identity in theory and practice". *The Sociological Review.* 33, 1, 22–46.

Knights, D. and H. Willmott. 1987. "Organizational culture as management strategy: a critique and illustration from the financial service industries". *International Studies of Management and Organization.* 17, 3, 40–63.

Knights, D. and H. Willmott. 1989. "Power and subjectivity at work". *Sociology.* 23, 4, 535–558.

Knights, D. and H. Willmott. 1992. "Conceptualizing leadership processes: a study of senior managers in a financial services company". *Journal of Management Studies.* 29, 761–782.

Knorr-Cetina, K. 1981. "Introduction. The micro-sociological challenge of macro-sociology: towards a reconstruction of social theory and methodology". In K. Knorr-Cetina and A. Cicourel (eds.). *Advances in Social Theory and Methodology.* Boston: Routledge and Kegan Paul.

Kuhn, T. S. 1970. *The Structure of Scientific Revolutions.* Chicago: University of Chicago Press.

Kunda, G. 1992. *Engineering Culture. Control and Commitment in a High-Tech Corporation.* Philadelphia: Temple University Press.

Latour, B. 1986. "The powers of association". In J. Law (ed.). *Power, Action and Belief: A New Sociology of Knowledge?* London: Routledge and Kegan Paul.

Laurent, A. 1978. "Managerial subordinancy". *Academy of Management Review.* 3, 220–230.

Law, J. 1994. *Organizing Modernity.* Oxford: Basil Blackwell.

Lindkvist, L. 1989. "Företagsintern styrning and informationsanvändning – en kontraktsansats". Paper. Ekonomiska inst., Linköpings Universitet:

Linstead, S. 1993. "From postmodern anthropology to deconstructive ethnography". *Human Relations.* 46, 1, 97–120.

Linstead, S. and R. Grafton-Small. 1992. "On reading organizational culture". *Organization Studies.* 13, 331–355.

Lukes, S. 1982. "Of gods and demons: Habermas and practical reason". In J. B. Thompson and D. Held (eds.). *Habermas. Critical Debates.* London: Macmillan.

Lyotard, J.-F. 1984. *The Postmodern Condition: A Report on Knowledge.* Manchester: Manchester University Press.

March, J. and J. Olsen. 1976 *Ambiguity and Choice in Organizations,* Bergen: Universitetsforlaget.

Marcus, G. and M. Fischer. 1986. *Anthropology as Cultural Critique.* Chicago: University of Chicago Press.

Marcuse, H. 1964. *One-dimensional Man.* Boston: Beacon Press.

Martin, J. 1992. *The Culture of Organizations. Three Perspectives.* New York: Oxford University Press.

Martin, J. and P. Frost. 1996. "The organizational culture wars: a struggle for intellectual dominance". In S. Clegg, C. Hardy and W. Nord (eds.). *Handbook of Organization Studies.* London: Sage.

Martin, J. and D. Meyerson. 1988. "Organizational cultures and the denial, channeling and acknowledgement of ambiguity". In L. R. Pondy et al. (eds.). *Managing Ambiguity and Change.* New York: Wiley.

Martin, J., M. Feldman, M. Hatch and S. Sitkin. 1983. "The uniqueness paradox in organizational stories". *Administrative Science Quarterly.* 28, 438–453.

Miller, P. and T. O´Leary. 1987. "Accounting and the construction of the governable person". *Accounting, Organizations and Society.* 12, 235–265.

Mintzberg, H. 1983. *Structure in Fives. Designing Effective Organizations.* Englewood Cliffs, NJ: Prentice-Hall.

Mintzberg, H. 1990. "The design school: reconsidering the basic premises of strategic management". *Strategic Management Journal.* 11, 171–195.

Mintzberg, H. and A. McHugh. 1985. "Strategy formation in an adhocracy". *Administrative Science Quarterly.* 30, 160–197.

Morgan, G. 1986. *Images of Organization.* London: Sage.

Moxnes, P. 1981. *Ångest och arbetsmiljö.* Stockholm: Natur och Kultur.

Mumby, D. 1988. *Communication and Power in Organizations: Discourse, Ideology and Domination.* Norwood, NJ: Ablex.

Mumby, D. 1991. "Communication, power and knowledge representation: the competing visions of Habermas and Foucault". Paper. Dept of Communication, Purdue University.

Mumby, D. and C. Stohl. 1991. "Power and discourse in organization studies: absence and the dialectic of control". *Discourse & Society.* 2, 313–332.

Nilson, G. 1976. *Sociodramer.* Göteborg: Korpen.

Ortner, S. 1984. "Theory in anthropology since the sixties". *Comparative Studies in Society and History.* 26, 126–166.

Ottmann, H. 1982. "Cognitive interests and self-reflection". In J. B. Thompson and D. Held (eds.). *Habermas. Critical Debates.* London: Macmillan.

Outhwaite, W. 1983. "Toward a realist perspective". In G. Morgan (ed.). *Beyond Method.* Beverly Hills: Sage.

Parker, M. and G. McHugh. 1991. "Five texts in search of an author: a response to John Hassard's 'Multiple paradigms and organizational analysis'". *Organization Studies.* 13, 451–456.

Payne, S. 1991. "A proposal for corporate ethical reform: the ethical dialogue group". *Business & Professional Ethics Journal.* 10, 1, 67–88.

Perrow, C. 1986. *Complex Organizations: A Critical Essay (3.rd ed.).* New York: Random House.

Peters, T. J. and R. H. Waterman. 1982. *In Search of Excellence.* New York: Harper and Row.

Pfeffer, J. 1978. "The ambiguity of leadership". In M. McCall and M. Lombardo (eds.) *Leadership: Where Else Can We Go?* Durham: Duke University Press.

Pfeffer, J. 1981a. "Management as symbolic action: the creation and maintenance of organizational paradigms". In L. L. Cummings and B. M. Staw (eds.). *Research in Organizational Behavior, Vol. 3.* Greenwich, CT: JAI Press.

Pfeffer, J. 1981b. *Power in Organizations.* Boston: Pitman.

Pfeffer, J. and G. R. Salancik. 1978. *The External Control of Organizations. A Resource Dependence Perspective.* New York: Harper & Row.

Pondy, L. R. 1983. "The role of metaphors and myths in organization and in the facilitation of change". In L. R. Pondy, P. J. Frost, G. Morgan and T. C. Dandridge (eds.). *Organizational Symbolism.* Greenwich, Conn: JAI Press Inc.

Potter, J. and M. Wetherell. 1987. *Discourse and Social Psychology. Beyond Attitudes and Behaviour.* London: Sage.

Putnam, L. 1983. "The interpretive perspective: an alternative to functionalism". In L. Putnam and M. Pacanowsky (eds.). *Communication and Organization.* Beverly Hills: Sage.

Putnam, L., C. Bantz, S. Deetz, D. Mumby and J. Van Maanen. 1993. "Ethnography versus critical theory. Debating organizational research". *Journal of Management Inquiry.* 2, 3, 221–235.

Putnam, L. and M. Pacanowsky (eds.). 1983. *Communication and Organization.* Beverly Hills: Sage.

Ranson, S., C. R. Hinings and R. Greenwood. 1980. "The structuring of organizational structures". *Administrative Science Quarterly.* 25, 1–17.

Rao, H. and W. Pasmore. 1989. "Knowledge and interests in organization studies: a conflict of interpretations". *Organization Studies.* 10, 225–240.

Ray, C. A. 1986. "Corporate culture: the last frontier of control". *Journal of Management Studies.* 23, 287–296.

Reed, M. 1985. *Redirections in Organizational Analysis.* London: Tavistock.

Reed, M. 1990. "From paradigms to images: the paradigm warrior turns post-modern guru". *Personnel Review.* 19, 3, 35–40.

Reed, M. 1993. "Organisations and modernity: continuity and discontinuity in organisation theory". In J. Hassard and M. Parker (eds.). *Post-modernism and Organizations.* London: Sage.

Riley, P. 1983. "A structurationist account of political cultures". *Administrative Science Quarterly.* 28, 414–437.

Rorty, R. 1989. *Contingency, Irony and Solidarity.* Cambridge: Cambridge University Press.

Rorty, R. 1992. "Cosmopolitism without emancipation". In S. Lash and J. Friedman (eds.). *Modernity & Identity.* Oxford: Blackwell.

Rosen, M. 1985. "Breakfirst at Spiro´s: dramaturgy and dominance". *Journal of Management.* 11, 2, 31–48.

Salancik, G. R. and J. Pfeffer. 1978. "A social information processing approach to job attitudes and task design". *Administrative Science Quarterly.* 23, 224–253.

Sandelands, L. and R. Drazin. 1989. "On the language of organization theory". *Organization Studies.* 10, 457–478.

Sandelands, L. and V. Srivatsan. 1993. "The problem of experience in the study of organizations". *Organization Studies.* 14, 1–22.

Sarup, M. 1988. *An Introductory Guide to Post-Structuralism and Postmodernism.* London: Harvester-Wheatsheaf.

Schein, E. 1985. *Organizational Culture and Leadership – A Dynamic View.* San Francisco, Ca: Jossey-Bass.

Sennett, R. 1980. *Authority.* New York: Vintage Books.

Shotter, J. and K. Gergen (eds.). 1989. *Texts of Identity.* London: Sage.

Shotter, J. and K. Gergen. 1994. "Social construction: knowledge, self, others, and continuing the conversation". In S. Deetz (ed.). *Communication Yearbook, Vol. 17.* Newbury Park: Sage.

Sievers, B. 1986. "Beyond the surrogate of motivation". *Organization Studies.* 7, 335–352.

Silverman, D. 1970. *The Theory of Organizations.* London: Heinemann.

Silverman, D. 1975. "Accounts of organizations – organizational ´structures´ and the accounting process". In J. McKinley (ed.). *Processing People – Cases in Organizational Behaviour*. London: Holt, Rinehart and Winston.

Silverman, D. 1985. *Qualitative Methodology & Sociology*. Aldershot: Gower.

Silverman, D. 1989. "Six rules of qualitative research: a post-romantic argument". *Symbolic Interaction*. 12, 2, 25–40.

Silverman, D. 1994. "On throwing away ladders: rewriting the theory of organisations". In J. Hassard and M. Parker. (eds.). *Towards a New Theory of Organization*. London: Routledge.

Simons, H. (ed.).1989. *Rhetoric in the Human Sciences*. London: Sage.

Sköldberg, K. 1992. "Through a glass, darkly. A critique of Sandelands and Drazin". *Organization Studies*. 12, 245–259.

Smircich, L. 1983. "Concepts of culture and organizational analysis". *Administrative Science Quarterly*. 28, 3, 339–358.

Smircich, L. and G. Morgan. 1982. "Leadership: the management of meaning". *The Journal of Applied Behavioural Science*. 18, 3, 257–273.

Steier, F. (ed.) 1991. *Research and Reflexivity*. London: Sage.

Therborn, G. 1980. *The Power of Ideology and the Ideology of Power*. London: Verso.

Thompson, J. B. 1982. "Universal pragmatics". In J. B. Thompson and D. Held (eds.). *Habermas. Critical Debates*. London: Macmillan.

Thompson, P. 1993. "Fatal distraction". In J. Hassard and M. Parker (eds.). *Postmodernism and Organizations*. London: Sage.

Townley, B. 1993. "Foucault, power/knowledge, and its relevance for human resource management". *Academy of Management Review*. 18, 518–545.

Townley, B. 1994. *Reframing Human Resource Management*. London: Sage.

Trice, H. and J. Beyer. 1985. "Using six organizational rites to change culture". In R. Kilmann et al. (eds.) *Gaining Control of the Corporate Culture*. San Francisco: Jossey Bass.

Van Maanen, J. and S. R. Barley. 1985. "Cultural organization. Fragments of a theory". In P. J. Frost et al. (eds.). *Organizational Culture*. Beverly Hills: Sage.

Walby, S. 1992. "Post-post-modernism? Theorizing social complexity". In M. Barrett and A. Phillips (eds.). *Destabilizing Theory*. Cambridge: Polity Press.

Walzer, M. 1986. "The politics of Michel Foucault". In D. Hoy (ed.) *Foucault. A Critical Reader*. Oxford: Basil Blackwell.

Watson, T. 1994. *In Search of Management*. London: Routledge.

Weaver, G. and D. Gioia 1994. "Paradigms lost: incommensurability versus structurationist inquiry". *Organization Studies*. 15, 565–589.

Weedon, C. 1987. *Feminist Practice & Poststructuralist Theory*. Oxford: Basil Blackwell.

Weick, K. E. and L. D. Browning. 1986. "Argument and narration in organizational communication". *Journal of Management*. 12, 243–259.

Weisbord, M. 1987. *Productive Workplaces*. San Francisco: Jossey-Bass.

Wellmer, A. 1985. "Reason, utopia and the dialectic of enlightenment". In R. J. Bernstein (ed.). *Habermas and Modernity*. Cambridge, Mass: MIT Press.

Wellmer, A. 1986. *Dialektiken mellan det moderna och det postmoderna*. Stockholm/Lund: Symposion.

Westley, F. (1990). "Middle managers and strategy: microdynamics of inclusion". *Strategic Management Journal*. 11, 337–351.

White, S. 1988. *The Recent Work of Jürgen Habermas*. Cambridge: Cambridge University Press.

Whittington, R. 1993. *What is Strategy – and Does it Matter?* London: Routledge.

Willmott, H. 1987. "Studying managerial work: a critique and a proposal". *Journal of Management Studies*. 24, 248–270.

Willmott, H. 1990. "Beyond paradigmatic closure in organisational inquiry". In J. Hassard and and D. Pym. (eds.). *The Theory and Philosophy of Organisations*. London: Routledge.

Willmott, H. 1993. "Strength is ignorance; slavery is freedom: managing culture in modern organizations". *Journal of Management Studies*. 30, 4, 515–552.

Willmott, H. 1994. "Theorizing human agency: responding to the crises of (post)modernity". In J. Hassard and M. Parker (eds.). *Towards a New Theory of Organizations*. London: Routledge.

Wrong, D. 1961. "The oversocialized conception of man in modern sociology". In R. Bocock (ed.). *An Introduction to Sociology*. Milton Keynes: The Open University Press.

Young, E. 1989. "On the naming of the rose: interests and multiple meanings as elements of organizational culture". *Organization Studies*. 10, 2, 187–206.

Østerberg, D. 1971. *Makt och materiell*. Göteborg: Korpen.

Author index

de Gruyter Studies in Organization

Alvesson, Mats
Management of Knowledge-Intensive Companies
1995. 23 × 15.5 cm. X, 367 pages. With 4 tables and 20 figures
Cloth. ISBN 3-11-012865-9
(de Gruyter Studies in Organization 61)

Billing, Yvonne Due / Alvesson, Mats
Gender, Managers, and Organizations
1994. 23 × 15.5 cm. X, 260 pages. Cloth. ISBN 3-11-012984-1
(de Gruyter Studies in Organization 50)

Alvesson, Mats / Berg, Per Olof
Corporate Culture and Organizational Symbolism
An Overview
1992. 23 × 15.5 cm. XII, 258 pages. With 10 figures and 1 table
Cloth. ISBN 3-11-012154-9, Paper. ISBN 3-11-013607-4
(de Gruyter Studies in Organization 34)

Alvesson, Mats
Organization Theory and Technocratic Consciousness
Rationality, Ideology and Quality of Work
1987. 23 × 15.5 cm. X, 286 pages. Cloth. ISBN 3-11-010574-8
(de Gruyter Studies in Organization 8)

Tamney, Joseph B.
The Struggle Over Singapore's Soul
Western Modernization and Asian Culture
1996. 23 × 15.5 cm. XII, 241 pages
Cloth. ISBN 3-11-014699-1, Paper. ISBN 3-11-014698-3
(de Gruyter Studies in Organization 70)

WALTER DE GRUYTER · BERLIN · NEW YORK
Genthiner Strasse 13, D-10785 Berlin, Tel. (030)26005-161, Fax: (030) 26005-222
200 Saw Mill Rivder Road, Hawthorne, N. Y. 10532, Tel. (914)747-0110, Fax (914)747-1326

de Gruyter Studies in Organization

Naschold, Frieder
New Frontiers in Public Sector Management. Trends and Issues in State and Local Government in Europe
Translated by Andrew Watt. With Case Studies by Robert Arnkil and Jaakko Virkkunen in Cooperation with Maarit Lahtonen and Claudius Riegler
1996. 23 × 15.5 cm. XVI, 329 pages. With 54 figures and 38 tables
Cloth. ISBN 3-11-015016-6
(de Gruyter Studies in Organization 69)

Brunstein, Ingrid (Editor)
Human Resource Management in Western Europe
1995. 23 × 15.5 cm. XVI, 342 pages
Cloth. ISBN 3-11-014274-0, Paper. ISBN 3-11-014275-9
(de Gruyter Studies in Organization 68)

Littek, Wolfgang / Charles, Tony (Editors)
The New Division of Labour
Emerging Forms of Work Organisation in International Perspective
1995. 23 × 15.5 cm. XIV, 514 pages. With 5 figures and 19 tables
Cloth. ISBN 3-11-013972-3
(de Gruyter Studies in Organization 67)

Warglien, Massimo / Masuch, Michael (Editors)
The Logic of Organizational Disorder
1996. 23 × 15.5 cm. X, 205 pages. Cloth. ISBN 3-11-013707-0
(de Gruyter Studies in Organization 66)

Grancelli, Bruno (Editor)
Social Change and Modernization
Lessons from Eastern Europe
1995. 23 × 15.5 cm. XII, 314 pages. Cloth. ISBN 3-11-014490-5
(de Gruyter Studies in Organization 65)

WALTER DE GRUYTER · BERLIN · NEW YORK
Genthiner Strasse 13, D-10785 Berlin, Tel. (030)26005-161, Fax: (030) 26005-222
200 Saw Mill Rivder Road, Hawthorne, N.Y. 10532, Tel. (914)747-0110, Fax (914)747-1326

L.-Brault

DATE DE RETOUR

Bibliofiche 297B